Developing IoT Projects with ESP32

Automate your home or business with inexpensive Wi-Fi devices

Vedat Ozan Oner

BIRMINGHAM—MUMBAI

Developing IoT Projects with ESP32

Group Product Manager: Wilson D'souza
Publishing Product Manager: Preet Ahuja
Senior Editor: Sangeeta Purkayastha
Content Development Editor: Nihar Kapadia
Technical Editor: Sarvesh Jaywant
Copy Editor: Safis Editing
Project Coordinator: Neil Dmello
Proofreader: Safis Editing
Indexer: Rekha Nair
Production Designer: Shankar Kalbhor

First published: August 2021

Production reference: 2131221

Published by Packt Publishing Ltd.
Livery Place
35 Livery Street
Birmingham
B3 2PB, UK.

ISBN 978-1-83864-116-0

www.packt.com

*For my daughters, Melis and Selin, and my wife, Ferah; how lucky
I am to have you!*

Contributors

About the author

Vedat Ozan Oner is an IoT product developer and software architect with a good blend of technical knowledge and experience. During his career, he participated in many IoT projects in different roles, which allowed him to see all aspects of developing successful IoT products in highly competitive markets. He holds a bachelor's degree in METU/computer engineering and holds several industry-recognized credentials and qualifications, including PMP®, ITIL®, and AWS Certified Developer.

Vedat started his limited company, Mevoo Ltd (https://mevoo.co.uk), in London in 2018 to provide consultancy services to his clients as well as develop his own IoT products. He still lives there with his family.

You can reach Vedat at https://www.linkedin.com/in/vedatozanoner/.

Special thanks to the Packt team for asking me to write this book. It was a great opportunity for me to share and to learn. I believe I did a good job together with the Packt team and the reviewers, Carlos and Tarik, to present the subjects to you in the most effective way possible. Their valuable feedback and efforts made this book worth publishing.

About the reviewers

Carlos Bugs is an electrical engineer with more than 15 years' experience of working with technology. He has experience in all the main stages of IoT product development, including preparation for large-scale production. He has undertaken projects in a variety of areas, including automotive, energy, instrumentation, medicine, and agriculture. Currently, he is the CTO of a tech company that integrates hardware projects (sensors, nodes, and gateways) with data science. He did the setup for large-scale production in China and thereafter in Brazil, where more than 70,000 sensors have been manufactured for big clients.

He has also undertaken many research projects and has won awards in Brazil and the United States. He can be reached on LinkedIn: `https://www.linkedin.com/in/carlos-bugs-6a272458/`

> *I would like to thank God for allowing me to contribute to this amazing book. I also wish to thank my family (my wife and son) for being my inspiration and for being patient during the review process. Finally, I would like to thank the author, Vedat, Neil, and the entire Packt team, who worked so hard on this book.*

Tarik Ceber is currently employed as a hardware development engineer at TechSat GmbH in Germany. He started his career as a self-learner in 2005 as a C++ developer and worked on various unmanned aerial vehicle projects. Because of his passion for embedded systems and avionics, he has also developed electronic printed circuit boards, including flight control computers, inertial navigation systems, battery management systems, and avionics test equipment for a vast arsenal of aerial platforms (small fixed-wing UAVs, tactical UAVs, quadcopters, and eVTOLs). Aside from the aviation business, he has also participated in IoT projects and designed printed circuit boards for smart home appliances, including BLE-enabled smart meters and RGB color bulbs.

> *I would like to thank the author for allowing me to be a technical reviewer of this informative and well-organized book, which truly fills a practice-oriented information source gap in the fast-growing IoT world.*

Table of Contents

3

Impressive Outputs with Displays

4

A Deep Dive into the Advanced Features

5

Practice – Multisensor for Your Room

9
Practice – Making Your Home Smart

Section 3: Cloud Communication

10
No Cloud, No IoT – Cloud Platforms and Services

11
Connectivity Is Never Enough – Third-Party Integrations

Preface

Internet of Things (IoT) technology has been in our lives for more than a decade now. When I first came across a single-board computer at an expo 20 years ago, I was fascinated, as a young computer engineer, by the possibilities that this device introduced. It was the gateway, in my eyes, to a smart home where you could know what was going on at home when you were miles away!

Since then, I have participated in many IoT projects in different positions, so I have had many chances to see IoT products from different perspectives. As developers, we mostly tend to forget about what the use of technology is while trying to solve a technical problem. However, as we develop an IoT product, the first question that we should ask is what is the value of this product, what benefit will people get from it? It doesn't matter if it is a consumer product or an industrial IoT solution; it should help people to solve real problems. In the last chapter of each part of this book, you will find a complete project that can help people in their daily lives.

There is no single driving force behind IoT, but we can count several strong enablers, such as the emergence of inexpensive silicon chips available in large quantities, mobile technologies, and cloud computing, to name just a few. I think ESP32 has contributed to this on its own terms. When it was launched in 2016 by Espressif Systems, I was working for a smart home company as a technical product manager. We had seen the opportunity immediately – that this chip could cut the cost of our home gateway to a quarter of the one that we had! There was no other Wi-Fi **system on a chip (SoC)** on the market as a complete computing solution with that price tag. I know it is not possible to discuss everything that we can do with ESP32, but I believe you will find this book quite useful before starting your next IoT project with ESP32.

Besides as a profession, it is my hobby to build new IoT devices together with my daughter at home. I always love sharing my knowledge and experience with her and with people around me, as well as learning from them. I hope you enjoy reading this book and developing the projects together with me.

Who this book is for

This book targets embedded software developers, IoT software architects/developers, and technologists who want to learn how to employ ESP32 effectively in their IoT projects. Hobbyists will also find the examples in this book useful when they need a powerful Wi-Fi SoC with professional features.

What this book covers

Chapter 1, *Getting Started with ESP32*, introduces you to IoT technology in general, the ESP32 hardware, and development environment options.

Chapter 2, *Talking to the Earth – Sensors and Actuators*, discusses different types of sensors and actuators and how to interface them with ESP32.

Chapter 3, *Impressive Outputs with Displays*, explains how to select and use different display types in ESP32 projects. FreeRTOS is also discussed in detail.

Chapter 4, A *Deep Dive into the Advanced Features*, covers audio/video applications with ESP32 and the power management subsystem for low-power requirements.

Chapter 5, *Practice – Multisensor for Your Room*, is the first reference project in the book, where several sensors are integrated as a single ESP32 device.

Chapter 6, *Good Old Friend – Wi-Fi*, shows how to use ESP32 in the station and access point modes of Wi-Fi. Some TCP/IP protocols are discussed in the context of ESP32.

Chapter 7, *Security First!*, explores the security features of ESP32 and provides examples of secure firmware updates and secure communication techniques.

Chapter 8, *I Can Speak BLE*, introduces the BLE basics and shows how to develop a BLE beacon, a GATT server, and BLE mesh nodes.

Chapter 9, *Practice – Making Your Home Smart*, builds a full-fledged smart home solution with a gateway, a light sensor, and a relay switch in a BLE mesh network.

Chapter 10, *No Cloud, No IoT – Cloud Platforms and Services*, discusses the important IoT protocols and introduces the IoT platforms from different providers with an example of AWS IoT integration.

Chapter 11, *Connectivity Is Never Enough – Third-Party Integrations*, focuses on integration with popular services such as voice assistants and IFTTT.

Chapter 12, *Practice – A Voice-Controlled Smart Fan*, converts an ordinary fan into an Alexa-enabled smart device as the last project of the book.

To get the most out of this book

IoT technology requires many different disciplines and skills to develop an IoT product. Fundamentally, you are expected to read Fritzing diagrams to set up the hardware prototypes in the examples, in addition to having programming capabilities with C and Python. It is also assumed that you have a familiarity with TCP/IP protocols and cryptography basics to follow the examples easily. In some chapters, there are reference books suggested for reading if you don't feel comfortable with the basics of the subject.

The necessary hardware components are listed before each example. However, you should have a breadboard, jumper wires, and a multimeter ready to be able to build the circuits. It is also advisable to have soldering equipment since many of the new modules need headers to be soldered in order to connect them to the breadboard.

As the development environment, you should have VS Code installed on your PC. The examples in this book are developed and tested on a Linux machine, but all should work regardless of the OS platform. The alternatives of the external tools are suggested for different platforms where necessary.

There are several mobile applications required for testing purposes. Therefore, you will need a mobile device while working on the examples. These mobile applications are available for both Android and iOS platforms.

To gain proficiency in a new subject requires a lot of practice. Each reference project at the end of the parts is for that purpose. After completing them, it would be highly beneficial to continue to work on the projects as suggested at the end of the chapters. Some more ideas are given for how to improve them further.

Software/hardware covered in the book	OS requirements
ESP32 and different additional hardware components	Windows, macOS, or Linux (any)
ESP-IDF and several external libraries	

If you are using the digital version of this book, we advise you to type the code yourself or access the code via the GitHub repository (link available in the next section). Doing so will help you avoid any potential errors related to the copying and pasting of code.

Download the example code files

You can download the example code files for this book from GitHub at `https://github.com/PacktPublishing/Internet-of-Things-with-ESP32`. If there's an update to the code, it will be updated on the existing GitHub repository.

We also have other code bundles from our rich catalog of books and videos available at `https://github.com/PacktPublishing/`. Check them out!

Code in Action

Code in Action videos for this book can be viewed at `https://bit.ly/2T0ynws`.

Download the color images

We also provide a PDF file that has color images of the screenshots/diagrams used in this book. You can download it here: `http://www.packtpub.com/sites/default/files/downloads/9781838641160_ColorImages.pdf`.

Conventions used

There are a number of text conventions used throughout this book.

`Code in text`: Indicates code words in text, database table names, folder names, filenames, file extensions, pathnames, dummy URLs, user input, and Twitter handles. Here is an example: "After installation, it integrates itself to the VSCode UI where you can find all the functionality that `idf.py` of ESP-IDF provides."

A block of code is set as follows:

```
#define GPIO_LED 2
#define GPIO_LED_PIN_SEL (1ULL << GPIO_LED)
#define GPIO_BUTTON 5
```

When we wish to draw your attention to a particular part of a code block, the relevant lines or items are set in bold:

```
static void button_handler(void *arg);


static void init_hw(void)
```

Any command-line input or output is written as follows:

```
$ ls -R
```

Bold: Indicates a new term, an important word, or words that you see on screen. For example, words in menus or dialog boxes appear in the text like this. Here is an example: "Click on the **New Project** button on the PIO home."

> Tips or important notes
> Appear like this.

Get in touch

Feedback from our readers is always welcome.

General feedback: If you have questions about any aspect of this book, mention the book title in the subject of your message and email us at customercare@packtpub.com.

Errata: Although we have taken every care to ensure the accuracy of our content, mistakes do happen. If you have found a mistake in this book, we would be grateful if you would report this to us. Please visit www.packtpub.com/support/errata, selecting your book, clicking on the Errata Submission Form link, and entering the details.

Piracy: If you come across any illegal copies of our works in any form on the internet, we would be grateful if you would provide us with the location address or website name. Please contact us at copyright@packt.com with a link to the material.

If you are interested in becoming an author: If there is a topic that you have expertise in and you are interested in either writing or contributing to a book, please visit authors.packtpub.com.

Share Your Thoughts

Once you've read *Developing IoT Projects with ESP32*, we'd love to hear your thoughts! Scan the QR code below to go straight to the Amazon review page for this book and share your feedback.

https://packt.link/r/1838641165

Your review is important to us and the tech community and will help us make sure we're delivering excellent quality content.

Section 1: Using ESP32

In this section, you will learn about the development platform/framework options for starting with ESP32 and how to use ESP32 in a project by interfacing with different sensors and actuators.

This part of the book comprises the following chapters:

- *Chapter 1, Getting Started with ESP32*
- *Chapter 2, Talking to the Earth – Sensors and Actuators*
- *Chapter 3, Impressive Outputs with Displays*
- *Chapter 4, A Deep Dive into the Advanced Features*
- *Chapter 5, Practice – Multisensor for Your Room*

1
Getting Started with ESP32

Espressif ESP32 is a powerful tool in the toolbox of a developer for many types of **Internet of Things (IoT)** projects. We are all developers, and we all know how important it is to select the right tool for a given problem in a domain. To solve the problem, we need to understand the domain, and we need to know the available tools and their features that are important for that specific problem in order to find the right one (or perhaps several combined). After selecting the tool, we eventually need to figure out how to use it in the most efficient and effective way possible so as to maximize the added value for end users.

In this chapter, I will discuss the technology, IoT, in general, what an IoT solution looks like in terms of basic architecture, and how ESP32 fits into those solutions as a tool. If you are new to IoT technology, or are thinking of using ESP32 in your next project, this chapter helps you to understand the big picture from the technology perspective by describing what ESP32 provides, its capabilities, and its limitations.

The main topics covered in this chapter are as follows:

- IoT as an emerging technology and its application areas with some examples
- The basic structure of IoT solutions, including security considerations
- An introduction to the ESP32 platform and modules
- Available development platforms and frameworks
- **Real-Time Operating System (RTOS)** options for ESP32

Technical requirements

In this book, we are going to have many practical examples where we can learn how to use ESP32 effectively in real-world scenarios. Although links to the examples are provided within each chapter, you can take a sneak peek at the online repository here: `https://github.com/PacktPublishing/Internet-of-Things-with-ESP32`. The examples are placed in their relative directories of the chapters for easy browsing. There is also a common source code directory that contains the shared libraries across the chapters.

We will use different software tools and hardware components throughout the book. Each chapter shows its own list of these tools and components.

IoT as an emerging technology

When I started my career 20 years ago, my first project involved collecting data regarding radio and TV stations by measuring some **Radio Frequency (RF)** parameters of broadcasted channels. The task was to design and develop a system in order to understand whether the stations comply with the existing regulations in the country. As a solution for this engineering problem, the technical leaders in the team designed a van with various equipment, including the following:

- A spectrum analyzer
- A TV demodulator
- Different types of antennas to measure those parameters
- An industrial PC to run the application software
- A radio transmitter to upload the measurements and some basic analysis to a data center

I was lucky that I participated in such a project in my very first job and saw how a complete data acquisition system was designed and developed to solve a real-world problem. This project was in the year just after Kevin Ashton introduced the term *Internet of Things* to technology literature in 1999.

When I first heard this term and was trying to understand what it actually means, I quickly noticed the similarities between an IoT solution and our monitoring van. We collected data from the environment by using some sensing devices, we had a processing unit, and we also transferred information to a central data storage and processing center. This last part was to access more processing and spot correlation between data coming from multiple vans. So, why not call it an IoT product? Well, not exactly. From that perspective, you could easily call any SCADA or PLC product an IoT system as well, so IoT would only then constitute a rebranding of existing technologies.

What is IoT?

Although the definition of IoT might change slightly from different viewpoints, there are some key concepts in the IoT world that differentiate it from other types of technologies:

- **Connectivity**: An IoT device is connected, either to the internet or to a local network. An old-style thermostat on the wall waiting for manual operation with basic programming features doesn't count as an IoT device.

- **Identification**: An IoT device is uniquely identified in the network so that data has a context identified by that device. In addition, the device itself is available for remote update, remote management, and diagnostics.

- **Autonomous operation**: IoT systems are designed for minimal or no human intervention. Each device collects data from the environment where it is installed, and it can then communicate the data with other devices to detect the current status of the system and respond as configured. This response can be in the form of an action, a log, or an alert if required.

- **Interoperability**: Devices in an IoT solution talk to one another, but they don't necessarily belong to a single vendor. When devices designed by different vendors share a common application-level protocol, adding a new device to that heterogeneous network is as easy as clicking on a few buttons on the device or on the management software.

- **Scalability**: IoT systems are capable of horizontal scalability to respond to an increasing workload. A new device is added when necessary to increase capacity instead of replacing the existing one with a superior device (vertical scalability).

- **Security**: I wish I could say that every IoT solution implements at least the minimal set of mandatory security measures, but unfortunately, this is not the case, despite a number of bad experiences, including the infamous Mirai botnet attack. On a positive note, I can say that IoT devices mostly have secure boot, secure update, and secure communication features to ensure confidentiality, integrity, and availability the (CIA triad).

Gartner added IoT in the 2011 hype cycle, with the expectation of more than 10 years to mainstream adoption. However, many related technologies, such as RFID, mesh networking, and Bluetooth, were already on the list many years before 2011, along with enablers such as mobile and cloud technologies. Since then, Gartner has added several other IoT technologies and applications to its list, including the following:

- IoT platform

- Connected home

- Smart dust

- Edge computing

- Low-cost, single-board computers at the edge

5G and embedded AI are other revolutionary technologies on the Gartner list that support IoT and expand its area of application.

Where do we apply IoT?

The application areas are vast, but conceptually speaking, we can group them into two basic categories:

- In the **consumer IoT** category, we can see mainly smart home and security systems, personal healthcare products, wearable technologies, and asset tracking applications.

- The **industrial IoT** category has more application areas, as you might expect. Every year, IoT Analytics publishes a top-10 trend list for industrial applications by reviewing thousands of new projects and the 2020 list contains manufacturing, transportation, energy, retail, cities, healthcare, supply chain, agriculture, and building applications in that order (`https://iot-analytics.com/top-10-iot-applications-in-2020`).

Since we have limited space in this book, I don't want to waste pages talking about each of these application areas. Instead, I'd like to share more interesting cases to show how the IoT technology can provide powerful solutions when incorporated with other cutting-edge technologies.

AI/ML on the edge

AI has been around for a long time and there are many successful examples of machine vision, **Natural Language Processing (NLP)**, speech recognition, and ML projects. However, they all require energy-hungry powerful hardware to be able to cope with CPU and memory-intensive calculations, which is not possible with humble sensor devices that have much less memory and processing power. TensorFlow Lite addresses this problem. Its converter can output a model, a set of rules to make predictions by running data through them, with a size as low as 14 KB to fit into any modern microcontroller, such as an ARM Cortex-M3 device with a very low power consumption, which enables you to have battery-operated sensor devices with ML capabilities. One interesting project comes from Benjamin Cabé (on Twitter: @kartben). In his project, he managed to train a model to discern different types of spirits with an accuracy of 92%. He used a Wio Terminal from SeeedStudio as the computing board, which has an ARM Cortex-M4F core running at 120 MHz.

Implications are enormous. Instead of a dummy sensor device, now we have the capability of developing a *real* smart device such that it can add meaning to data it collects and can react based not only on data, but also the meaning. Benjamin employed a simple gas sensor to detect various gases, such as carbon monoxide (CO), nitrogen dioxide (NO_2), ethyl alcohol (C_2H_5CH), and some other types. But the device itself can understand what it actually *smells*, thanks to the ML model it uses in its firmware. Without such a capability, the device would have to send its data to another more powerful machine or a cloud to make this analysis and then wait for a reply to decide what to do next. Moreover, if it loses its network connectivity somehow, nothing could be done more until connectivity is restored.

This subject definitely deserves another book, but if you want to do some experiments, ESP32 is also on the list of supported platforms on the TensorFlow Lite website.

> **Important note**
>
> You can have a look at the supported platforms for TensorFlow Lite at
> the following link: `https://www.tensorflow.org/lite/`
> `microcontrollers`.

Energy harvesting

A vital discussion and research subject for **Wireless Sensor Networks** (**WSNs**) has always been the energy consumption of sensor nodes. Obviously, less is better. If you have some experience with the development of battery-operated wireless devices, you know the concept of *run to sleep*, which means do the job and go into sleep mode as soon as possible to preserve the most valuable resource, energy. Nonetheless, whatever you do, sensor nodes must consume energy and the user will have to replace the batteries after a while. An interesting technology comes to your aid at this point – energy harvesting, which has been around since the days of Nikola Tesla. The energy can be harvested from various ambient sources, including light, vibration, and wireless energy sources. To do that, a harvesting solution first needs to access that ambient energy by means of various components, depending on the energy type.

It is an RF antenna if the energy comes from an RF source, or a photovoltaic cell if light is the source. Then, this *raw* electrical energy has to be converted with the help of an integrated circuit in order to store it in a capacitor or a battery. But you know that this is easier said than done. Although there are several **Power Management Integrated Circuits** (**PMICs**) from different silicon vendors on the market, it is hard to say whether they solve this problem efficiently. The major challenges are very low levels of energy to harvest, the need to boost the very low voltage to higher logic levels, the need for multiple external components to operate, and a large chip footprint on the PCB. Therefore, these challenges have prevented vendors from producing high-performance energy harvesting chips. One product does sound promising, though.

Nowi Energy promotes its NH2D0245 PMIC as the most efficient and the smallest footprint power management IC compared to other semiconductor giants on the market. To prove their arguments, they launched a hybrid smartwatch module together with the module company MMT, such that a watch with that module requires no charge to operate during its lifetime. Energy harvesting is a hot topic, so there are, of course, competitors, such as e-peas semiconductors from Belgium. You might want to try one of those PMICs in your next WSN project.

Nanorobotics

Before we move on, we should look at one last project, a research project from Cornell University. The result of this research has been published in *Nature Journal* in August 2020 as an article named *Electronically integrated, mass-manufactured, microscopic robots*. They invented actuators on a nano scale that you literally cannot see with your eyes. The super tiny structure has two solar cells on it to move the legs, and when laser beams are dropped on those solar cells, they generate enough voltage to activate the legs. Although not ready for any practical application as yet, this research is definitely on my follow-up list as a technologist and IoT expert.

> **Important note**
> If you want to see them in action, there is a video on YouTube: `https://www.youtube.com/watch?v=2TjdGuBK9mI`.

These examples are certainly extremes in terms of technology application, but I hope they provide a glimpse of the future in terms of IoT technologies and inspire you in your next IoT project. Let's now continue with some common features of IoT solutions.

Understanding the basic structure of IoT solutions

An IoT solution combines many different technologies into a single product, starting from a physical device and covering all layers up to end user applications. Each layer of the solution aims to implement the same vision set by the business, but requires a different approach while designing and developing. We definitely cannot talk about one-size-fits-all solutions in IoT projects, but we still can apply an organized approach to develop products. Let's see which layers a solution has in a typical IoT product:

- **Device hardware**: Every IoT project requires hardware with a **System-On-Chip (SoC)** or **Microcontroller Unit (MCU)** and sensors/actuators to interact with the physical world. In addition to that, every IoT device is connected, so we need to select the optimal communication medium, such as wired or wireless. Power management is also another consideration under this category.

- **Device firmware**: We need to develop device firmware to run on the SoC in order to fulfill the project's requirements. This is where we collect data and transfer it to the other components in the solution.

- **Communication**: Connectivity issues are handled in this category of the solution architecture. The physical medium selection corresponds to one part of the solution, but we still need to decide on the protocol between devices as a common language for sharing data. Some protocols may provide a whole stack of communication by defining both the physical medium up to the application layer. If this is the case, you don't need to worry about anything else, but if your stack leaves the context management at the application layer up to you, then it is time to decide on what IoT protocol to use.

- **Backend system**: This is the backbone of the solution. All data is collected on the backend system and provides the management, monitoring, and integration capabilities of the product. Backend systems can be implemented on on-premises hardware or cloud providers, again depending on the project requirements. Moreover, this is where IoT encounters other disruptive technologies. You can apply big data analytics to extract deeper information from data coming from sensors, or you can use AI algorithms to feed your system with more smart features, such as anomaly detection or predictive maintenance.

- **End user applications**: You will very likely require an interface for your end users to let them access the functionality. 10 years ago, we were only talking about desktop, web, or mobile applications. But today we have voice assistants. You can think of them as a modern interface for human interaction, and it might be a good idea to add voice assistant integration as a feature, especially in the consumer segment.

The following diagram depicts the general structure of IoT solutions:

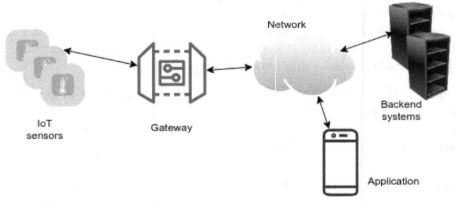

Figure 1.1 – Basic structure

This is the list of aspects, more or less, that we need to take into account in many types of IoT projects before starting.

IoT security

One important consideration that remains is security. Actually, it is all about security. I cannot overemphasize its importance whatever I write. IoT devices are connected to the real world and any security incident has the potential for serious damage in the immediate environment, let alone other cybersecurity crimes. Therefore, it should always be in your checklist while designing any hardware or software components of the solution. Although security, as a subject, definitely deserves a book by itself, I can list some golden rules for devices in the field:

- Always look to reduce the attack surface for both hardware and firmware.
- Prevent physical tampering wherever possible. No physical port should be open if this is not necessary.
- Keep secret keys on a secure medium.
- Implement secure boot, secure firmware updates, and encrypted communication.
- Do not use default passwords; TCP/IP ports should not be open unnecessarily.
- Put health check mechanisms in place along with anomaly detection where possible.

We should embrace secure design principles in general as IoT developers. Since an IoT product has many different components, end-to-end security becomes the crucial point while designing the product. A risk impact analysis should be done for each component to decide on the security levels of data in transit and data at rest. There are many national/international institutions and organizations that provide standards, guidelines, and best practices regarding cybersecurity. One of these, which works specifically on IoT technology is the IoT Security Foundation. They are actively developing guidelines and frameworks on the subject and publishing many of those guidelines, which are freely available.

> **Important note**
> If you want to check those guidelines, you can visit the IoT Security Foundation website for their publications here: `https://www.iotsecurityfoundation.org/best-practice-guidelines/`.

Now, that we are equipped with sufficient knowledge of IoT and its applications, we can propel our journey with ESP32, a platform perfectly suited for beginner-level projects as well as end products. In the remaining sections of this chapter, we are going to talk about the ESP32 hardware, development frameworks, and RTOS options available on the market.

Introduction to ESP32 platform and modules

The first ESP32 chip was launched in 2016 when I was working for a smart home company as a technical product manager. The wireless communication technology that we had chosen for our product line was Z-wave on account of its technical features (sub-gigahertz wireless communication, mesh networking, interoperability, and suchlike) and market status (many vendors, thousands of certified products, and so on).

The vision was not to be yet another device vendor, but to be a platform where every other vendor meets with end users. The most crucial step was to develop the most affordable Z-wave gateway on the market such that any smart home enthusiast would prefer our gateway as the access point of other Z-wave devices in their home. Our first prototype was a high-performance, embedded Linux board with an ARM-CortexA SoC; however, in terms of pricing, it was certainly not the most affordable one in our segment. Then we discovered ESP32 from Espressif. This was a game-changer.

ESP32 allowed us to slash the price of the gateway to a quarter of what it was originally. Having an ESP32 as the main computing unit, we attached a Z-wave module to it as the network co-processor. The other end was Wi-Fi, a built-in feature of ESP32, to connect the backend system. We didn't worry about security requirements because there was a cryptographic hardware accelerator in the ESP32 chip for encryption/decryption purposes. That was all that we needed. However, as always, life is not that easy. The Z-wave library that we procured from the market had targeted Linux-based boards, not a resource-constrained SoC like ESP32. So we started to port the whole Z-wave library for ESP32 and succeeded. Finally, we had the most compact and most affordable Z-wave gateway on the market.

Why ESP32?

IoT technologies have proven their worth over the years and, as developers, we have a great many tools available to us today for developing exceptional IoT products compared to 5 or 10 years ago. ESP32 is definitely one of those tools and there are many reasons as to why this is so:

- Its price tag and availability
- Wi-Fi and Bluetooth in a single SoC

- Great hardware features with many peripheral interfaces, different power modes, and cryptographic hardware acceleration

- Variants for different requirements, in terms of both chips and modules

- Advanced development platforms and frameworks

- A huge community

- And finally, native integration with top cloud infrastructures

These are the reasons for putting ESP32 at the top of your SoC selection list if you require a Wi-Fi SoC in your project.

ESP32 features

Since the introduction of the first ESP32 on the market, Espressif launched several variants of ESP32 and most recently, in 2020, they introduced ESP32-S2 series chips. The ESP32 family is a general-purpose, feature-rich, and versatile SoC solution that you can use in many different types of IoT projects where you require Wi-Fi connectivity. Let's have a quick look at the main features:

- **CPU and memory**: 32-bit Xtensa® LX6 microprocessor with a clock frequency/ MIPS of up to 240 MHz/600 MIPS. Single- or dual-core variants. 448 KB ROM, 520 KB SRAM, and 16 KB RTC memory. Support for external SPI flash and SPI RAM for module variants. DMA for peripherals.

- **Connectivity**: Wi-Fi 802.11 n (2.4 GHz) up to 150 Mbps (STA and softAP modes) and Bluetooth-compliant with Bluetooth v4.2 BR/EDR and BLE specifications.

- **Peripheral interfaces**: GPIOs, ADC, DAC, SPI, I2C, I2S, UART, eMMC/SD (chip variants), CAN, IR, PWM, touch sensor, and hall sensor.

- **Security**: Cryptographic hardware acceleration (random number, hash, AES, RSA, and ECC), 1024-bit OTP, secure boot, and flash encryption.

- **Power modes**: Different power modes with the help of an **Ultra-Low-Power** (**ULP**) co-processor and a **Real-Time Clock** (**RTC**). 100 µA power consumption in deep-sleep mode (ULP active).

The new ESP32-S2 series is a bit different, with some notable differences including the following:

- Single core.

- No Bluetooth.

- No support for SD/eMMC, but USB OTG has been added.

- Enhanced security features.

To make hardware design easier, Espressif provides different ESP32 modules with different configurations. Variable parameters for the modules are the ESP32 chip variant, external flash (4, 8, or 16 MB), external SRAM, and the antenna type. We can select among modules with a PCB antenna, or there is an external antenna option realized with the help of a U.FL/IPEX connector. On the ESP32-S2 side, we have only one module option as of the time of writing this book. Most of the time, it is enough to choose one of those modules in your projects. However, if you require a specific ESP32 chip, for example, one with high-temperature operation, then you need to use a corresponding chip variant such as ESP32-U4WDH and design your PCB accordingly. You can find available modules on the Espressif website here: `https://docs.espressif.com/projects/esp-idf/en/latest/esp32/hw-reference/index.html`.

The following photo shows an ESP32-WROOM-32D module with an integrated onboard antenna:

Figure 1.2 – ESP32-WROOM-32D module

As a development kit, we can find many boards from different vendors on the market. We can easily start to develop with such a kit without the need for the actual hardware design and prototype of the final product. All models integrate a USB-UART bridge chip and a USB port, so we only need to plug the kit into our development PC to flash and test the firmware:

Figure 1.3 – DOIT ESP32 Devkit v1

Following this introduction to the hardware, we can continue with the firmware development platforms and frameworks.

Development platforms and frameworks

ESP32 is quite popular. Therefore, there are a good number of options that you can select as your development platform and framework.

The first one, of course, comes directly from Espressif itself. They call it the **Espressif IoT Development Framework (ESP-IDF)**. It supports all three main OS environments – Windows, macOS, and Linux. After installing some prerequisite packages, you can download the ESP-IDF from the GitHub repository, and install it on your development PC. They have collected all the necessary functionality into a single Python script, named `idf.py`, for developers. You can configure project parameters and a final binary image by using this command-line tool. You can also use it in every step of your project, starting from the build phase to connecting and monitoring your ESP32 board from the serial port of your computer. But as I said, it is a command-line tool, so if you are a more graphical UI person, then you need to install Visual Studio Code and install an ESP-IDF extension in it. Here is the link to ESP-IDF: `https://docs.espressif.com/projects/esp-idf/en/latest/esp32/get-started/index.html`.

The second option is the Arduino IDE. As you might expect. Arduino provides its own library to work with ESP32 boards. If you have experience with the Arduino IDE, you know how easy it is to use. However, it comes at the cost of development flexibility compared to ESP-IDF. You are constricted in terms of what Arduino allows you to do and you need to obey its rules.

The third alternative you can choose is PlatformIO. This is not a standalone IDE or tool, but comes as an extension in Visual Studio Code as an open source embedded development environment. It supports many different embedded boards, platforms, and frameworks, including ESP32 boards and ESP-IDF. Following installation, it integrates itself with the VSCode UI, where you can find all the functionality that `idf.py` of ESP-IDF provides. In addition to VSCode IDE features, PlatformIO has an integrated debugger, unit testing support, static code analysis, and remote development tools for embedded programming. PlatformIO is a good choice for balancing ease of use and development flexibility.

The programming language for those three frameworks is C/C++, so you need to know C/C++ in order to develop within those frameworks. However, C/C++ is not the only programming language for ESP32. You can use MicroPython for Python programming or Espruino for JavaScript programming. They both support ESP32 boards, but to be honest, I wouldn't use them to develop any product to be launched on the market. Although you may feel more comfortable with them because of your programming language preferences, you won't find ESP-IDF capabilities in any of them.

RTOS options

Basically, an RTOS provides a deterministic task scheduler. Although the scheduling rules change depending on the scheduling algorithm, we know that the task we create will complete in a certain time frame within those rules. The main advantages of using an RTOS are the reduction in complexity and improved software architecture for easier maintenance.

The main real-time operating system supported by ESP-IDF is FreeRTOS. ESP-IDF uses its own version of the Xtensa port of FreeRTOS. The fundamental difference compared with the vanilla FreeRTOS is the dual-core support. In ESP-IDF FreeRTOS, you can choose one of two cores to assign a task or you can let FreeRTOS choose it. Other differences compared with the original FreeRTOS mostly stem from the dual-core support. FreeRTOS is distributed under an MIT license: `https://docs.espressif.com/projects/esp-idf/en/latest/esp32/api-reference/system/freertos.html`.

If you want to connect your ESP32 to the **Amazon Web Services (AWS)** IoT infrastructure, you can do that by using Amazon FreeRTOS as your RTOS choice. ESP32 is in the AWS partner device catalog and officially supported. Amazon FreeRTOS has the necessary libraries to connect to the AWS IoT and other security-related features, such as TLS, OTA updates, secure communication with HTTPS, WebSockets, and MQTT, pretty much everything to develop a secure connected device: `https://docs.aws.amazon.com/freertos/latest/userguide/getting_started_espressif.html`.

Zephyr is another RTOS option with a permissive free software license, Apache 2.0. Zephyr requires an ESP32 toolchain and ESP-IDF installed on the development machine. Then, you need to configure Zephyr with them. When the configuration is ready, we use the command-line Zephyr tool, "west," for building, flash, monitoring, and debugging purposes: `https://docs.zephyrproject.org/latest/boards/xtensa/esp32/doc/index.html`.

The last RTOS that I want to share here is Mongoose OS. It provides a complete development environment with its web UI tool, **mos**. It has native integration with several cloud IoT platforms, namely, AWS IoT, Google IoT, Microsoft Azure, and IBM Watson, as well as any other IoT platform that supports MQTT or REST endpoints if you need a custom platform. Mongoose OS comes with two different licenses, one being an Apache 2.0 community edition, and the other an enterprise edition with a commercial license: `https://mongoose-os.com/mos.html`.

Summary

In this chapter, we covered all the necessary background information regarding the IoT technology and ESP32 as a hardware platform for developing IoT products.

To add value to our end users, we, as developers, should know the ground. It is not enough to come up with a solution; it has to be the right solution, which requires us to learn more about the technologies and tools available. When it comes to IoT technology, things may become more difficult because an IoT product has several components, starting from sensor/actuator devices to end user applications, allowing end users to interact with the solution. In this manner, learning ESP32 is an important professional skill to be acquired by an IoT developer.

Following the background information in this chapter, upcoming chapters are going to focus on how to use ESP32 effectively in our projects. With the help of practical examples and explanations, we will see different aspects of ESP32 for different use cases and apply them in the projects at the end of each part. We will begin by using sensors and actuators in the next chapter.

2
Talking to the Earth – Sensors and Actuators

As we have discussed in *Chapter 1, Getting Started with ESP32*, **Internet of Things (IoT)** devices interact with the physical world. They collect data from the immediate environment and react based on a condition or schedule in the form of a physical action, a log, or maybe a trigger of another event in its operating environment. How they do this is by means of sensors and actuators.

In this chapter, we're going to use several sensors and actuators by interfacing with an ESP32 **development kit** (**devkit**) and will learn about different types of communication protocols.

We'll cover the following topics:

- Toolchain installation, programming, and debugging ESP32

- Warming up: **Basic input/output** (**I/O**) with buttons, **potentiometers** (**pots**), and **light-emitting diodes** (**LEDs**)

- Working with sensors
- Working with actuators

Technical requirements

Throughout the book, we're going to use **Visual Studio Code (VS Code)** as the **integrated development environment (IDE)**. If you don't have it, you can find it here: `https://code.visualstudio.com/`.

As the ESP32 devkit, I have **ESP32-DevKitC V4** from AZ-Delivery. However, the examples will compile and run successfully for most—if not all—of the ESP32 devkits with an ESP32 series chip. You can buy one from the *AZ-Delivery* website or from online marketplaces such as Amazon or eBay.

I have used many sensors and actuators in the examples. You will see their types and models under the related topics, so you can order them from online marketplaces as well. You will also need a breadboard, jumper wires, and resistors for prototyping.

The source code in the examples is located in the repository found at this link: `https://github.com/PacktPublishing/Internet-of-Things-with-ESP32/tree/main/ch2`

Check out the following video to see the code in action: `https://bit.ly/3hK33Kx`

Toolchain installation, programming, and debugging ESP32

There are several options for the development environment. Among them, I will use the **PlatformIO** IDE throughout the book, except for some examples where I have to use **Espressif IoT Development Framework (ESP-IDF)** tools directly. PlatformIO supports many different platforms, architectures, and frameworks with modern development capabilities. It comes as an extension in VS Code, and so is very easy to install and configure with just a few clicks.

PlatformIO installation

Let's start with the installation. After launching VS Code, go to **Extensions** (*Ctrl + Shift + X*) and search for `platformio` in the marketplace. This appears at the first place in the match list. Click on the **Install** button, and that is it. In a few minutes, the installation completes and we have PlatformIO installed in the VS Code IDE, as illustrated in the following screenshot:

Figure 2.1 – PlatformIO installation

After the installation, you will see the PlatformIO icon in the activity bar on the left. This is the link to the PlatformIO world.

The first program

Let's go step by step through our first program. Our goal in this program is just to print `hello world` over the serial port and monitor it by using the PlatformIO serial monitor tool. Proceed as follows:

1. Click on the PlatformIO icon in the left bar. It lists PlatformIO (or PIO for short) quick access links.

2. Select **PIO Home/Open** to navigate to the PlatformIO home page, as illustrated in the following screenshot:

Figure 2.2 – PlatformIO Home

3. Click on the **New Project** button on the PlatformIO home page.

4. PlatformIO pops up a dialog for your project settings, where you set your project name and select board, framework, and project location.

5. Set the project name as my_first_project (no space, please), then select your ESP32 board type and ESP-IDF as the framework. PlatformIO supports both ESP-IDF and Arduino frameworks for ESP32 development. ESP-IDF is going to be our framework selection for the rest of the book. You can choose any location on your machine for the project location or just leave it as the default, which is $HOME/Documents/PlatformIO/Projects. The project settings are shown in the following screenshot:

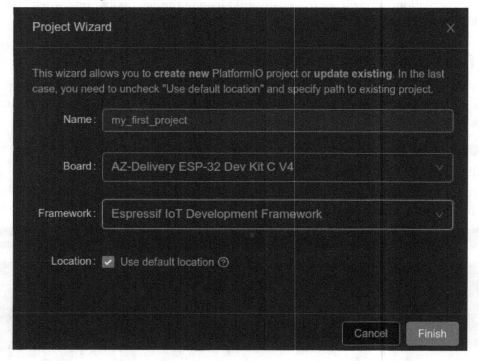

Figure 2.3 – Project settings for the first project

When you click on the **Finish** button, PlatformIO does several things at that point, and these may take several minutes to complete. These tasks are listed as follows:

- Creates the project folder
- Downloads the framework sources and other tools from the PlatformIO repository into the $HOME/.platformio/packages folder when it is your first project with the selected framework

- Downloads the board sources into `<project_folder>/.pio/build`
- Generates some configuration and build files, as illustrated in the following screenshot:

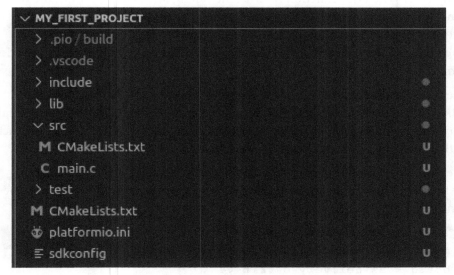

Figure 2.4 – Folder structure of a new project

The generated files are outlined here:

- `CmakeLists.txt` files are for CMake build configurations of ESP-IDF.
- `sdkconfig` contains ESP-IDF project configurations. There is a tool to edit this file, but you may prefer to edit it manually if you do not feel comfortable with those configurations.
- `platform.ini` corresponds to the PlatformIO project configuration.
- `main.c` is the first source code file in our project.

Let's get back to the steps, as follows:

1. Edit `main.c`, like this:

```
#include <stdio.h>
void app_main()
{
    printf("hello world\n");
    fflush(stdout);
}
```

app_main is the function where ESP-IDF passes the control to your application after the bootloader runs. Actually, there is a FreeRTOS task that calls app_main behind the scenes after the bootloader runs and the hardware initialization is completed. When this function returns, the calling task is deleted from the **real-time operating system (RTOS)** scheduler and the application ends. For more information about the boot process, see the following link: https://docs.espressif.com/projects/esp-idf/en/latest/esp32/api-guides/general-notes.html.

The printf output is directed to the serial port of the ESP32 board in the sdkconfig file by default, so we should be able to see the output over the serial port when we connect to it from any serial monitoring app. However, we are lucky in that PIO has one integrated that we will use for this purpose.

2. The default serial baud rate in the sdkconfig file is 115200, so we need to set the same value in the platform.ini file as for the monitoring. Here is the configuration to do this:

```
[env:az-delivery-devkit-v4]
platform = espressif32
board = az-delivery-devkit-v4
framework = espidf


monitor_speed = 115200
```

3. I've only added the last line to set the baud rate. The previous lines are generated based on my selections in the **Project Wizard** dialog box when I first created the project.

4. It's time to compile and upload the firmware. At the bottom of the IDE, there is another toolbar, where PlatformIO inserts its buttons for compiling, uploading, cleaning, and monitoring. You can see the toolbar in the following screenshot:

Figure 2.5 – The bottom toolbar

You can either compile your code first or, if you have your ESP32 devkit attached, you can choose to upload the code directly. PlatformIO will create the binary and flash the devkit if there is no error in your code. If there is an error, you will see it on the terminal. PlatformIO should detect the serial port that ESP32 is connected to automatically, but if it fails then you may need to check serial drivers for your development machine.

> **Tip**
> If you encounter any errors regarding CMake configuration while compiling, you can try to clean and recompile the project. Most of the time, this solves such compile errors. I suggest you keep this in mind while working on the examples throughout the book and apply it when necessary.

5. To connect the devkit serially, you can click on the **Serial Monitor** button of the bottom PlatformIO toolbar. It will start the **miniterm** serial monitoring tool that comes with PlatformIO, with the baud rate that we have specified in the `platformio.ini` configuration file. Press the reset button of the devkit to reboot it. After the bootloader messages, we finally see the output of our very first ESP32 application. Congratulations!

> **Tip**
> PlatformIO should detect the serial port automatically when you connect the devkit. If it doesn't, make sure the serial driver is installed properly and try another port if necessary. If you have two ESP32 devkits connected to your development PC, you can specify the port of the one that you work on by adding the `upload_port` directive into `platformio.ini`.

As we see, PlatformIO handles most tasks for us behind the scenes. It creates a neat folder structure, then downloads the ESP-IDF and its tools, and finally configures the project for the board type that we provide. With PlatformIO, we can directly get into coding without any configuration hassle. The next step is how to debug the application.

Debugging the application

ESP32 supports a **Joint Test Action Group (JTAG)** hardware interface as debugging technology. To be able to debug with JTAG, you need to have another type of hardware tool, named a **JTAG probe**. JTAG is an industry standard, so you can find many JTAG probes from different vendors in the market, but there is a list on the PlatformIO website about supported JTAG probes for ESP32. The list can be viewed here: `https://docs.platformio.org/en/latest/plus/debugging.html#tools-debug-probes`.

After obtaining one of those probes, you can use it to debug your application.

> **Important note**
>
> Wiring is important. Basically, a JTAG serial bus has four signals: **Test Clock (TCK)**, **Test Mode Select (TMS)**, **Test Data Input (TDI)**, and **Test Data Output (TDO)**. However, it doesn't mean all JTAG probes have the same type connector. You need to check the datasheet of your JTAG probe to understand how to connect it to your ESP32 devkit.

When you have connected your JTAG probe, you also need to specify it in the `platformio.ini` file—for example, this would be the configuration parameter for an **ESP-prog** JTAG probe:

```
debug_tool = esp-prog
```

Now, you're ready to debug your application. The only thing to do is to start the debug by pressing the **Run** button (*Ctrl + Shift + D*) of the VS Code IDE, and this will employ the PlatformIO debug for you. The PlatformIO debug integrates the **Open On-Chip Debugger (OpenOCD)** behind the scenes. OpenOCD corresponds to the software side of the JTAG hardware interface to manage the debugging process.

The rest is no different from any software debugging. You can put breakpoints, add variables to the watchlist, run the debug, and step in, step out, and step over, as all IDEs provide. Since it is an embedded application, you also need to see registers, memory, and disassembly of firmware, and this part is on the PlatformIO debug, as can be seen in the following screenshot:

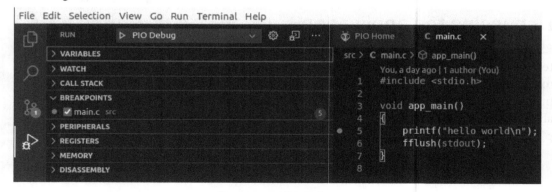

Figure 2.6 – PIO Debug

There is a nice tutorial about ESP32 debugging in the PlatformIO documentation here: `https://docs.platformio.org/en/latest/tutorials/espressif32/espidf_debugging_unit_testing_analysis.html`.

We have now learned how to create an ESP32 project in PlatformIO and debug the application, and we will apply these steps throughout the book. It is time to practice with an example.

Warming up – Basic I/O with buttons, pots, and LEDs

Fundamentally, a sensor is any device that generates some sort of output when exposed to a phenomenon—say, temperature, humidity, light, vibration, and so on. In our case, this output is an electrical signal. However, it is usually not possible to read this electrical signal directly by connecting to an input pin of a microcontroller, so sensor designers integrate another circuitry, called a signal conditioner, to filter this electrical signal and convert it into a form ready to be processed as input to the microcontroller.

Actuators are on the output side of IoT solutions. They change their state according to an analog or digital signal coming from the microcontroller and generate output to the environment. Some examples are a buzzer to make sound, an LED to emit light, a relay to switch on/off, or a motor to create motion.

The most basic skill with any embedded development is to use **general-purpose I/O (GPIO)** pins to read from sensors and control actuators. In the next example, we will configure ESP32 pins for I/O and use them.

> **Tip**
>
> Keep the pinout diagram of your devkit board close at hand all the time so that you can easily see which pin is where and see the functions of the pins, and so on. A pinout diagram shows pin numbers and designated functions of pins, which is quite handy as a quick reference during development.

Example: Turning an LED on/off by using a button

The goal of this example is to toggle the state of an LED when a button is pressed. Press the button, then the LED is on; another press, the LED is off. So, the button is the sensor in this example, and the LED is the actuator.

The hardware components are listed here:

- An LED, 5 **millimeters (mm)**
- A resistor, >220 ohm
- A tactile switch

Here is a *Fritzing* diagram of the circuitry:

Figure 2.7 – Fritzing diagram of the circuitry

The terminals of the button are connected to GPIO5 and GND. We will set the internal pull-up resistor of the GPIO5 pin while configuring it so that when the button is pressed, it will read a LOW value.

The LED is on GPIO2 as an output pin. We use a resistor to limit the current and protect the LED.

> **Tip**
> Make sure the shorter leg (cathode) of the LED is connected to the GND side and the longer leg (anode) is connected to GPIO2. If it is wired in reverse, it won't work.

Let's create a new PlatformIO project and edit the source code in main.c, as follows:

```c
#include <stddef.h>
#include "driver/gpio.h"
#include "freertos/FreeRTOS.h"
#include "freertos/task.h"
```

ESP-IDF defines the GPIO functionality, such as configuring pins, setting pin values, and attaching an **interrupt service routine (ISR)** to them to read values, in the driver/ gpio.h header file. Traditionally, function names in an ESP-IDF library start with their header filename, so we will see GPIO function names with the gpio prefix.

We also include two FreeRTOS headers to support our program with some timing functions for proper operation.

> **Important note**
>
> As we have discussed in *Chapter 1, Getting Started with ESP32*, FreeRTOS is the official RTOS supported by ESP-IDF, so we will use many functions of FreeRTOS in the examples, especially task management functions. We are going to talk about FreeRTOS in detail in *Chapter 4, A Deep Dive into the Advanced Features*, where there is a separate section devoted to it.

Next, some macros are defined to use the pins, as follows:

```
#define GPIO_LED 2
#define GPIO_LED_PIN_SEL (1ULL << GPIO_LED)
#define GPIO_BUTTON 5
#define GPIO_BUTTON_PIN_SEL (1ULL << GPIO_BUTTON)
#define ESP_INTR_FLAG_DEFAULT 0
```

We define the connected GPIOs for the LED and the button as well as the bit masks, to configure them in the hardware initialization. ESP_INTR_FLAG_DEFAULT is the ISR configuration flag with a default value of 0. The hardware initializing function comes next, as illustrated in the following code snippet:

```
static void button_handler(void *arg);

static void init_hw(void)
{
    gpio_config_t io_conf;

    io_conf.mode = GPIO_MODE_OUTPUT;
    io_conf.pin_bit_mask = GPIO_LED_PIN_SEL;
    io_conf.intr_type = GPIO_INTR_DISABLE;
    io_conf.pull_down_en = 0;
    io_conf.pull_up_en = 0;
    gpio_config(&io_conf);
```

```
    io_conf.mode = GPIO_MODE_INPUT;
    io_conf.pin_bit_mask = GPIO_BUTTON_PIN_SEL;
    io_conf.intr_type = GPIO_INTR_NEGEDGE;
    io_conf.pull_up_en = 1;
    gpio_config(&io_conf);

    gpio_install_isr_service(ESP_INTR_FLAG_DEFAULT);
    gpio_isr_handler_add(GPIO_BUTTON, button_handler, NULL);
}
```

In `init_hw`, I configured the LED as output and the button as input with its button-pressed handling ISR.

`gpio_config_t` is the structure that is used to set configuration parameters of a GPIO pin. First, I set the configuration values for the LED in the `io_conf` variable, which I passed as a parameter of the `gpio_config` library function to let ESP-IDF know about the LED pin configuration. Then, I used the same variable for the button configuration. The interesting point here is that I set the **internal pull-up resistor** to read a normally high value from the button GPIO pin. When the button is pressed, the signal goes from high to low since the other terminal is connected to the ground. This triggers the ISR because I configured the interrupt type as `GPIO_INTR_NEGEDGE`. You can say rising edge or any change as well.

> **Important note**
> Not all GPIO pins have internal pull-up or pull-down resistors. When you need to use them, please refer to the datasheet first.

Finally, I initialized the ISR service with the `gpio_install_isr_service` function and added the button handler with the `gpio_isr_handler_add` function. The add function requires the pin number, handling function, and parameter to the handling function as parameters so that when a pin change is detected as configured, the handling function is called by the ESP-IDF. So, let's define the `button_handler` function, as follows:

```
static TickType_t next = 0;
static bool led_state = false;

static void IRAM_ATTR button_handler(void *arg)
{
    TickType_t now = xTaskGetTickCountFromISR();
```

```
    if (now > next)
    {
        led_state = !led_state;
        gpio_set_level(GPIO_LED, led_state);
        next = now + 500 / portTICK_PERIOD_MS;
    }
}
```

While defining button_handler, we need to use the IRAM_ATTR attribute to instruct the compiler to place this piece of code in the internal **random-access memory (RAM)** of ESP32. The reason is that this function is an ISR and it must be short and quick as an interrupt handler, which implies that it has to be in the RAM when needed. Otherwise, the hardware will try to load code from the flash, which might cause your application to crash. This stems from how the ESP32 processor is designed.

xtaskGetTickCountFromISR is a function from the FreeRTOS task.h library. It returns a count of ticks since the FreeRTOS scheduler has started. We need this information to prevent a button-debouncing effect. Debouncing would cause flickering of the LED when we pressed the button, and we don't want this. The idea is to put a time buffer between two presses to make sure they are separate, intentional button presses rather than debouncing. There is a better solution to prevent this effect, but our solution is good enough for now. The time buffer is 500 **milliseconds (ms)** in our case. portTICK_PERIOD_MS tells us the value of the tick period in ms so that we can convert 500 ms to ESP32 ticks. This is defined in the ESP32 port of FreeRTOS.

If it is not a debounce, we invert the value of the led_state variable and call the gpio_set_level function to set the LED state with the new value, as follows:

```
void app_main()
{
    init_hw();

    vTaskSuspend(NULL);
}
```

We finish with the app_main function, which is called by the main application task of the ESP-IDF. First, we initialize the hardware by our init_hw function that we've implemented before, and then call the vTaskSuspend function of FreeRTOS to suspend the main task and prevent our application from exiting. That's it—you can now set up the hardware and upload the code to test the application. Enjoy it.

Example – LED dimmer

This example is about using a pot to adjust the brightness of an LED. The idea is to read the pot value, which is connected to an **analog-to-digital converter** (**ADC**) pin, and then dim the LED by using a **pulse-width modulation** (**PWM**) technique.

Analog-to-digital conversion is a basic technique in electronics to convert any analog signal, which is continuous, to a digital representation with a resolution. For example, an analog input voltage in a range of 0-3.3 V can be digitized by an ADC with a resolution of 10 bits, which provides a value between 0 and 1,023. ESP32 integrates two 12-bit ADCs with 18 channels (GPIO pins to connect an analog signal).

PWM creates the reverse effect. It is not a true **digital-to-analog conversion** (**DAC**), but when you generate a high-frequency digital signal and change its on-off ratio (duty cycle) in a unit of time, the output power is reduced by that ratio, so on an LED—for example—this creates a dimming effect. A 100% duty cycle means the output signal is on all the time, and 50% means it is on only half of the time. You can also use PWM to control **direct current** (**DC**) motors. On ESP32, all output pins support PWM.

Let's try these techniques on ESP32. The hardware components are listed here:

- An LED and a resistor (>220 ohm) to protect it

- A pot

The *Fritzing* diagram of the circuitry looks like this:

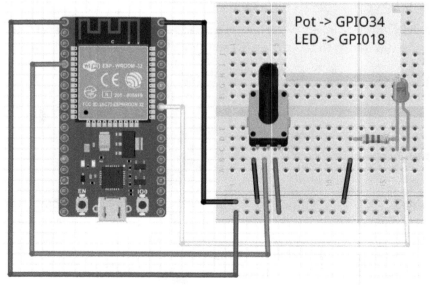

Figure 2.8 – Fritzing diagram of the circuitry

We can now create a new PlatformIO project and edit `main.c` to develop the application, as follows:

```
#include <stdio.h>
#include <stdlib.h>
#include "freertos/FreeRTOS.h"
#include "freertos/task.h"
#include "driver/adc.h"
#include "driver/ledc.h"
```

There are two new header files included. `driver/adc.h` is for the ADC definitions and functions (hence the name), and `driver/ledc.h` is for the PWM control of LEDs or motors. The global variables and macro definitions can be seen in the following snippet:

```
#define SAMPLE_CNT 32
static const adc1_channel_t adc_channel = ADC_CHANNEL_6;


#define LEDC_GPIO 18
static ledc_channel_config_t ledc_channel;
```

In this example, we will use `ADC_CHANNEL_6` of the **ADC-1 unit** for sampling the pot. This channel corresponds to the **GPIO34** pin of my devkit board. To have a better approximation, we will not read a single value from the ADC channel, but rather get `SAMPLE_CNT` samples in a single run and then calculate the average.

Then, we define the LED control channel, `ledc_channel`, and the GPIO pin to use with it, as follows:

```
static void init_hw(void)
{
    adc1_config_width(ADC_WIDTH_BIT_10);
    adc1_config_channel_atten(adc_channel, ADC_ATTEN_DB_11);

    ledc_timer_config_t ledc_timer = {
        .duty_resolution = LEDC_TIMER_10_BIT,
        .freq_hz = 1000,
        .speed_mode = LEDC_HIGH_SPEED_MODE,
        .timer_num = LEDC_TIMER_0,
        .clk_cfg = LEDC_AUTO_CLK,
    };
```

```
    ledc_timer_config(&ledc_timer);

    ledc_channel.channel = LEDC_CHANNEL_0;
    ledc_channel.duty = 0;
    ledc_channel.gpio_num = LEDC_GPIO;
    ledc_channel.speed_mode = LEDC_HIGH_SPEED_MODE;
    ledc_channel.hpoint = 0;
    ledc_channel.timer_sel = LEDC_TIMER_0;
    ledc_channel_config(&ledc_channel);
}
```

In the init_hw function, we will initialize the ADC and the LED control channel.

First, we set the capture width of the ADC-1 unit to ADC_WIDTH_BIT_10, which means the readings will be in the range of 0-1,023. The maximum resolution is 12 bits, so we will use 2^12 values for ADC sampling. Then, the channel attenuation is configured to support 3.3 V input by passing the value of ADC_ATTEN_DB_11 since the third terminal of the pot is connected to 3.3 V of the devkit board. The ADC configuration was easy.

To configure the LED control channel we need to use a timer, as expected. LEDC_TIMER_0 will be used for this purpose, providing 1,000 **hertz (Hz)** frequency to drive the LED. We have also configured the duty cycle resolution to 10 bits so that we can use the pot reading directly to set the duty cycle value with that reading. The maximum resolution here is 20 bits.

> **Important note**
> ESP32 has four 64-bit hardware timers with 16-bit prescalers and up/down counters.

Then comes the LED control channel configuration. This is LEDC_CHANNEL_0 (eight channels are available in total) on LEDC_GPIO, which is GPIO18 and uses LEDC_TIMER_0, which we have configured before. Now, the hardware is ready and we can use it to achieve the goal, as follows:

```
void app_main()
{
    init_hw();
```

```
    while (1)
    {
        uint32_t adc_val = 0;
        for (int i = 0; i < SAMPLE_CNT; ++i)
        {
            adc_val += adc1_get_raw(adc_channel);
        }
        adc_val /= SAMPLE_CNT;

        ledc_set_duty(ledc_channel.speed_mode, ledc_channel.
channel, adc_val);
        ledc_update_duty(ledc_channel.speed_mode, ledc_channel.
channel);

        vTaskDelay(500 / portTICK_RATE_MS);
    }
}
```

In the app_main function, we first initialize the hardware as always, by calling init_hw. Then, the while loop starts. In the loop, we get samples from the ADC channel with the help of the adc1_get_raw function and calculate the average to have a better approximation. We use this average value to set the duty cycle of the LED control channel (ledc_set_duty). This setting, however, doesn't take effect until we update the channel for that duty cycle (ledc_update_duty).

After these basic examples of I/O systems, we're ready to get into sensors.

Working with sensors

To relate to the physical world, we use sensors. For example, a button or a pot are sensors, but when we need to measure different phenomena—let's say temperature—we can use a temperature sensor with a more advanced communication interface rather than a simple GPIO or ADC interface. In this section, we'll cover plenty of sensors with different communication interfaces to get familiar with those interfaces. Let's start with a popular temperature and humidity sensor, **DHT11**.

Reading ambient temperature and humidity with DHT11

DHT11 is a basic temperature and humidity sensor with a very low price tag. The operational voltage is between 3 and 5 V, so we can use it by directly connecting to our ESP32 without a need for a level shifter. The temperature range is 0-50°C, with ±2°C accuracy and 1°C resolution. We can also use it to measure humidity between 20% and 90% with ±5% accuracy. It already comes calibrated, so we don't need to worry about calibration. It also incorporates a simple 8-bit processor, which enables it to implement a basic single-wire serial communication protocol. The following figure shows a DHT11 module that you can find online:

Figure 2.9 – DHT11 module

It has three pins for **ground (GND)**, **Voltage Common Collector (VCC)**, and signal. We use that signal pin to communicate with it. Let's use it in a simple example. The hardware components are listed here:

- DHT11 module
- Active buzzer module

I have a sensor kit from ELEGOO with many different types of sensors. These two modules come with it, but you can use any such modules you have to hand. You can see the following *Fritzing* diagram for connections:

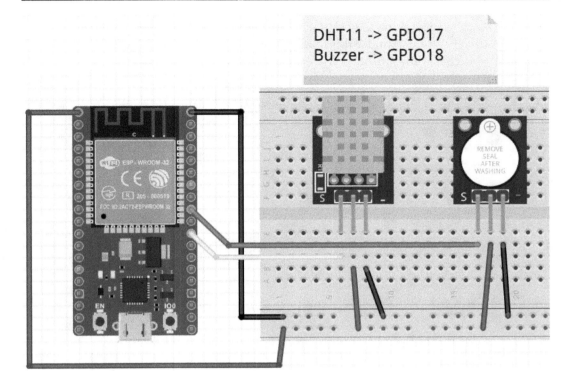

Figure 2.10 – Fritzing diagram of DHT11 example

We will use an external library for DHT11 communication. This is included in the book repository and can be found at this link: `https://github.com/PacktPublishing/Internet-of-Things-with-ESP32/tree/main/common/esp-idf-lib`.

The original library is here: `https://github.com/UncleRus/esp-idf-lib`. It is a great work by many developers for the community.

In this example, we are going to read temperature and humidity values from the DHT11 module, and if any of those values exceed the threshold, the buzzer will start an alarm sound pattern.

After creating the PlatformIO project, we first need to edit the `platformio.ini` file to set the serial monitor baud rate and the external library, as follows:

```
monitor_speed = 115200
lib_extra_dirs =
    ../../esp-idf-lib/components
```

The lib_extra_dirs option tells PlatformIO where to search for external libraries. The DHT11 driver is located under this folder. Now, we can proceed with the code in the main.c source file, as follows:

```
#include <stdio.h>
#include <freertos/FreeRTOS.h>
#include <freertos/task.h>
#include <dht.h>
#include "driver/gpio.h"

#define DHT11_PIN 17
#define BUZZER_PIN 18
#define BUZZER_PIN_SEL (1ULL << BUZZER_PIN)

#define HUM_THRESHOLD 800
#define TEMP_THRESHOLD 250

static void init_hw(void)
{
    gpio_config_t io_conf;

    io_conf.mode = GPIO_MODE_OUTPUT;
    io_conf.pin_bit_mask = BUZZER_PIN_SEL;
    io_conf.intr_type = GPIO_INTR_DISABLE;
    io_conf.pull_down_en = 0;
    io_conf.pull_up_en = 0;
    gpio_config(&io_conf);
}
```

We include the dht.h header file to use DHT11. driver/gpio.h is only for the buzzer configuration. DHT11 returns 10 times of the ambient values it measures, so HUM_THRESHOLD and TEMP_THRESHOLD values denote 10 times of the actual threshold values for easy comparison—so, 80% of humidity and 25°C temperature are the threshold values in our program. In the init_hw function, we only initialize BUZZER_PIN for alarm output. We do not have any specific DHT11 initialization functions in the library.

Next comes a function to generate an alarm sound as in the following snippet:

```
static void beep(void *arg)
{
    int cnt = 2 * (int)arg;
    bool state = true;
    for (int i = 0; i < cnt; ++i, state = !state)
    {
        gpio_set_level(BUZZER_PIN, state);
        vTaskDelay(100 / portTICK_PERIOD_MS);
    }
    vTaskDelete(NULL);
}
```

beep simply sets the BUZZER_PIN level to on and off every 100 ms for a given number of times in the function parameter. This function will be called from a FreeRTOS task every time a threshold is exceeded, and it deletes the task when the job is finished.

Then, we check the alarm state. The code is shown in the following snippet:

```
static int16_t temperature;
static bool temp_alarm = false;
static int16_t humidity;
static bool hum_alarm =false;

static void check_alarm(void)
{
    bool is_alarm = temperature >= TEMP_THRESHOLD;
    bool run_beep = is_alarm && !temp_alarm;
    temp_alarm = is_alarm;
    if (run_beep)
    {
        xTaskCreate(beep, "beep", configMINIMAL_STACK_SIZE,
(void *)3, 5, NULL);
        return;
    }

    is_alarm = humidity >= HUM_THRESHOLD;
    run_beep = is_alarm && !hum_alarm;
```

```
    hum_alarm = is_alarm;
    if (run_beep)
    {
        xTaskCreate(beep, "beep", configMINIMAL_STACK_SIZE,
(void *)2, 5, NULL);
    }
}
```

We have four global variables to hold ambient readings and alarm states. The
check_alarm function checks for a new alarm for both temperate and humidity, and
if there is one, it then creates a new beep task by calling the xTaskCreate function
of FreeRTOS. It takes six parameters for the following:

- Function to be called.
- Task name.
- Task local stack size in bytes. We need to reserve enough memory to run a task
  properly.
- Function parameter(s).
- Task priority.
- A pointer for the task handle, if needed. For this example, we don't need to keep
  track of beep tasks—just fire and forget.

We will discuss the FreeRTOS functions in detail in the next chapter. Let's continue with
the app_main function, as follows:

```
int app_main()
{
    init_hw();

    while (1)
    {
        if (dht_read_data(DHT_TYPE_DHT11, (gpio_num_t)DHT11_
PIN, &humidity, &temperature) == ESP_OK)
        {
            printf("Humidity: %d%% Temp: %dC\n", humidity / 10,
temperature / 10);
            check_alarm();
        }
        else
```

```
        {
            printf("Could not read data from sensor\n");
        }
        vTaskDelay(2000 / portTICK_PERIOD_MS);
    }
}
```

In the app_main function, we do initialization with init_hw and then start a while loop to read from the DHT11 sensor periodically. dht_read_data is the function to do that. It needs a DHT sensor type (which is DHT_TYPE_DHT11 in our project), the GPIO pin that the sensor is connected to, and the addresses of the variables to write readings. It returns ESP_OK if all goes well and we print the values on the serial port, then check for an alarm case. Lastly, we set a 2-second delay between readings.

> **Important note**
>
> The sampling rate of DHT11 should not exceed 1 Hz (that is, one reading per second). Otherwise, the sensor gets hot and the readings will be inaccurate.

DHT11 is a low-cost, easy-to-use temperature sensor but when we need a higher resolution, we can use DS18B20, as in the following example.

Using DS18B20 as temperature sensor

DS18B20 is a high-resolution, programmable thermometer from Maxim Integrated. Its measurement range is -55°C to +125°C and it provides ±0.5°C accuracy between -10°C and +85°C, which makes it a strong candidate for many types of applications. DS18B20 uses a **1-Wire** bus system and communication protocol with 64-bit addressing so that multiple DS18B20s can share the same communication line.

It is manufactured in different packages. The following figure shows a DS18B20 sensor in a TO-92 package:

Figure 2.11 – DS18B20 sensor

In this example, we simply scan a line to find out connected DS18B20 sensors and then query them to get temperature readings. The hardware components are listed as follows:

- DS18B20 sensor. I will use a single DS18B20 module from my ELEGOO kit, but you can connect many sensors on the same bus if you have them.

- A 4.7 kΩ pull-up resistor for the data leg of the sensor.

A driver exists in the same external library from the previous example. We are going to include it to drive the sensor. Here is the link for the library: `https://github.com/PacktPublishing/Internet-of-Things-with-ESP32/tree/main/common/esp-idf-lib`.

You can see the connections in the following *Fritzing* diagram:

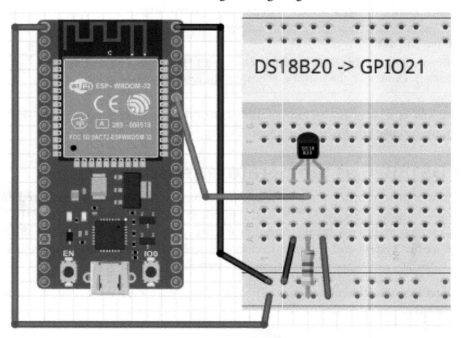

Figure 2.12 – DS18B20 connections

After setting up the circuitry, we can continue with the code. First, we edit the `platformio.ini` file and add the external library path, as follows:

```
monitor_speed = 115200
lib_extra_dirs =
    ../../esp-idf-lib/components
```

Now, we can write our application in `main.c`, like this:

```c
#include <stdio.h>
#include <freertos/FreeRTOS.h>
#include <freertos/task.h>
#include <ds18x20.h>


#define SENSOR_PIN 21


#define MAX_SENSORS 8
static ds18x20_addr_t addrs[MAX_SENSORS];
static int sensor_count = 0;
static float temps[MAX_SENSORS];
```

We include the `ds18x20.h` header file for the driver functions and type definitions. For instance, `ds18x20_addr_t` is the type for addressing, which is simply a 64-bit unsigned integer defined in this header file.

In our example, we allocate arrays of size 8 to hold addresses and temperature readings. Then, the hardware initialization is as follows:

```c
static void init_hw(void)
{
    while (sensor_count == 0)
    {
        sensor_count = ds18x20_scan_devices((gpio_num_t)SENSOR_PIN, addrs, MAX_SENSORS);
        vTaskDelay(1000 / portTICK_PERIOD_MS);
    }
    if (sensor_count > MAX_SENSORS)
    {
        sensor_count = MAX_SENSORS;
    }
}
```

In the `init_hw` function, we scan the 1-wire bus for sensors by calling `ds18x20_scan_devices`. This takes the GPIO pin where the sensors are connected and fills the `addrs` array with sensor addresses. Now, we can define the `app_main` function as illustrated in the following code snippet:

```
void app_main()
{
    init_hw();

    while (1)
    {
        ds18x20_measure_and_read_multi((gpio_num_t)SENSOR_PIN,
addrs, sensor_count, temps);
        for (int i = 0; i < sensor_count; i++)
        {
            printf("sensor-id: %08x temp: %fC\n", (uint32_t)
addrs[i], temps[i]);
        }

        vTaskDelay(1000 / portTICK_PERIOD_MS);
    }
}
```

The `app_main` function contains a `while` loop where we read from the sensors. The name of the library function to query temperature values from the sensors is `ds18x20_measure_and_read_multi`, and this takes the GPIO pin where all sensors are connected, along with the addresses and the array to store readings.

> **Tip**
> If you have a single DS18B20 sensor connected to your ESP32 then you can use another function from this library, named `ds18x20_read_temperature`, with the sensor address of `ds18x20_ANY`. This eliminates the need of a bus scan to discover addresses.

Sensing light with TSL2561

If we want to measure ambient light level, then we can use **TSL2561** from AMS. It provides illuminance in lux over the **Inter-Integrated Circuit** (I²C or IIC) interface to the connected microcontroller with 16-bit resolution. There are many example use cases, such as automatic keyboard illumination where optimum viewing condition is needed.

I²C is another serial communication bus that supports multiple devices on the same line. Devices on the bus use 7-bit addressing. Two lines are needed for the I²C interface: clock (CLK) and serial data (SDA). The master device provides the clock to the bus.

An example light sensor is shown in the following figure:

Figure 2.13 – Adafruit TSL2561 light sensor

In this example, we are going to set the LED level according to the ambient light-level data coming from a TSL2561 module—a high level of ambient light, low LED duty, and vice versa. The hardware components are listed here:

- A TSL2561 module (for example, from Adafruit)
- An LED
- 330 ohm resistor

The following *Fritzing* diagram shows the connections in our setup:

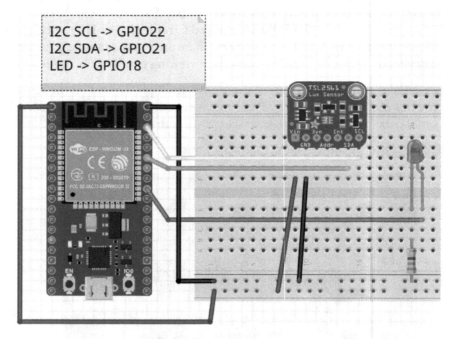

Figure 2.14 – Fritzing diagram of TSL2561 example

Let's code the application. As always, we first update `platformio.ini` for any additional settings, as follows:

```
monitor_speed = 115200
lib_extra_dirs =
  ../../esp-idf-lib/components

build_flags =
  -DCONFIG_I2CDEV_TIMEOUT=100000
```

This time, in addition to the external library path, we add a CONFIG_I2CDEV_TIMEOUT definition as a build flag required by the TSL2561 library. After updating the `platformio.ini` file, we can continue with our program, as follows:

```
#include <stdio.h>
#include <string.h>
#include <freertos/FreeRTOS.h>
#include <freertos/task.h>
```

```
#include <tsl2561.h>
#include "driver/ledc.h"


#define SDA_GPIO 21
#define SCL_GPIO 22
#define ADDR TSL2561_I2C_ADDR_FLOAT
static tsl2561_t light_sensor;


#define LEDC_GPIO 18
static ledc_channel_config_t ledc_channel;
```

The tsl2561.h header file contains all definitions and functionality to drive a TSL2561 sensor. We use GPIO21 as the I²C data pin and GPIO22 as the I²C clock, as designated pins of the devkit board. The I²C address is defined as TSL2561_I2C_ADDR_FLOAT and we access the sensor through a variable of type tsl2561_t.

> **Important note**
>
> A TSL2561 sensor can have three different I²C addresses. It is determined by the status of the ADDR-SEL pin of the sensor, and can be connected to either VCC, GND, or left float.

Then, we define the hardware initialization function as in the following code snippet:

```
static void init_hw(void)
{
    i2cdev_init();


    memset(&light_sensor, 0, sizeof(tsl2561_t));
    light_sensor.i2c_dev.timeout_ticks = 0xffff / portTICK_
PERIOD_MS;


    tsl2561_init_desc(&light_sensor, ADDR, 0, SDA_GPIO, SCL_
GPIO);
    tsl2561_init(&light_sensor);


    ledc_timer_config_t ledc_timer = {
        .duty_resolution = LEDC_TIMER_10_BIT,
        .freq_hz = 1000,
```

```
        .speed_mode = LEDC_HIGH_SPEED_MODE,
        .timer_num = LEDC_TIMER_0,
        .clk_cfg = LEDC_AUTO_CLK,
    };
    ledc_timer_config(&ledc_timer);

    ledc_channel.channel = LEDC_CHANNEL_0;
    ledc_channel.duty = 0;
    ledc_channel.gpio_num = LEDC_GPIO;
    ledc_channel.speed_mode = LEDC_HIGH_SPEED_MODE;
    ledc_channel.hpoint = 0;
    ledc_channel.timer_sel = LEDC_TIMER_0;
    ledc_channel_config(&ledc_channel);
}
```

The initialization of TSL2561 requires several steps. First, we initialize the I²C bus with the i2cdev_init function and set its timeout_ticks field to 0xffff in ms. Then, we call the tsl2561_init_desc and tsl2561_init functions to initialize the TSL2561 sensor itself. The tsl2561_init_desc function takes the sensor address and I²C pins as parameters to communicate with the sensor. Next, we initialize the LED pin as PWM output (ledc_channel_config_t) in order to control its brightness.

We also need a function to set the LED brightness. Here it is:

```
static void set_led(uint32_t lux)
{
    uint32_t duty = 1023;
    if (lux > 50)
    {
        duty = 0;
    }
    else if (lux > 20)
    {
        duty /= 2;
    }
```

```
    ledc_set_duty(ledc_channel.speed_mode, ledc_channel.
channel, duty);
    ledc_update_duty(ledc_channel.speed_mode, ledc_channel.
channel);
}
```

In the set_led function, we change the brightness of the LED according to its lux parameter. For lux levels higher than 50, we set the duty variable to 0 so that the LED turns off. If the lux level is more than 20, then half duty, else full duty for full brightness of the LED. You can play with the lux value comparisons according to your ambient light to get a better result.

Lastly, we define the app_main function. The code is shown in the following snippet:

```
void app_main()
{
    init_hw();

    uint32_t lux;
    while (1)
    {
        vTaskDelay(500 / portTICK_PERIOD_MS);
        if (tsl2561_read_lux(&light_sensor, &lux) == ESP_OK)
        {
            printf("Lux: %u\n", lux);
            set_led(lux);
        }
    }
}
```

The while loop of the app_main function is where we read from the light sensor periodically and set the LED brightness. The tsl2561_read_lux function sets the lux parameter value when called.

That's it. We can add light-sensing capability to our IoT device with a TSL2561 sensor, as we did in this example. The next example uses another popular I²C device: BME280.

Employing BME280 in your project

BME280 is a high-resolution temperature, humidity, and barometric pressure sensor from Bosch. The temperature range is -40°C-85 °C with ±1.0 °C accuracy, the humidity range is 0-100% with ±3% accuracy, and the pressure range is 300-1100 **hectopascal pressure unit (hPa)** with ±1.0 hPa accuracy. It supports both **Serial Peripheral Interface (SPI)** and I²C communication interfaces. It can be operated in three different modes, as follows:

- Sleep mode
- Normal mode
- Forced mode

In sleep mode, measurements are disabled and its power consumption is as low as 0.1 µA. Therefore, it is a good option for battery-operated devices such as smart watches since its power mode can be programmatically controllable.

There are many BME280 modules on the market, so you can buy and use any of them in your projects. A BME280 module is shown in the following figure:

Figure 2.15 – A BME280 module

In this example, we are going to read from BME280 and print it on the serial monitor of PlatformIO. The only hardware component is a BME280 module. The following *Fritzing* diagram shows the connections:

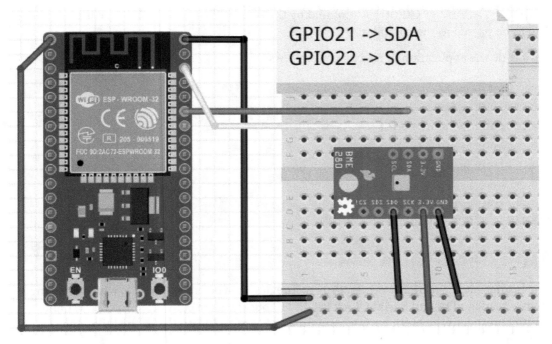

Figure 2.16 – Fritzing diagram of BME280 example

We are ready to continue with the application. After creating the project, we need to update the platformio.ini file, as follows:

```
[env:az-delivery-devkit-v4]
platform = espressif32
board = az-delivery-devkit-v4
framework = espidf

monitor_speed = 115200
lib_extra_dirs =
    ../../esp-idf-lib/components

build_flags =
    -DCONFIG_I2CDEV_TIMEOUT=100000
```

CONFIG_I2CDEV_TIMEOUT is required by the sensor library, and we define it as a build flag to be passed to the compiler.

Let's code the application in main.c, as follows:

```
#include <stdio.h>
#include <freertos/FreeRTOS.h>
#include <freertos/task.h>
#include <bmp280.h>
#include <string.h>


#define SDA_GPIO 21
#define SCL_GPIO 22


static bmp280_t temp_sensor;
```

The header file for BME280 is bmp280.h. The device type is bmp280_t, which is defined in this header. SDA and **Serial Clock (SCL)** I²C bus lines are connected to GPIO21 and GPIO22 respectively. Next, we initialize the hardware, as illustrated in the following code snippet:

```
static void init_hw(void)
{
    i2cdev_init();

    memset(&temp_sensor, 0, sizeof(bmp280_t));
    temp_sensor.i2c_dev.timeout_ticks = 0xffff / portTICK_
PERIOD_MS;

    bmp280_params_t params;
    bmp280_init_default_params(&params);

    bmp280_init_desc(&temp_sensor, BMP280_I2C_ADDRESS_0, 0,
SDA_GPIO, SCL_GPIO);
    bmp280_init(&temp_sensor, &params);
}
```

In the hardware initialization function, we first initialize the I²C bus with `i2cdev_init`, and then the sensor. The `bmp280_init_desc` function sets the I²C parameters of the BME280 module by passing the address and the I²C pins. Then, the default parameters are set in `bmp280_init`—these are the normal power mode operation and the 4 Hz sampling rate (one reading in 250 ms) in this library.

> **Important note**
> There are two I²C addressing options for BME280, for when the SDO pin of BME280 is connected to GND and for when it is connected to VCC. In this example, it is connected to GND.

Now, we can code the `app_main` function, as follows:

```
void app_main()
{
    init_hw();

    float pressure, temperature, humidity;
    while (1)
    {
        vTaskDelay(500 / portTICK_PERIOD_MS);
        if (bmp280_read_float(&temp_sensor, &temperature,
&pressure, &humidity) == ESP_OK)
        {
            printf("%.2f Pa, %.2f C, %.2f %%\n", pressure,
temperature, humidity);
        }
    }
}
```

In the `app_main` function, we simply read values from the BME280 module by calling `bmp280_read_float`, and print on the serial monitor every 500 ms.

This was the last example for sensor devices. In the next section, we are going to use actuators.

Working with actuators

An IoT device acts on the physical world by using actuators, hence the name. The device generates an output as decided by the internal states of the application, which can be a reading from a sensor or a scheduled operation. The trigger for an action can also be an external command received from an external entity such as another device in the network, or perhaps its human user with a mobile application. Let's start with relays.

Using an electromechanical relay to control switching

An **electromechanical relay** (**EMR**) is an electronic device that switches its output on and off according to its input control signal. The input signal level is low voltage, so it can be driven by using a microcontroller unit or a **system on a chip** (**SoC**), such as ESP32. The output of an EMR is electrically isolated from its input and switches' high-voltage/ high-current load connected to it. The power source of the load can be **alternating current** (**AC**) and/or DC. It is possible to control the power source of a home appliance by using an EMR. Most **solid-state drives** (**SSDs**) specify their I/O specifications on their packages, so it is easy to understand what you can drive with it when you have one at hand. For example, I have the following EMR module that comes within an ELEGOO sensor kit:

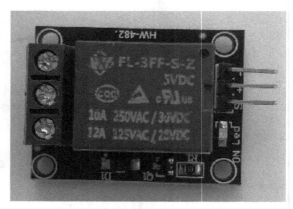

Figure 2.17 – An EMR module

As we can see in *Figure 2.17*, this EMR can drive a 10A/250VAC or 10A/30VDC load with a 5 V input control signal.

Important note

An EMR is used to drive high voltage/high current loads, therefore take maximum precaution while using it. Make sure it is not connected to the mains while setting up any circuitry—there is no short circuit and there are no open wires on the high-voltage end for your safety.

In this example, we will use this EMR module to simply switch on and off without connecting any load, to stay safe. It is easy to understand whether switching has been successful or not because the EMR makes a click sound when it flips its output. The hardware components of the example are listed here:

- An EMR module
- A 5 V power module
- A level converter for 5V-3.3 V logic-level conversion
- A **passive infrared** (**PIR**) motion detection module

The goal of the example is to have an application in order to switch the relay on when a move is detected from a PIR motion detection sensor. The following *Fritzing* diagram shows the connections:

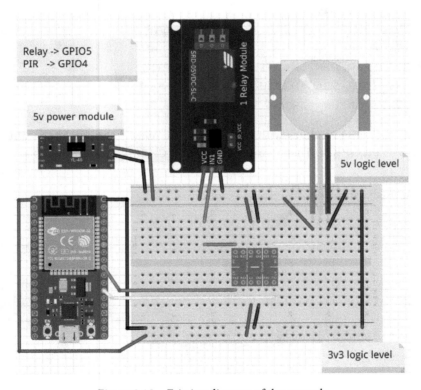

Figure 2.18 – Fritzing diagram of the example

This diagram requires some explanation. We need to divide the breadboard into two parts for two logic levels, 3.3 V and 5 V. ESP32 operates at a 3.3 V logic level. On the other hand, the relay module and the PIR module need a 5 V logic level to operate. Therefore, the 3.3 V – 5 V logic converter in the middle connects to the ESP32 devkit on the 3.3 V end and to the relay and PIR modules on the 5 V end. We need an extra 5 V power supply for the modules.

After setting up this circuitry, we can move on to the coding, as follows:

```
#include <stddef.h>
#include "freertos/FreeRTOS.h"
#include "freertos/task.h"
#include "driver/gpio.h"


#define RELAY_PIN 4
#define GPIO_RELAY_PIN_SEL (1ULL << RELAY_PIN)
#define PIR_PIN 5
#define GPIO_PIR_PIN_SEL (1ULL << PIR_PIN)
#define ESP_INTR_FLAG_DEFAULT 0
#define STATE_CHECK_PERIOD 10000
```

We are going to drive the modules with GPIO pins. The relay is connected to GPIO4 and the PIR module is on GPIO5. Then, we define `STATE_CHECK_PERIOD` as 10 seconds for relay.

We implement the hardware initialization as follows:

```
static void pir_handler(void *arg);


static void init_hw(void)
{
    gpio_config_t io_conf;

    io_conf.mode = GPIO_MODE_OUTPUT;
    io_conf.pin_bit_mask = GPIO_RELAY_PIN_SEL;
    io_conf.intr_type = GPIO_INTR_DISABLE;
    io_conf.pull_down_en = 0;
    io_conf.pull_up_en = 0;
    gpio_config(&io_conf);
```

```
    io_conf.mode = GPIO_MODE_INPUT;
    io_conf.pin_bit_mask = GPIO_PIR_PIN_SEL;
    io_conf.intr_type = GPIO_INTR_POSEDGE;
    io_conf.pull_up_en = 1;
    gpio_config(&io_conf);

    gpio_install_isr_service(ESP_INTR_FLAG_DEFAULT);
    gpio_isr_handler_add(PIR_PIN, pir_handler, NULL);
}
```

The next thing is to configure the pins in the `init_hw` function. The PIR pin is for input and the relay pin is for output. We also configure an ISR service handler for the PIR sensor, `pir_handler`, which is called when a motion is detected, as illustrated in the following code snippet:

```
static TickType_t next = 0;
const TickType_t period = STATE_CHECK_PERIOD / portTICK_PERIOD_
MS;

static void IRAM_ATTR pir_handler(void *arg)
{
    TickType_t now = xTaskGetTickCountFromISR();

    if (now > next)
    {
        gpio_set_level(RELAY_PIN, 1);
    }
    next = now + period;
}
```

The `next` global variable denotes the tick time for opening the relay. `pir_handler` pushes it forward every time it is called. If the current time, `now`, has already passed `next`, it switches the relay on. The `xtaskGetTickCountFromISR` function of FreeRTOS is used to get the current tick time.

We also need to implement a function to switch the relay off. The code is illustrated in the following snippet:

```
static void open_relay(void *arg)
{
    while (1)
    {
        TickType_t now = xTaskGetTickCount();
        if (now > next)
        {
            gpio_set_level(RELAY_PIN, 0);
            vTaskDelay(period);
        }
        else
        {
            vTaskDelay(next - now);
        }
    }
}
```

The open_relay function monitors the next value to decide whether to switch the relay off. If the time is over, then the relay pin level is set to 0. The xtaskGetTickCount function of FreeRTOS is used this time to get the current time since the call is from a task, not from an ISR.

Finally, we develop the app_main function. The code is illustrated in the following snippet:

```
void app_main()
{
    init_hw();
    xTaskCreate(open_relay, "openrl", configMINIMAL_STACK_SIZE,
NULL, 5, NULL);
}
```

app_main simply calls the init_hw function and passes the control to open_relay by creating a FreeRTOS task.

The second actuator example is to use a stepper motor, in the next section.

Running a stepper motor

There are many different types of motors grouped in terms of technology and use cases. One of them is a stepper motor. Stepper motors are used where precise positioning and speed control are needed, such as with printers, plotters, or **computer numerical control** (**CNC**). There is an additional component to drive a stepper motor—an open-loop stepper driver chip in between the stepper motor and a microcontroller unit. The microcontroller commands that stepper driver chip to set the intended position and speed. A drawback of a stepper motor is that it always draws the maximum current to operate regardless of whether it is rotating or not, so the power source is an important factor to use it effectively. The following figure shows a stepper motor that you can buy online:

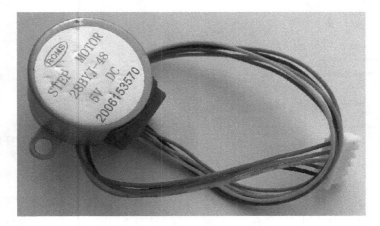

Figure 2.19 – 28BYJ-48 stepper motor

In this example, we will drive a stepper motor with a rotary encoder. You can think of a rotary encoder as a positional sensor that provides direction (clockwise or counter-clockwise) and position in that direction as step counts. The following figure shows a rotary encoder:

Figure 2.20 – A rotary encoder

The hardware components of this example are listed here:

- A 28BYJ-48 stepper motor

- An A4988 motor driver module

- A pull-up resistor (4.7 k ohm)

- A decoupling capacitor (100uF)—this is optional

- A rotary encoder

Before coding, we need to set up the circuitry as usual. The *Fritzing* diagram of the circuitry is shown here:

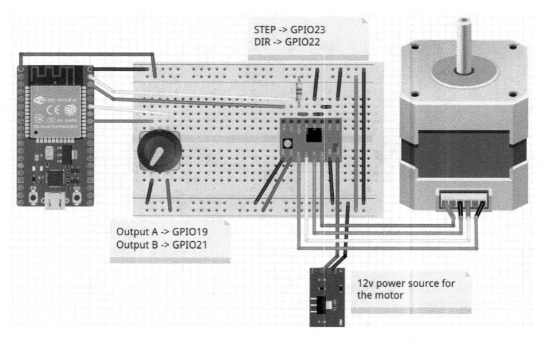

STEP -> GPIO23
DIR -> GPIO22

Output A -> GPIO19
Output B -> GPIO21

12v power source for the motor

Figure 2.21 – Fritzing diagram of the stepper-motor circuitry

We see the rotary encoder on the left part of the breadboard. A rotary encoder provides two outputs to a microcontroller: **Output A** (or **CLK**) and **Output B** (or **DT**). By reading those outputs from the connected GPIO pins of the microcontroller, we can understand the direction and the position of the rotary encoder. The connections of the rotary encoder in this diagram are listed here:

- Output A to GPIO19

- Output B to GPIO21

The other module on the breadboard is the A4988 motor driver module. It is not possible to drive any motor directly by any of the pins of a microcontroller because of the power requirements of motors. We use an intermediary chip for this purpose, which is called a motor driver chip. It provides interfaces for both the microcontroller and the motor. The connections of the motor driver module for the ESP32 are listed here:

- Pin-1 (EN) to LOW
- Pin-2 (MS1) , Pin-3 (MS2), and Pin-4 (MS3) to LOW
- Pin-5 (RST) and Pin-6 (SLP) to HIGH
- Pin-7 (STEP) to ESP32/GPIO23
- Pin-8 (DIR) to ESP32/GPIO22
- Pin-9 (GND) to GND
- Pin-10 (VDD) to 3.3 V

For the motor side connections, we basically need to check the datasheet of the motor or working examples online. There are different color codes for the coils of different stepper motors. For our case, (28BYJ-48) the following applies:

- Pin-11 (1B) to motor/orange
- Pin-12 (1A) to motor/yellow
- Pin-13 (2A) to motor/pink
- Pin-14 (2B) to motor/blue
- Pin-15 (GND) to GND
- Pin-16 (VMOT) to 12 V

There are some important precautions that we need to take before using the A4988 motor driver module, which are outlined here:

- Make sure the motor is connected (four pins) correctly and firmly to the module pins before powering on or using the A4988 module.
- The module has a current-limiting feature. It has a pot on it to set the current limit. The datasheet of the module explains how to use this pot with the correct settings for your motor. A safe value of the reference voltage is around 0.10 V.

- You can put a decoupling capacitor, typically 100 uF, between VMOT and GND to protect the module from voltage spikes. If you are using a well-regulated power source, then you might not need it.

- A heatsink can be attached onto the A4988 chip to protect it from overheating. Usually, it is delivered with the module.

After our hardware setup is ready, we can continue with the project. Before starting to develop the application, we need a library from the GitHub repository to be copied under the project lib directory. It is the rotenc library to drive the rotary encoder. You can download the library files from this link if you haven't cloned the whole repository before: https://github.com/PacktPublishing/Internet-of-Things-with-ESP32/tree/main/ch2/rotenc_motor_ex/lib/rotenc.

Let's edit the application in main.c, as follows:

```
#include <stdio.h>
#include <stddef.h>
#include "driver/gpio.h"
#include "freertos/FreeRTOS.h"
#include "freertos/task.h"
#include "rotenc.h"
#include "driver/mcpwm.h"
#include "soc/mcpwm_periph.h"


#define ROTENC_CLK_PIN 19
#define ROTENC_DT_PIN 21


#define MOTOR_DIR_PIN 22
#define MOTOR_STEP_PIN 23
```

We include the necessary header files and define the pins. The rotary encoder driver functionality is defined in the rotenc.h file. To drive the motor, we will use the **Motor Control PWM (MCPWM)** library of ESP-IDF.

Then, we initialize the hardware. The code can be seen in the following snippet:

```
static void init_hw(void)
{
    rotenc_init(ROTENC_CLK_PIN, ROTENC_DT_PIN);
```

```
gpio_config_t io_conf;
io_conf.mode = GPIO_MODE_OUTPUT;
io_conf.intr_type = GPIO_INTR_DISABLE;
io_conf.pull_down_en = 0;
io_conf.pull_up_en = 0;
io_conf.pin_bit_mask = 0;
io_conf.pin_bit_mask |= (1ULL << MOTOR_DIR_PIN);
gpio_config(&io_conf);

mcpwm_gpio_init(MCPWM_UNIT_0, MCPWM0A, MOTOR_STEP_PIN);
mcpwm_config_t pwm_config;
pwm_config.frequency = 250;
pwm_config.cmpr_a = 0;
pwm_config.cmpr_b = 0;
pwm_config.counter_mode = MCPWM_UP_COUNTER;
pwm_config.duty_mode = MCPWM_DUTY_MODE_0;
mcpwm_init(MCPWM_UNIT_0, MCPWM_TIMER_0, &pwm_config);
}
```

In the init_hw function, we initialize the GPIO pins of both the rotary encoder and the motor driver. rotenc_init configures the rotary encoder pins as input. We set MOTOR_DIR_PIN as output. Then, we initialize the MCPWM signal pin by calling mcpwm_gpio_init. This function takes the following three parameters:

- The MCPWM unit. ESP32 has two PWM peripherals that we can use.
- The output channel. Each MCPWM unit has three pairs of output channels.
- The GPIO pin to attach to the specified channel.

We only need one channel to drive the motor by connecting the associated GPIO pin to the direction signal of the motor.

The mcpwm_init function initializes the MCPWM peripheral itself by providing default values. In addition to the MCPWM unit, we also specify which timer is to be used with the unit.

Next, we implement the callback function for the position change:

```
static int rotenc_pos = 0;
static int motor_pos = 0;

static void print_rotenc_pos(void *arg)
{
    while (1)
    {
        rotenc_pos = rotenc_getPos();
        printf("pos: %d\n", rotenc_pos);
        vTaskSuspend(NULL);
    }
}
```

There are two global variables for the position. rotenc_pos holds the current rotary encoder position, as returned by rotenc_getPos, in print_rotenc_pos. The print_rotenc_pos function is actually a task function that is resumed by the ISR of the rotary encoder input pins. The motor_pos variable is for the motor position, hence the name.

Finally, we implement the app_main function. The code is illustrated in the following snippet:

```
void app_main()
{
    init_hw();
    rotenc_setPosChangedCallback(print_rotenc_pos);

    mcpwm_set_duty_in_us(MCPWM_UNIT_0, MCPWM_TIMER_0, MCPWM_
GEN_A, 4000);
    int steps;
    int step_delay = 100;

    while (1)
    {
        if (motor_pos == rotenc_pos)
        {
            vTaskDelay(100);
```

```
            continue;
        }
        steps = rotenc_pos - motor_pos;
        motor_pos = rotenc_pos;

        gpio_set_level((gpio_num_t)MOTOR_DIR_PIN, steps > 0);
        vTaskDelay(10);

        mcpwm_set_duty(MCPWM_UNIT_0, MCPWM_TIMER_0, MCPWM_
GEN_A, 50);
        mcpwm_set_duty_type(MCPWM_UNIT_0, MCPWM_TIMER_0, MCPWM_
GEN_A, MCPWM_DUTY_MODE_0);
        vTaskDelay(step_delay * abs(steps) / portTICK_PERIOD_
MS);
        mcpwm_set_signal_low(MCPWM_UNIT_0, MCPWM_TIMER_0,
MCPWM_GEN_A);
    }
}
```

In the app_main function, we set the position changed callback function by calling rotenc_setPosChangedCallback so that we can keep track of the rotary encoder position. Then, we call mcpwm_set_duty_in_us to set the PWM duty duration to 4 ms—the shorter the duration, the faster the motor. The motor takes one step at each duty.

In the while loop, we track the rotary encoder position, and we will get the motor to the same position by using MCPWM. First, we set the direction by checking the sign of steps. In order to start the PWM, we call two functions, which are mcpwm_set_duty and mcpwm_set_duty_type. Calling these two functions triggers MCPWM to generate the signal on the step signal pin for step_delay * abs(steps) / portTICK_PERIOD_MS ms. Since the duty cycle is 4 ms in our application, we can easily find how many steps the motor takes by dividing the delay duration by 4. This value shows the real steps taken by the motor. After the delay, we simply call mcpwm_set_signal_low to stop MCPWM and the motor.

This was the last example of the chapter. You can find all of the code in the GitHub repository, as provided earlier.

Summary

In this chapter, we have seen many sensors and actuators that we can use in real-world projects. Starting from a simple button and LED driving, we have reached a point where we can use stepper motors to design our very own 3D printers. Although the main focus was sensors and actuators, we have also learned how to use peripherals such as GPIO pins, ADC, and PWM, and different communication protocols such as 1-Wire or I²C, which you can apply anytime you need to use a different sensor or actuator not listed in this book. Some useful FreeRTOS functions have also been added to our knowledge base to be employed in our projects.

The next chapter is about more advanced features of ESP32. We are going to test different types of displays and discuss their features. We will continue to use different peripherals such as **Inter-IC Sound (I2S)** and a **universal asynchronous receiver-transmitter (UART)** for different purposes. One interesting feature of ESP32 is its **ultra-low power (ULP)** co-processor that can be used while the main processors are in sleep mode. We will see how to program the ULP co-processor for our battery-operated devices in the next chapter.

Questions

Let's try to answer the following questions to review what we have learned in this chapter:

1. If you want to change an ESP-IDF project configuration value, which file do you need to edit?

   a) `platformio.ini`

   b) `sdkconfig`

   c) `CMakeLists.txt`

   d) `main.c`

2. When you need to measure temperature, which of these is not an option to use with ESP32?

   a) BME280

   b) TSL2561

   c) DHT22

   d) DHT11

3.   Which of these is not an actuator?

    a) Motor

    b) Relay

    c) Button

    d) LED

4.   Which of the following is not a serial communication method of communicating with a sensor?

    a) I^2C

    b) SPI

    c) PWM

    d) GPIO

5.   What are the signals to drive an I^2C device?

    a) Data and clock

    b) A GPIO pin

    c) MOSI and MISO

    d) TX and RX

3
Impressive Outputs with Displays

Some IoT products require an immediate visual output to end users; for example, a smart thermostat needs to have a display to show setpoints. In this chapter, we will talk about different display types that we can use together with ESP32 and how to select a display for a given set of requirements by discussing the pros and cons. There are several display technologies available on the market with different features and it is important to know about them so as to select the right one when necessary.

Another subject that we are going to learn is FreeRTOS, which is the official RTOS supported by ESP32. In actual fact, we have already used several FreeRTOS functions in the examples, but there is more to learn with a view to developing real-world products.

In this chapter, we're going to cover the following main topics:

- Using LCDs
- Interfacing with OLED displays
- TFT displays for superior graphics
- Using FreeRTOS

Technical requirements

In this chapter, we are going to need an LCD, an OLED display, and a TFT display to be used with our devkit in the examples. All other sensors and actuators will be listed in each example, so you can easily follow the Fritzing diagrams.

On the software side, we will continue with the existing toolchain and development tools, but new driver libraries are introduced for the displays. The links for the driver libraries are provided in the examples.

The source codes for the chapter are located here: `https://github.com/PacktPublishing/Internet-of-Things-with-ESP32/tree/main/ch3`.

Check out the following video to see the code in action: `https://bit.ly/3dXRFto`

Liquid Crystal Displays (LCDs)

Usually, IoT products come with a mobile or web application to let users interact with the product. However, we may sometimes need to display direct information on the device itself. For such products, we can integrate a display with ESP32.

LCDs are a common type of display that we can use in our IoT projects. They are highly available on the market with a low price tag. They come in a variety of sizes, in other words, columns and rows, that we can select; for example, 16x2, which means there are 16 columns and 2 rows on that type of LCD, with a total of 32 characters to display at a time. There is one such LCD shown in the following figure:

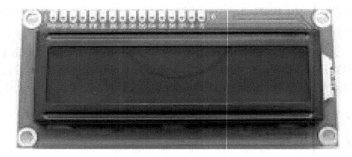

Figure 3.1 – 16x2 LCD

An LCD can operate in 4-bit mode or 8-bit mode, which defines the number of data lines to drive the LCD. However, it is too costly in terms of the GPIO resources on ESP32. Therefore, it is a good idea to use an I²C adapter module to reduce the number of pins to two, which are **serial data (SDA)** and **serial clock (SCL)**. An example of that adapter module is shown here:

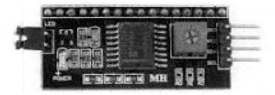

Figure 3.2 – I²C adapter for an LCD

There are also some LCD screens delivered with an I²C adapter already soldered on the LCD for ease of use.

In this example, we will develop a simple temperature sensor with an LCD screen. The hardware components are as follows:

- A 16x2 LCD (HD44780 controller chip) with I²C adapter
- A logic converter, 3.3 V-5 V
- A 5 V power source for the screen
- DHT11

Before starting to code, we need to connect the components as follows:

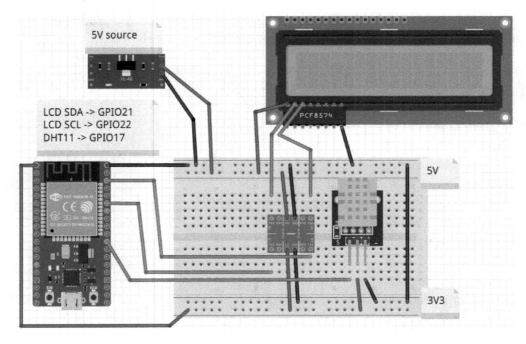

Figure 3.3 – Fritzing diagram for the LCD example

The upper section of the breadboard is for 5 V logic, and the lower section is for 3.3 V logic. Therefore, we have to make sure that all the pins of the ESP32 devkit are connected to the lower section. We are now ready for the application code.

`platformio.ini` needs to be updated for the libraries that we use to drive both the LCD screen and the DHT11 sensor. I have provided the LCD library along with the project codes here: `https://github.com/PacktPublishing/Internet-of-Things-with-ESP32/tree/main/common/ESP32-HD44780`. The original library comes from this repository on GitHub: `https://github.com/maxsydney/ESP32-HD44780`.

Let's update `platformio.ini` as follows:

```
build_flags =
    -DCONFIG_I2CDEV_TIMEOUT=100000

monitor_speed = 115200
lib_extra_dirs =
    ../../common/ESP32-HD44780/components
    ../../common/esp-idf-lib/components
```

The LCD library requires a timeout value for the I²C communication. We provide it as a build flag, `CONFIG_I2CDEV_TIMEOUT`. The next step is to edit the `main.c` file:

```
#include <freertos/FreeRTOS.h>
#include <freertos/task.h>
#include <string.h>
#include <stdio.h>
#include <driver/i2c.h>
#include <HD44780.h>
#include <dht.h>

#define LCD_ADDR 0x27
#define SDA_PIN 21
#define SCL_PIN 22
#define LCD_COLS 16
#define LCD_ROWS 2

#define DHT11_PIN 17
```

```
static void init_hw(void)
{
    LCD_init(LCD_ADDR, SDA_PIN, SCL_PIN, LCD_COLS, LCD_ROWS);
}
```

The header file of the LCD library is HD44780.h. We also define some macros, which will be used for the I²C communication with the LCD module. In the init_hw function, we only initialize the LCD module by using LCD_init, which takes the I²C bus address of the module, the I²C data and clock pins, and the LCD size as the number of columns and rows.

The following show_dht11 function is the task callback to show the temperature and humidity readings from DHT11:

```
void show_dht11(void *param)
{
    char buff[17];
    int16_t temperature, humidity;
    uint8_t read_cnt = 0;

    while (true)
    {
        vTaskDelay(2000 / portTICK_PERIOD_MS);
        LCD_clearScreen();

        if (dht_read_data(DHT_TYPE_DHT11, (gpio_num_t)DHT11_
PIN, &humidity, &temperature) == ESP_OK)
        {
            temperature /= 10;
            humidity /= 10;

            memset(buff, 0, sizeof(buff));
            sprintf(buff, "Temp: %d", temperature);
            LCD_home();
            LCD_writeStr(buff);

            memset(buff, 0, sizeof(buff));
            sprintf(buff, "Hum: %d", humidity);
```

```
        LCD_setCursor(0, 1);
        LCD_writeStr(buff);
    }
```

In the `while` loop, we clear the screen with `LCD_clearScreen` and read from DHT11 every 2 seconds. The main approach to write on the screen is to go to the write location first and then send text to the LCD module. To display the temperature, for example, we use the `LCD_home` function to move the cursor to the (column = 0, row = 0) location and call `LCD_writeStr` with the temperature string as a parameter. The function to locate the cursor on any location is `LCD_setCursor`, which takes column and row positions as parameters. Then, we handle the DHT11 read failures as follows:

```
        else
        {
            LCD_home();
            memset(buff, 0, sizeof(buff));
            sprintf(buff, "Failed (%d)", ++read_cnt);
            LCD_writeStr(buff);
        }
    }
}
```

If we can't read from DHT11, we show an error message on the LCD.

We have implemented the display function and we can code the `app_main` function next:

```
void app_main(void)
{
    init_hw();
    xTaskCreate(show_dht11, "dht11", configMINIMAL_STACK_SIZE *
4, NULL, 5, NULL);
}
```

`app_main` is quite simple. We first initialize the hardware and then start a task with `show_dht11`, which displays readings from DHT11 on the LCD. That is all.

The code is completed and ready to test. After flashing the devkit, we can observe that the LCD updates every 2 seconds with a new reading from DHT11.

The next example involves using another type of display, an OLED display.

Organic Light-Emitting Diode Displays (OLEDs)

Organic Light-Emitting Diode (**OLED**) displays have a number of advantages over LCDs, most notably the following:

- Lower energy usage since there is no need for a backlight.
- A fast response time.
- Integrated I²C communication.
- It is thinner in depth.

Those advantages make it a strong option in many products. However, it is a relatively new technology, so prices are a bit higher. You can see an image of an OLED display in the following figure:

Figure 3.4 – 1.3" OLED with 128x64 pixels

This time, we will develop the same temperature application with an OLED display. The hardware components that we need are as follows:

- A 1.3" OLED display with an SH1106 driver chip (I have one from AZ-Delivery)
- DHT11

The driver chip supports 3.3 V logic level and we can directly interface it with ESP32. Moreover, we don't require any external power source, thanks to its low power consumption rate, which is less than 11 mA. The connection with the ESP32 devkit is very straightforward, as demonstrated in the following figure:

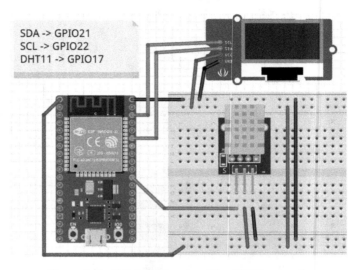

Figure 3.5 – Fritzing diagram of the OLED example

As usual, we update the platformio.ini file first:

```
monitor_speed = 115200
lib_extra_dirs =
    ../../common/components
    ../../common/esp-idf-lib/components
```

The original driver library for OLED displays is from this repository: https://github.com/lexus2k/ssd1306. However, I had to change the directory structure to make it compatible with PlatformIO. You can find the updated library in the book's source repository here: https://github.com/PacktPublishing/Internet-of-Things-with-ESP32/tree/main/common/components/ssd1306. Following correct configuration, we can continue with the code file. We need to rename it as main.cpp to make PlatformIO use the C++ compiler, since the OLED library is developed in C++. Let's start as follows:

```
#include "dht.h"
#include "ssd1306.h"
#include <freertos/FreeRTOS.h>
```

```
#include <freertos/task.h>
#include <stdio.h>

#define DHT11_PIN 17
#define OLED_CLK 22
#define OLED_SDA 21

extern "C" void app_main(void);

static void init_hw(void)
{
    ssd1306_128x64_i2c_initEx(OLED_CLK, OLED_SDA, 0);
}
```

We include ssd1306.h to drive the OLED display and define the pins. One important point is that we need to mark the app_main function as extern "C" so that the C++ compiler doesn't mangle the name of it since this is the entry point of our application once ESP32 boots up.

ssd1306_128x64_i2c_initEx initializes the OLED driver with I²C information. 128x64 in the function name denotes the width and height of the OLED in pixels. The last parameter is for the I²C bus address, and passing it as zero (0) makes the library use the default address of the OLED display.

Next, we have the display functions to show readings:

```
static void draw_screen(void)
{
    ssd1306_clearScreen();
    ssd1306_setFixedFont(ssd1306xled_font8x16);
    ssd1306_printFixed(0, 0, "Temp", STYLE_NORMAL);
    ssd1306_printFixed(0, 32, "Hum", STYLE_NORMAL);
}

static void display_reading(int temp, int hum)
{
    char buff[10];
    ssd1306_setFixedFont(ssd1306xled_font6x8);
    sprintf(buff, "%d", temp);
```

```
    ssd1306_printFixedN(48, 0, buff, STYLE_BOLD, 2);

    sprintf(buff, "%d", hum);
    ssd1306_printFixedN(48, 32, buff, STYLE_BOLD, 2);
}
```

draw_screen prints the labels on the screen. First, we clear the screen with the help of ssd1306_clearScreen and set the font to ssd1306xled_font8x16 by calling ssd1306_setFixedFont for text until the next time it is called with another font. Then we call ssd1306_printFixed to print a Temp string at the location of (column = 0, row = 0) in pixels. Similarly, we print Hum at the location of (column = 0, row = 32) in the middle position of the height.

We use the display_reading function to update the screen with the latest temperature and humidity values. When it is called, the font is updated to ssd1306xled_font6x8 first, and then the values are printed on the screen by calling ssd1306_printFixedN. The last parameter of this function scales the font size by N, which is 2 in our case.

Next, we implement a function to read from DHT11. It is given in the following code snippet:

```
static void read_dht11(void* arg)
{
    int16_t humidity = 0, temperature = 0;
    while(1)
    {
        vTaskDelay(2000 / portTICK_PERIOD_MS);
        dht_read_data(DHT_TYPE_DHT11, (gpio_num_t)DHT11_PIN,
&humidity, &temperature);
        display_reading(temperature / 10, humidity / 10);
    }
}
```

read_dht11 is the task callback to read from DHT11 every 2 seconds. In the while loop, it then calls the display_reading function to display the values on the OLED screen.

We complete the application by coding the `app_main` function as provided next.

```
void app_main()
{
    init_hw();
    draw_screen();

    xTaskCreate(read_dht11, "dht11", configMINIMAL_STACK_SIZE *
8, NULL, 5, NULL);
}
```

The `app_main` function initializes the hardware, draws the labels, and finally passes the control to the `read_dht11` function by creating a task with it.

The coding is now finished and we can test the application by flashing it into our devkit.

Our last display example is with a TFT screen, as follows.

Thin Film Transistor Displays (TFTs)

The color alternative for other types of displays is a TFT display. Actually, TFT is a type of LCD, but the technology is enhanced to lower the power consumption to a level that is comparable to OLED. It still uses backlight, which is the main reason for power consumption, but its graphic capabilities come to play when we need a better user experience. A TFT display is shown in the following figure:

Figure 3.6 – 1.8" TFT screen with 128x160 pixels

In this example, we will use a TFT display for our temperature sensor. The components are as follows:

- A 1.8" TFT with an ST7735 driver chip (for example, one from AZ-Delivery)
- DHT11

The connections in the setup are shown in the following Fritzing diagram:

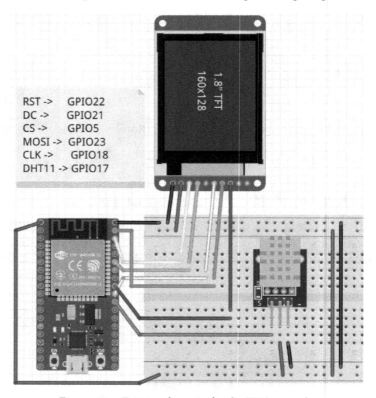

Figure 3.7 – Fritzing diagram for the TFT example

The TFT display uses a **Serial Peripheral Interface** (**SPI**) bus to communicate with an MCU. The purpose is the same as with I²C, but SPI communication requires four signal lines instead of two, as I²C uses SDA and SCL. Those signal lines are as follows:

- Clock, CLK
- Master Output Slave Input, MOSI
- Master Input Slave Output, MISO
- Slave select or Chip select, SS or CS

An SPI bus supports multiple slave devices, but each slave requires a reserved line, SS, to enable it. The master takes the SS line to low before talking to a slave. Therefore, the more the slaves, the more lines used on the MCU.

Going back to our example, the TFT display requires 3 pins of the SPI interface as CLK, MOSI, and CS. It doesn't need an MISO line since it doesn't send any data to the devkit; it just receives from it. Instead, another pin is required, which is for data/command select, or DC in short. The driver chip uses this pin to understand whether bits coming from MOSI are for data or command purposes.

Let's move on to the code. We will use the same library of the OLED example to drive the TFT screen. That library supports both. We specify the paths in `platformio.ini`:

```
monitor_speed = 115200
lib_extra_dirs =
    ../../common/components
    ../../common/esp-idf-lib/components
```

The TFT library is located here: `https://github.com/PacktPublishing/Internet-of-Things-with-ESP32/tree/main/common/components/ssd1306`.

As for the source code file, our application resides in `main.cpp` to make PlatformIO use the C++ compiler:

```cpp
#include "dht.h"
#include "ssd1306.h"
#include <freertos/FreeRTOS.h>
#include <freertos/task.h>
#include <stdint.h>

#define DHT11_PIN 17
#define TFT_CS_PIN 5
#define TFT_DC_PIN 21
#define TFT_RST_PIN 22

#define TFT_ROTATE_CW90 (1 & 0x03)

extern "C" void app_main(void);
```

We include the header files and define the pins on ESP32 for the hardware connection. `TFT_ROTATE_CW90` is the macro to define the command code to rotate the TFT screen 90 degrees clockwise. We forward declare `app_main` as a C function to prevent the C++ compiler from name mangling. Next, we implement the hardware initialization function:

```
static void init_hw(void)
{
    st7735_128x160_spi_init(TFT_RST_PIN, TFT_CS_PIN, TFT_DC_
PIN);
    ssd1306_setMode(LCD_MODE_NORMAL);
    st7735_setRotation(TFT_ROTATE_CW90);
}
```

The SPI initialization function of the screen, `st7735_128x160_spi_init`, requires the CS, DC, and RST pin numbers as input. It uses the defaults for MOSI and CLK as the designated pins of SPI lines, which are GPIO23 and GPIO18, respectively. `st7735` in the name shows the driver chip model of the screen, and `128x160` denotes the screen size in pixels. Then, `ssd1306_setMode` is called with `LCD_MODE_NORMAL` to enable RGB. `st7735_setRotation` commands the TFT screen to rotate 90 degrees clockwise, so the orientation becomes landscape in our application.

Let's see how we format the screen next:

```
static void draw_screen(void)
{
    ssd1306_clearScreen8();
    ssd1306_setFixedFont(ssd1306xled_font8x16);
    ssd1306_setColor(RGB_COLOR8(255, 255, 255));
    ssd1306_printFixed8(5, 5, "Temperature", STYLE_NORMAL);
    ssd1306_printFixed8(10, 21, "(C)", STYLE_NORMAL);
    ssd1306_printFixed8(5, 64, "Humidity", STYLE_NORMAL);
    ssd1306_printFixed8(10, 80, "(%)", STYLE_NORMAL);
}
```

The `draw_screen` function prints the labels on the screen. First, `ssd1306_clearScreen8` clears it, and then `ssd1306_setFixedFont` sets the font. We have a new function, `ssd1306_setColor`, to be used with TFT, which sets the font color to white (255,255,255). `ssd1306_printFixed8` goes to the position of (5,5) and writes the text in `STYLE_NORMAL`. The 8 at the end of functions means that that function belongs to an 8-bit RGB class for color devices.

In the `display_reading` function, we write the temperature and humidity values on the TFT screen as follows:

```
static void display_reading(int temp, int hum)
{
    char buff[10];
    ssd1306_setFixedFont(comic_sans_font24x32_123);
    ssd1306_setColor(RGB_COLOR8(255, 0, 0));

    sprintf(buff, "%d", temp);
    ssd1306_printFixed8(80, 21, buff, STYLE_BOLD);

    sprintf(buff, "%d", hum);
    ssd1306_printFixed8(80, 80, buff, STYLE_BOLD);
}
```

First, we update the font to `comic_sans_font24x32_123` and set the color to red (255,0,0). We use `ssd1306_printFixed8` to print the text in the buffer, this time in the style of `STYLE_BOLD`.

The driver library has many other functions, such as for drawing lines or 2D shapes. To learn more about this library, you can visit its documentation here: `https://github.com/lexus2k/ssd1306/wiki`.

We have all the display functions ready. We complete the application by implementing the DHT11 read function and `app_main` as follows:

```
static void read_dht11(void* arg)
{
    int16_t humidity = 0, temperature = 0;
    while(1)
    {
        vTaskDelay(2000 / portTICK_PERIOD_MS);
        dht_read_data(DHT_TYPE_DHT11, (gpio_num_t)DHT11_PIN,
&humidity, &temperature);
        display_reading(temperature / 10, humidity / 10);
    }
}

void app_main()
```

```
{
    init_hw();
    draw_screen();

    xTaskCreate(read_dht11, "dht11", configMINIMAL_STACK_SIZE *
8, NULL, 5, NULL);
}
```

In read_dht11, we read from DHT11 every 2 seconds and show the values on the TFT display by calling display_reading.

app_main first initializes the hardware, then calls draw_screen to print the value labels on the TFT display, and finally, creates a FreeRTOS task to read from DHT11.

Having the application ready, we can flash the devkit and see how the readings are shown on the TFT display.

This was the last example of the displays section. You will find many other displays on the market, but most of them have a common set of driver chips. Therefore, you can also easily use them in your projects as the examples in this chapter.

In the next topic, we will discuss FreeRTOS in detail to understand how we can use it in our projects more effectively.

Using FreeRTOS

As we know, FreeRTOS is the official real-time OS supported by ESP32. FreeRTOS was originally designed for single-core architectures. However, ESP32 has two cores, and therefore this port of FreeRTOS is revised to handle 2-core systems as well. Most of the differences between the vanilla FreeRTOS and ESP-IDF FreeRTOS stem from this reason. For those who have some experience with FreeRTOS, it would be enough to skim through these differences:

- Creating a new task: We have a new function where we can specify on which core to run a new task; it is xTaskCreatePinnedToCore. This function takes a parameter to set the task affinity to the specified core. If a task is created by the original xTaskCreate, it doesn't belong to any core, and any core can choose to run it at the next tick interrupt.

- Scheduler suspension: The vTaskSuspendAll function call only suspends the scheduler on the core on which it is called. The other core continues its operation. Therefore, it is not the right way to suspend the scheduler for protecting shared resources.

- Critical sections: Entering a critical section stops the scheduler and interrupts only on the calling core. The other core continues its operation. However, the critical section is still protected by a mutex, preventing the other core from running the critical section until the first core exits. We can use `portENTER_CRITICAL_SAFE(mux)` and `portEXIT_CRITICAL_SAFE(mux)` macros for this purpose.

> **Important note**
>
> Dual-core ESP32 names its cores as **PRO_CPU (cpu0)** and **APP_CPU (cpu1)**. PRO_CPU starts when ESP32 is first powered and executes all the initialization, including APP_CPU activation. `app_main` is called from the main task running on PRO_CPU.

If you are new to FreeRTOS, there is some great documentation available on its website here: `https://www.freertos.org/`.

Espressif also explains in detail what is different in the ESP-IDF version of FreeRTOS here: `https://docs.espressif.com/projects/esp-idf/en/latest/esp32/api-guides/freertos-smp.html`.

Let's see an example of how to protect shared resources in FreeRTOS.

Counting touch sensor

In this example, we will enable interrupts on two of the touch sensor channels to count touches on the pins and print statistics in a periodic FreeRTOS task. We use two hook-up wires with male pins for this purpose. They are simply connected to GPIO32 (Touch 9) and GPIO33 (Touch 8) of the ESP32 devkit.

We can just move on to the source code to discuss how we implement this application:

```c
#include "freertos/FreeRTOS.h"
#include "freertos/task.h"

#include "driver/touch_pad.h"
#include <string.h>

static portMUX_TYPE mut = portMUX_INITIALIZER_UNLOCKED;

typedef struct
{
    int pin_num;
```

```
        TickType_t when;
} touch_info_t;

#define TI_LIST_SIZE 10
static volatile touch_info_t ti_list[TI_LIST_SIZE];
static volatile size_t ti_cnt = 0;

static const TickType_t check_period = 500 / portTICK_PERIOD_
MS;
```

driver/touch_pad.h contains functions and type definitions for using touch pad peripherals. We use a mutex, mut, of the portMUX_TYPE type, to guard shared resources from concurrent access. The mutex type definition is specific to ESP-IDF. Our shared resources are ti_list and ti_cnt, which need to be protected by mut. Next, the ISR comes for the touch pad:

```
static void IRAM_ATTR tp_handler(void *arg)
{
    uint32_t pad_intr = touch_pad_get_status();
    touch_pad_clear_status();

    touch_info_t touch = {
        .pin_num = (pad_intr >> TOUCH_PAD_NUM8) & 0x01 ? TOUCH_
PAD_NUM8 : TOUCH_PAD_NUM9,
        .when = xTaskGetTickCountFromISR()};
```

tp_handler is the ISR for the touch peripheral. If any of the two channels detect a touch, this ISR will run. In tp_handler, we read from the touch peripheral (called touch_pad) by calling touch_pad_get_status to understand which pin is touched and save this information in the variable of touch, along with the time in ticks. We use xTaskGetTickCountFromISR of FreeRTOS for this.

> **Important note**
>
> FreeRTOS provides two versions of some functions. If a function ends with the FromISR suffix, it is the ISR version of that function. If there is no suffix, it is meant to be called from a task.

Let's continue to develop the touch pad handler:

```
    portENTER_CRITICAL_SAFE(&mut);
    if (ti_cnt < TI_LIST_SIZE)
    {
        bool skip = (ti_cnt > 0) &&
((touch.when - ti_list[ti_cnt - 1].when) < check_period) &&
(touch.pin_num == ti_list[ti_cnt - 1].pin_num);
        if (!skip)
        {
            ti_list[ti_cnt++] = touch;
        }
    }
    portEXIT_CRITICAL_SAFE(&mut);
}
```

Then, we enter the critical section by calling the portENTER_CRITICAL_SAFE macro with the mutex address. This section is critical because we will modify ti_list and ti_cnt values and they must be consistent. To achieve consistency, we have to prevent any access to those variables while modifying it in the ISR. After completing the update, we call portEXIT_CRITICAL_SAFE to free the mutex, and so the shared resources are free to access from any other task.

In the next function, we will print the touch information on the serial monitor:

```
static void monitor(void *arg)
{
    touch_info_t ti_list_local[TI_LIST_SIZE];
    size_t ti_cnt_local;

    while (1)
    {
        vTaskDelay(10000 / portTICK_PERIOD_MS);
        ti_cnt_local = 0;

        portENTER_CRITICAL_SAFE(&mut);
        if (ti_cnt > 0)
        {
            memcpy((void *)ti_list_local, (const void *)ti_
```

```
list, ti_cnt * sizeof(touch_info_t));
            ti_cnt_local = ti_cnt;
            ti_cnt = 0;
    }

        portEXIT_CRITICAL_SAFE(&mut);
```

monitor is the task function where we print collected touch information every 10
seconds. In the while loop, we again use the portENTER_CRITICAL_SAFE and
portEXIT_CRITICAL_SAFE pair to access the global ti_list and ti_cnt values by
shielding them with the mutex. The crucial point here is that we copy the values of those
shared resources into local variables, ti_list_local and ti_cnt_local, to keep
the critical section as short as possible so as to make the shared resources available for
the interrupt handler in the shortest time. In the rest of the function, we simply print the
statistics that we have copied into the local variable:

```
        if (ti_cnt_local > 0)
        {
            int t8_cnt = 0;
            for (int i = 0; i < ti_cnt_local; ++i)
            {
                if (ti_list_local[i].pin_num == TOUCH_PAD_NUM8)
                {
                    ++t8_cnt;
                }
            }
            printf("First touch tick: %u\n", ti_list_local[0].
when);
            printf("Last touch tick: %u\n", ti_list_local[ti_
cnt_local - 1].when);
            printf("Touch8 count: %d\n", t8_cnt);
            printf("Touch9 count: %d\n", ti_cnt_local - t8_
cnt);
        }
        else
        {
            printf("No touch detected\n");
        }
```

```
        }
    }
```

If we detect any touch, we print the first detection tick, the last detection tick, and the counts on each pin. If there is no touch, we print this information on the serial monitor, too.

Let's initialize the hardware next:

```
static void init_hw(void)
{
    touch_pad_init();
    touch_pad_set_fsm_mode(TOUCH_FSM_MODE_TIMER);
    touch_pad_set_voltage(TOUCH_HVOLT_2V7, TOUCH_LVOLT_0V5,
TOUCH_HVOLT_ATTEN_1V);

    touch_pad_config(TOUCH_PAD_NUM8, 0);
    touch_pad_config(TOUCH_PAD_NUM9, 0);
    touch_pad_filter_start(10);
```

In the init_hw function, we only initialize the touch peripheral. We first initialize the driver, and then the finite state machine mode of the peripheral and the voltage reference values. The next thing to do is to calibrate the touch pins 8 and 9 with threshold values as the interrupt trigger. During calibration, we have to make sure that there is no contact with these pins. We need to read from each touch pad and set a threshold value accordingly. The next code snippet shows how to implement calibration:

```
    uint16_t val;
    touch_pad_read_filtered(TOUCH_PAD_NUM8, &val);
    touch_pad_set_thresh(TOUCH_PAD_NUM8, val * 0.2);
    touch_pad_read_filtered(TOUCH_PAD_NUM9, &val);
    touch_pad_set_thresh(TOUCH_PAD_NUM9, val * 0.2);

    touch_pad_isr_register(tp_handler, NULL);
}
```

Finally, we set tp_handler as the ISR of the touch interrupt and complete the hardware initialization.

Now we can continue with the application entry point, `app_main`:

```c
void app_main(void)
{
    init_hw();


    TaskHandle_t taskh;
    if (xTaskCreatePinnedToCore(monitor,
                                "monitor",
                                1024,
                                NULL,
                                2,
                                &taskh,
                                APP_CPU_NUM) == pdPASS)
    {
        printf("info: monitor started\n");
    }
    else
    {
        printf("err: monitor task couldn't start\n");
    }
    char buffer[128];
    vTaskList(buffer);
    printf("%s\n", buffer);


    touch_pad_intr_enable();
}
```

After calling `init_hw` to initialize the touch peripheral, we create the monitor task with the help of `xTaskCreatePinnedToCore`. It takes seven parameters, which are as follows:

- The function to run as a task. This is the `monitor` function.

- The name of the task for diagnostic purposes.

- The stack size to reserve for the task in bytes. This differs from the vanilla FreeRTOS since it takes this parameter in words. If we don't set this value greater than the amount the task needs, the application is going to crash.

- The void* parameter to pass to the task function. monitor doesn't need any, so NULL is passed.

- The priority of the task. Low value means low priority.

- The address of the task handle. If provided, xTaskCreate* functions set its value and we can use the task handle to manage the task, such as suspending, resuming, or deleting.

- The core to run the task. This parameter is specific to xTaskCreatePinnedToCore, which exists only in the ESP-IDF FreeRTOS. We provide APP_CPU_NUM as the core.

We can see the existing tasks in our application by calling vTaskList with a buffer as the parameter. Our monitor task is also listed in its output. The last thing in app_main is to enable touch interrupts.

Before compiling the code, we need to edit platformio.ini, too, to add some definitions in order to enable vTaskList as follows:

```
monitor_speed = 115200
build_flags =
     -DCONFIG_FREERTOS_USE_TRACE_FACILITY=1
     -DCONFIG_FREERTOS_USE_STATS_FORMATTING_FUNCTIONS=1
```

We are now ready to compile and flash our ESP32 devkit. To test the application, we only need to touch the hookup wires. We can see that the monitor task prints the touch statistics on the serial monitor every 10 seconds.

In the next example, we will look at how to use a FreeRTOS queue.

Using several sensors as producers

The purpose of this example is to collect data from several digital sensors and process them in a FreeRTOS task as the consumer. They all use a single FreeRTOS queue to pass data between them.

FreeRTOS queues are a convenient way of sharing data between interrupts and tasks where the data rate is not high. The queue mechanism is implemented as a by-copy method. This means that when a data element is pushed into the queue, it is copied to a memory location in the queue. Similarly, the consumer provides a memory location when it takes data out of the queue. In this way, there is no concern about data corruption or data synchronization, which makes the software design simple and clear.

Let's see the example. The sensors are as follows:

- A tilt sensor (from the Elegoo sensor kit)
- A tap sensor
- A shock sensor

The following photo shows the sensors:

Figure 3.8 – Tilt, tap, and shock sensors

The wiring is given in the following Fritzing diagram:

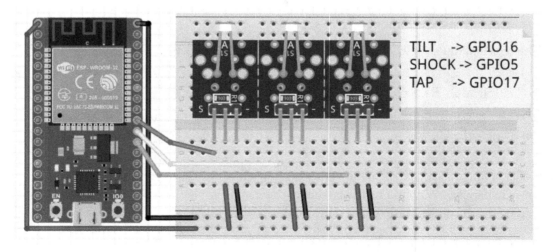

Figure 3.9 – Fritzing diagram of the example

After setting up the hardware, we create a PlatformIO project with the following platformio.ini configuration file:

```
[env:az-delivery-devkit-v4]
platform = espressif32
board = az-delivery-devkit-v4
framework = espidf


monitor_speed = 115200
```

Let's now edit main.c to develop the code:

```c
#include <inttypes.h>
#include <stdio.h>
#include "freertos/FreeRTOS.h"
#include "freertos/task.h"
#include "freertos/queue.h"
#include "driver/gpio.h"
#include "esp_timer.h"

#define TILT_SWITCH_PIN 16
#define SHOCK_SWITCH_PIN 5
#define TAP_SWITCH_PIN 17

#define MS_100 100000

typedef struct
{
    gpio_num_t pin;
    int64_t time;
} queue_data_t;

static QueueHandle_t sensor_event_queue = NULL;

static bool filter_out(queue_data_t *);
```

We begin by including the header files. The FreeRTOS queue API is provided in `freertos/queue.h`. Then we define the pin numbers of the sensors. `queue_data_t` is the data type of elements to be pushed into the FreeRTOS queue, and the next line contains the queue variable, `sensor_event_queue`. All data coming from the sensors will be retained in it. `filter_out` is a function for eliminating some of the data before processing.

Next, we define the producer as an ISR handler:

```
static void IRAM_ATTR producer(void *arg)
{
    queue_data_t data = {
        .pin = (uint32_t)arg,
        .time = esp_timer_get_time()};
    xQueueSendToBackFromISR(sensor_event_queue, &data, NULL);
}
```

`producer` is the function where we push the sensor data to the back of the queue. We define the `data` variable and set its fields. Then, we queue it as an element in `sensor_event_queue` by calling `xQueueSendToBackFromISR`, to be processed in a FreeRTOS task later. All sensor interrupts will be attached to this handler while configuring the GPIO.

`consumer` is defined as a FreeRTOS task function in the following code block:

```
static void consumer(void *arg)
{
    queue_data_t data;
    while (1)
    {
        if (xQueueReceive(sensor_event_queue, &data, portMAX_
DELAY))
        {
```

We first define a variable to hold a data element. Then we call `xQueueReceive` to remove an element from the front of the queue. This function blocks the task until a data element is available in the queue. Once a sensor data has been pushed, `xQueueReceive` runs and stores this data in the `data` variable:

```
            if (filter_out(&data))
            {
```

```
                continue;
            }
            switch (data.pin)
            {
            case SHOCK_SWITCH_PIN:
                printf("> shock sensor");
                break;
            case TILT_SWITCH_PIN:
                printf("> tilt sensor");
                break;
            case TAP_SWITCH_PIN:
                printf("> tap sensor");
                break;
            default:
                break;
            }
            printf(" at %" PRId64 "(us)\n", data.time);
        }
    }
    vTaskDelete(NULL);
}
```

After having a data element in data, we can proceed with processing it, in our case,
filtering first and printing the sensor event on the serial monitor.

A simple filter is implemented in the following code block:

```
static bool filter_out(queue_data_t *d)
{
    static int64_t tilt_time = 0;
    static int64_t tap_time = 0;
    static int64_t shock_time = 0;

    switch (d->pin)
    {
    case TILT_SWITCH_PIN:
        if (d->time - tilt_time < MS_100)
        {
```

```
        return true;
    }
    tilt_time = d->time;
    break;
```

The `filter_out` function receives a queue element as the only parameter. In the `switch` statement, we start with the tilt event. We compare its timestamp with the previous event of the tilt sensor. If the time difference is less than 100 ms, it returns `true` to signal the caller to skip this data point:

```
case TAP_SWITCH_PIN:
    if (d->time - tap_time < MS_100)
    {
        return true;
    }
    tap_time = d->time;
    break;
case SHOCK_SWITCH_PIN:
    if (d->time - shock_time < MS_100)
    {
        return true;
    }
    shock_time = d->time;
    break;
default:
    break;
}

    return false;
}
```

We do the same comparison for the other two sensors. Returning `false` means the data is good to process.

Let's implement the hardware initialization next:

```
static void init_hw(void)
{
    uint64_t pin_select = 0;
```

```
    pin_select |= (1ULL << SHOCK_SWITCH_PIN);
    pin_select |= (1ULL << TILT_SWITCH_PIN);
    pin_select |= (1ULL << TAP_SWITCH_PIN);

    gpio_config_t io_conf;
    io_conf.intr_type = GPIO_PIN_INTR_POSEDGE;
    io_conf.pin_bit_mask = pin_select;
    io_conf.mode = GPIO_MODE_INPUT;
    io_conf.pull_up_en = 1;
    gpio_config(&io_conf);

    gpio_install_isr_service(0);
    gpio_isr_handler_add(SHOCK_SWITCH_PIN, producer, (void *)
SHOCK_SWITCH_PIN);
    gpio_isr_handler_add(TILT_SWITCH_PIN, producer, (void *)
TILT_SWITCH_PIN);
    gpio_isr_handler_add(TAP_SWITCH_PIN, producer, (void *)
TAP_SWITCH_PIN);
}
```

In init_hw, we first configure the sensors' pins as input. Then the important part comes, where we attach producer as the ISR handler of all the sensor pins. In this way, we set all of the sensors as data sources of the queue.

Finally, we implement app_main as follows:

```
void app_main(void)
{
    init_hw();
    sensor_event_queue = xQueueCreate(20, sizeof(queue_
data_t));
    xTaskCreate(consumer, "consumer", 2048, NULL, 10, NULL);
}
```

After initializing the hardware, we call xQueueCreate to create the queue with a capacity of 20 elements. Before we exit app_main, we pass the control to consumer by creating a FreeRTOS task with it.

We have completed the code. Now, we can test it by flashing on the devkit. When we shake the sensors, they generate data that is queued to be printed on the serial monitor unless filtered out.

This was the final example in the chapter. We have covered many important features of FreeRTOS, although it does have more, such as a semaphore API for task synchronization or a software timer API for periodic tasks. The FreeRTOS website shares some very nice examples of these APIs that you can experiment with by using ESP32.

Summary

In this chapter, we have learned about a number of popular display technologies and how to use them in our ESP32 projects when an immediate output to end users is required. It is important to know the differences between those technologies to select the right display type in a project. FreeRTOS was an important subject of this chapter as well. It is the official real-time operating system of ESP32, supported by Espressif. We have discussed the differences between the vanilla FreeRTOS and the ESP-IDF versions with the help of examples.

We will talk about the advanced features of ESP32 in the next chapter, including multimedia peripherals and power management subsystems. When a battery-operated device is to be designed, the ULP co-processor of ESP32 can be very handy for achieving low power consumption. All these subjects will be covered next.

Questions

Here are some questions to reiterate the topics in this chapter:

1. Which is not a display technology?

    a) OLED

    b) LCD

    c) OECD

    d) TFT

2. If energy consumption is an important factor for a project, in which order would you evaluate the display options?

    a) OLED, TFT, LCD

    b) LCD, TFT, OLED

    c) LCD, OLED, TFT

    d) TFT, LCD, OLED

3. If graphic capabilities are an important factor for a project, in which order would you evaluate the display options?

    a) LCD, OLED, TFT

    b) LCD, TFT, OLED

    c) TFT, OLED, LCD

    d) TFT, LCD, OLED

4. What is the most fundamental difference between the vanilla FreeRTOS and the ESP-IDF FreeRTOS?

    a) The vanilla FreeRTOS is designed for a single core, whereas ESP-IDF supports multiple cores.

    b) ESP-IDF FreeRTOS doesn't use a configuration header

    c) In the vanilla FreeRTOS, you don't need to specify a core; this is handled automatically.

    d) ESP-IDF has improved functionality.

5. Which macro/function pair can be used to protect a shared resource in FreeRTOS?

    a) xTaskCreate/vTaskDelete

    b) portENTER_CRITICAL_SAFE/portEXIT_CRITICAL_SAFE

    c) xQueueSendToBack/xQueueReceive

    d) xTaskCreateStaticPinnedToCore/vTaskDelete

4

A Deep Dive into the Advanced Features

ESP32 is a full-fledged hardware platform for **Internet of Things (IoT)** projects. We started our journey with basic features and peripherals to integrate with elementary sensors and actuators. This was just the tip of the iceberg. In this chapter, we are going to use more of its peripherals to experiment with advanced devices such as a speaker and a camera.

Battery-powered products require the use of the energy-saving features of ESP32. We can put ESP32 in sleep mode so that the battery has a longer lifespan. For the purpose of computation even if it is in sleep mode, an **Ultra-Low-Power (ULP)** coprocessor is integrated into ESP32. The ULP coprocessor has access to some peripherals for sensor integration so that the device can still function while the main processors are in sleep mode. This chapter is the right place to check out if you need your ESP32 device to be battery-powered in your project.

In this chapter, we will cover the following main topics:

- UART communication
- Adding a speaker with I2S
- Developing a camera application
- Power management, deep sleep, and ULP

Technical requirements

In this chapter, we will continue with the existing toolchain and development environment. However, the examples will require new libraries. The links for all new libraries will be provided in the corresponding sections.

In addition to our existing ESP32 devkit, we will need one more for the **Universal Asynchronous Receiver-Transmitter** (**UART**) example where we connect two devkits to communicate with each other.

The camera example is implemented with a special kit, AiThinker ESP32-CAM. We use this devkit because it has an integrated camera sensor port and microSD card slot, so we don't need to worry about pin connections. Moreover, the devkit comes with a camera sensor that can be easily attached to the port.

All other sensors and actuators will be listed in each example so that you can easily follow the Fritzing diagrams.

The source codes of the examples in this chapter are located at `https://github.com/PacktPublishing/Internet-of-Things-with-ESP32/tree/main/ch4`.

Check out the following video to see the code in action: `https://bit.ly/36nrbgI`

Communicating over UART

UART is an asynchronous communication technique in which parties use a predetermined data transmission rate or **baud rate** for communication. I2C and SPI are called synchronous because there is a common clock provided by the bus master, which is usually an MCU, and all other devices in the bus use this common clock to send/receive data. On the contrary, in UART communication, the parties have their own independent clocks and data transmission is achieved by the common UART settings in the applications running on the devices. Those settings or UART parameters are as follows:

- Baud rate: This is the speed at which parties exchange data. For example, 9600 baud means 9,600 bits of data can be sent in a second.
- A packet definition.

A packet definition shows the following:

- The number of bits in a packet.
- Whether the parity bit exists. Parity is to ensure that no bit is changed during the transmission.
- The number of stop bits: 1 or 2.

For instance, when we see a UART communication defined as *9600, 8N1*, we understand that the baud rate is 9,600, there are 8 bits in a packet, there is no parity, and 1 stop bit.

I2C and SPI both support bus communication, that is, there can be more than two devices on the line. However, UART protocol defines only two parties in the communication. As signal lines, we have a transmit, **TX**, and a receive, **RX**. Both ends are connected to each other, as demonstrated in the following diagram:

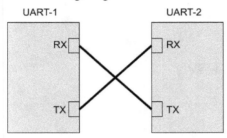

Figure 4.1 – UART communication

ESP32 integrates three UART controllers, which means we can have three different UART connections at the same time on the same hardware setup. When using an ESP32 devkit, one of these UART controllers is reserved for serial communication with a PC over USB for programming purposes and the serial print. The `printf` function in our applications uses this UART controller.

In this example, we need two devkit boards, which we will connect to via UART. One has a DHT11 attached to it and it will send temperature readings to the other devkit. The second devkit will print this reading over USB, and we can monitor it with the integrated serial monitor of PlatformIO. The following figure shows the Fritzing diagram:

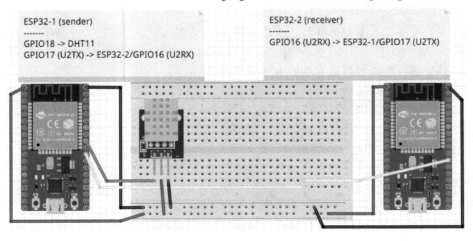

Figure 4.2 – A Fritzing diagram of the UART example

We need to develop two different applications for ESP32-1 (the sender) and ESP32-2 (the receiver). ESP32-1 will read from DHT11 and transmit the reading over the UART2-TX pin. ESP32-2 will be waiting for the data from its UART2-RX pin and will print the reading on the serial monitor when it has been received. Let's start with the ESP32-1 application:

```
#include "dht.h"
#include <freertos/FreeRTOS.h>
#include <freertos/task.h>
#include <stdint.h>
#include "driver/uart.h"


#define DHT11_PIN 18


#define UART_PORT UART_NUM_2
#define TXD_PIN 17
#define RXD_PIN 16
#define UART_BUFF_SIZE 1024
```

Here, we include `driver/uart.h` for UART functionality. Then, we define which UART controller we wish to use; in this scenario, it is `UART_NUM_2`. We also define the transmit and receive pins, which are 17 and 16, respectively. Additionally, we define the receive buffer size. Although we are not going to use it at all since this application is for the sender, the UART driver still requires it.

Next, we initialize the hardware:

```
static void init_hw(void)
{
    const uart_config_t uart_config = {
        .baud_rate = 9600,
        .data_bits = UART_DATA_8_BITS,
        .parity = UART_PARITY_DISABLE,
        .stop_bits = UART_STOP_BITS_1,
        .flow_ctrl = UART_HW_FLOWCTRL_DISABLE,
        .source_clk = UART_SCLK_APB,
    };
    uart_driver_install(UART_PORT, UART_BUFF_SIZE, 0, 0, NULL,
0);
```

```
    uart_param_config(UART_PORT, &uart_config);
    uart_set_pin(UART_PORT, TXD_PIN, RXD_PIN, UART_PIN_NO_
CHANGE, UART_PIN_NO_CHANGE);
}
```

In `init_hw`, we define a configuration variable, `uart_config`, which contains the setting required for UART communication; this is *9600,8N1*. The `uart_driver_install` function reserves the UART controller and RX/TX buffer memories. We pass `0` (zero) as the buffer size for TX, which makes the transmit function block the calling task until all of the data has been sent. That is fine for our purposes in this example. Then, we set the UART communication parameters by calling `uart_param_config` with the variable of `uart_config`, which we defined earlier. Finally, we set the RX/TX pins with the `uart_set_pin` function. Now, we are ready to send DHT11 readings to the receiving ESP32 over UART:

```
static void read_dht11(void *arg)
{
    int16_t humidity = 0, temperature = 0;
    char buff[1];


    while (1)
    {
        vTaskDelay(2000 / portTICK_PERIOD_MS);
        dht_read_data(DHT_TYPE_DHT11, (gpio_num_t)DHT11_PIN,
&humidity, &temperature);
        buff[0] = (char)(temperature / 10);
        uart_write_bytes(UART_PORT, buff, 1);
    }
}


void app_main()
{
    init_hw();


    xTaskCreate(read_dht11, "dht11", configMINIMAL_STACK_SIZE *
8, NULL, 5, NULL);
}
```

In `read_dht11`, we read the temperature value from DHT11 every 2 seconds. We update the buffer with the temperature value that has just been read and call `uart_write_bytes` with the UART channel, the buffer, and buffer size as parameters. In `app_main`, we simply call `init_hw` and create a task to pass the control to `read_dht11`. That is all for the sender. Now, we can move onto the receiving end, ESP32-2:

```c
#include <freertos/FreeRTOS.h>
#include <freertos/task.h>
#include <stdint.h>
#include "driver/uart.h"
#include <stdio.h>

#define UART_PORT UART_NUM_2
#define TXD_PIN 17
#define RXD_PIN 16
#define UART_BUFF_SIZE 1024

static void init_hw(void)
{
    const uart_config_t uart_config = {
        .baud_rate = 9600,
        .data_bits = UART_DATA_8_BITS,
        .parity = UART_PARITY_DISABLE,
        .stop_bits = UART_STOP_BITS_1,
        .flow_ctrl = UART_HW_FLOWCTRL_DISABLE,
        .source_clk = UART_SCLK_APB,
    };
    uart_driver_install(UART_PORT, UART_BUFF_SIZE, 0, 0, NULL, 0);
    uart_param_config(UART_PORT, &uart_config);
    uart_set_pin(UART_PORT, TXD_PIN, RXD_PIN, UART_PIN_NO_CHANGE, UART_PIN_NO_CHANGE);
}
```

As you can see, every piece of initialization code for the receiver is the same as the sender. In fact, we could set a different UART controller, such as UART_NUM_1, or use other pins for TX and RX. As long as the baud rate, the data bits, and the parity and stop bit configuration parameters are the same as the sender, it doesn't matter what hardware is used.

Let's implement a function to read from the UART port:

```
static void read_uart(void *arg)
{
    uint8_t buff[UART_BUFF_SIZE];

    while (1)
    {
        if (uart_read_bytes(UART_PORT, buff, UART_BUFF_SIZE,
2000 / portTICK_PERIOD_MS) > 0)
        {
            printf("temp: %d\n", (int)buff[0]);
        }
    }
}
```

In the read_uart function, we call uart_read_bytes with the buff parameter into which the received data will be written. The uart_read_bytes function waits for 2 seconds, and if anything has been received, this is printed on the serial monitor. We could set the timeout value to anything; however, we know that the sender sends a temperature reading every 2 seconds, so this timeout value works for us.

In the app_main function, we simply initialize the hardware and start a FreeRTOS task with read_uart, as follows:

```
void app_main()
{
    init_hw();

    xTaskCreate(read_uart, "uart", configMINIMAL_STACK_SIZE *
8, NULL, 5, NULL);
}
```

Now we have completed the code and it is ready to run. When we connect to the receiver via the serial monitor, we will see that a temperature reading is printed on the screen every 2 seconds.

UART communication is very useful when we need to connect two different MCUs to exchange data between them. They don't have to be the same model or type; it is just enough to use the same UART configuration.

In the next section, we are going to learn how to add sound capabilities to our ESP32 projects.

Adding a speaker with I²S

Inter-IC Sound (I²S) is another type of data interface but for audio. Essentially, it has three lines for the following:

- Data, **Data-In (DIN)**, or **Data-Out (DOUT)**
- Clock or **bit clock (BCLK)**
- Channel select, **word select (WS)**, or **left-right clock (LRCLK)**

The interface is a standard; however, the naming is not, as we see above. The data line carries stereo audio data for both the left (channel 0) and right (channel 1) channels. The channel select signal indicates which channel data is currently being transferred: it is a low level for the left channel and a high level for the right channel. Finally, the clock line is a common clock for both ends provided by the master, which is usually the sending party in this type of communication.

ESP32 provides two I²S peripherals that can be configured as input or output. When configured as input, a mic can be used to sample the sound data and store it on the flash for later use. If it is configured as an output, then a speaker can be connected to produce the sound.

In this example, we are going to use MAX98357 from Maxim Integrated as an I2S sound amplifier between ESP32 and a speaker. In the following figure, you can see a breakout board with a MAX98357 chip:

Figure 4.3 – The MAX98357 module

This module is a low-cost, highly efficient amplifier that can be used with a 3.3 V output from an ESP32 module without the need for any external power source. It can output 3.2W of power to a 4Ω speaker, which is more than enough for our purposes. For more information, you can check out its datasheet on the Maxim Integrated website at `https://datasheets.maximintegrated.com/en/ds/MAX98357A-MAX98357B.pdf`.

Our example has been divided into two parts to make things easier to follow. In the first part, we will define the partitions on the ESP32 flash memory and upload a *WAV* file to the data partition as audio data. The second part contains the real application, where we play the audio file on a speaker. Let's start by uploading a file.

Uploading a sound file to the flash memory

Although it is not hard, uploading a file requires some attention. So, let's follow it step by step:

1. After creating the PlatformIO project, add the partition definition file, `partitions.csv`, in the root folder of the project:

```
# Name,     Type, SubType, Offset,    Size, Flags
nvs,        data, nvs,     ,          0x6000,
phy_init,   data, phy,     ,          0x1000,
factory,    app,  factory, ,          1M,
spiffs,     data, spiffs,  0x210000,      1M,
```

This is the file in which we can define partitions of the flash memory. The bootloader always looks for a `factory` partition where the application has been stored. The audio file will be in the `spiffs` data partition. `partitions.csv` also contains other information such as the offset from the flash start and the size of a partition. If an offset is not provided, then *ESP-IDF* calculates it based on the information coming from `sdkconfig` and the sizes, as provided in `partitions.csv`. Here, we have to provide all sizes. In this example, the `spiffs` partition starts from `0x210000` and its size is 1 megabyte.

Since we want to customize the flash partitions, we need to specify the definition file, `partitions.csv`, in both `platformio.ini` and `sdkconfig`.

2. Edit `platformio.ini` to specify the partition file:

```
monitor_speed = 115200
board_build.partitions = partitions.csv
```

3. Start a command line and activate the Python virtual environment for the `pio` command-line tool:

```
$ source ~/.platformio/penv/bin/activate
(penv)$ pio --version
PlatformIO, version 5.1.0
```

4. Edit `sdkconfig` using the `pio` tool. As discussed earlier, `sdkconfig` contains all of the application settings for an ESP32 project. In this case, we will set the custom partitions file in `sdkconfig`:

```
(penv)$  pio run -t menuconfig
```

The preceding command shows the following interface:

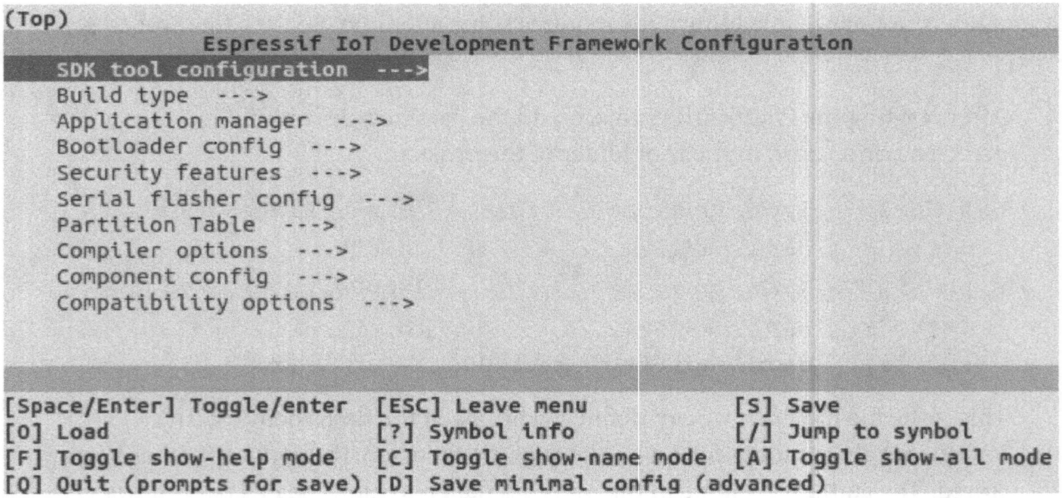

```
(Top)
              Espressif IoT Development Framework Configuration
    SDK tool configuration  --->
    Build type  --->
    Application manager  --->
    Bootloader config  --->
    Security features  --->
    Serial flasher config  --->
    Partition Table  --->
    Compiler options  --->
    Component config  --->
    Compatibility options  --->




[Space/Enter] Toggle/enter   [ESC] Leave menu        [S] Save
[O] Load                     [?] Symbol info         [/] Jump to symbol
[F] Toggle show-help mode    [C] Toggle show-name mode  [A] Toggle show-all mode
[Q] Quit (prompts for save)  [D] Save minimal config (advanced)
```

Figure 4.4 – ESP-IDF menuconfig

`menuconfig` is a menu-driven user interface, which is used to edit configuration files that are based on the **Kconfig** configuration system. ESP-IDF adopts `menuconfig` to edit `sdkconfig`, and we use `pio` to run `menuconfig`.

> **Tip**
>
> You can also use the *K* and *J*, or + and -, key pairs on your keyboard to navigate up and down in menuconfig if the *Up* and *Down* arrow keys don't work.

5. Set the name of the partition file in sdkconfig by selecting **Partition Table | Partition Table | Custom partition table CSV**:

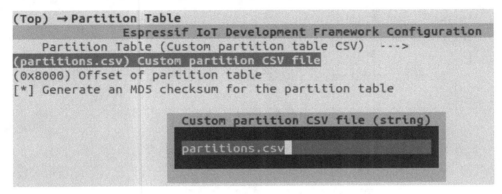

Figure 4.5 – Custom partition CSV filename

Enter the name of the file as partitions.csv in the textbox.

6. Let's go back to the top level and navigate to **Component Config | SPIFFS Configuration** to set the maximum number of partitions to 5. This will support the number of partitions that we have defined in the custom partition file:

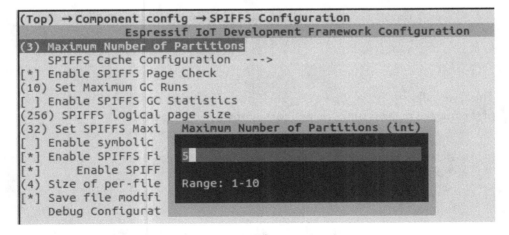

Figure 4.6 – The maximum number of partitions

Press *Q* to quit. It will prompt you to save.

7. Now we are ready to test whether the `spiffs` partition will be created. To do this, run a simple application, as follows:

```c
#include <stdio.h>
#include <sys/stat.h>
#include "esp_spiffs.h"
#include "esp_err.h"

void app_main(void)
{
    printf("Initializing SPIFFS\n");

    esp_vfs_spiffs_conf_t conf = {
        .base_path = "/spiffs",
        .partition_label = NULL,
        .max_files = 5,
        .format_if_mount_failed = true};
```

In `app_main`, we first create a configuration variable to register the `spiffs` partition:

```c
    esp_err_t ret = esp_vfs_spiffs_register(&conf);
    if (ret != ESP_OK)
    {
        printf("Failed to initialize SPIFFS (%s)\n", esp_
err_to_name(ret));
        return;
    }
```

Then, we call `esp_vfs_spiffs_register` with that variable. When the code first runs, the register function will format the `spiffs` partition:

```c
    size_t total = 0, used = 0;
    ret = esp_spiffs_info(conf.partition_label, &total,
&used);
    if (ret == ESP_OK)
    {
        printf("Partition size: total: %d, used: %d\n",
total, used);
    }
```

```
    else
    {
        printf("Failed to get SPIFFS partition
information (%s)\n", esp_err_to_name(ret));
    }
}
```

Here, esp_spiffs_info will read the partition information. And, if everything goes well, we will see the partition size printed on the serial monitor.

8. Having seen that the spiffs partition is ready, create the data folder in the project root and copy the sound file, rooster.wav. This file is provided in the code repository, but you can use any *WAV* file that has the parameters supported by the sound module:

```
(penv)$ mkdir data && cp ~/Downloads/rooster.wav data/
```

9. Generate the SPIFFS image by using the pio tool. The pio tool requires the data folder and uses the files inside this folder to generate the partition image:

```
(penv)$ pio run -t buildfs
```

10. Upload the image to the spiffs partition, again by using pio:

```
(penv)$ pio run -t uploadfs
```

11. Let's update the code file, main.c. Add the following code snippet to the end of the app_main function to check whether the file is in the partition. Then, rerun the application:

```
struct stat st;
if (stat("/spiffs/rooster.wav", &st) == 0)
{
    printf(">> rooster.wav found. %ld\n", st.st_size);
}
else
{
    printf(">> rooster.wav NOT found\n");
}
```

12. Connect to the serial monitor to see whether the sound file exists on the flash memory:

```
Initializing SPIFFS
Partition size: total: 956561, used: 100400
>> rooster.wav found. 99286
```

> **Important note**
>
> pio employs mkspiffs and esptool.py from Espressif behind the scenes to create and upload SPIFFS image files. If you want to customize the file upload process, you can use these tools. The latest mkspiffs tool is available at https://github.com/igrr/mkspiffs, and esptool.py is located in your $HOME/.platformio folder.

Finally, we are ready to play this WAV file on a speaker. Let's discuss this next.

Playing the sound file

After adding a sound file to the spiffs partition, we first need to set up the prototype on the breadboard, as usual. The components are as follows:

- A MAX98357 amplifier module
- A speaker (impedance >= 4 ohm)

The following figure shows the Fritzing diagram of our setup:

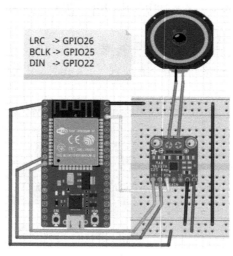

Figure 4.7 – A Fritzing sketch of the sound example

Here is the application code:

```c
#include "app.h"
#include <stdio.h>
#include <stdint.h>
#include <stdio.h>
#include <sys/stat.h>
#include "esp_spiffs.h"
#include "esp_err.h"
#include "driver/i2s.h"
#include "hal/i2s_types.h"

#define BCLK_PIN 25
#define LRC_PIN 26
#define DIN_PIN 22

static const int i2s_num = I2S_NUM_0;
static uint8_t buff[1024];
static FILE *wav_fp;
```

The header file for the I2S driver is driver/i2s.h. We define I2S pins and a constant for the I2S peripheral with the value of I2S_NUM_0. We also create variables for the sound file and the sound data buffer that will be used in the application.

In the init_hw function, we only initialize the spiffs partition, as follows:

```c
static esp_err_t init_hw(void)
{
    printf("Initializing SPIFFS\n");

    esp_vfs_spiffs_conf_t conf = {
        .base_path = "/spiffs",
        .partition_label = NULL,
        .max_files = 5,
        .format_if_mount_failed = true};

    return esp_vfs_spiffs_register(&conf);
}
```

We need a function to open the sound file. Let's continue with that function:

```c
static esp_err_t open_file(wav_header_t *header)
{
    wav_fp = fopen("/spiffs/rooster.wav", "rb");
    if (wav_fp == NULL)
    {
        printf("err: no file\n");
        return ESP_ERR_INVALID_ARG;
    }

    fread((void *)header, sizeof(wav_header_t), 1, wav_fp);
    printf("Wav format:\n");
    printf("bit_depth: %d\n", header->bit_depth);
    printf("num_channels: %d\n", header->num_channels);
    printf("sample_rate: %d\n", header->sample_rate);

    return ESP_OK;
}
```

In open_file, we open the sound file stored inside the spiffs partition and read the WAV header within the file. Every WAV file contains metadata information about the actual sound data. We are going to use some information enclosed in this header while configuring the I2S peripheral for output. This information is as follows:

- The sample rate or the number of samples in a second
- The bit depth or the number of bits per sample (ADC resolution)
- The number of channels; a single channel or two channels for left and right

We should initialize the I2S peripheral to play the sound file. Here is the initialization function:

```c
static esp_err_t init_i2s(wav_header_t *header)
{
    esp_err_t err;

    i2s_config_t i2s_config = {
        .mode = I2S_MODE_MASTER | I2S_MODE_TX,
```

```
        .sample_rate = header->sample_rate,
        .bits_per_sample = header->bit_depth,
        .communication_format = I2S_COMM_FORMAT_I2S_MSB,
        .channel_format = header->num_channels == 2 ? I2S_
CHANNEL_FMT_RIGHT_LEFT : I2S_CHANNEL_FMT_ONLY_LEFT,
        .intr_alloc_flags = 0,
        .dma_buf_count = 2,
        .dma_buf_len = 1024,
        .use_apll = 1,
    };
```

The init_i2s function takes the sound metadata coming from the file as the argument. In the function, we create a configuration variable of the i2s_config_t type. This configuration variable has various fields regarding how we will use the I2S peripheral and the properties of the sound file to be played. We also specify that the I2S peripheral will use **direct memory access (DMA)** for fast data processing directly from the DMA buffer. After preparing the configuration variable, we use i2s_driver_install to configure the driver with this configuration:

```
    err = i2s_driver_install(i2s_num, &i2s_config, 0, NULL);
    if (err != ESP_OK)
    {
        return err;
    }
```

The next thing to do is to set the pins to be used with the I2S peripheral by calling i2s_set_pin:

```
    i2s_pin_config_t pin_config = {
        .bck_io_num = BCLK_PIN,
        .ws_io_num = LRC_PIN,
        .data_out_num = DIN_PIN,
        .data_in_num = I2S_PIN_NO_CHANGE,
    };
    err = i2s_set_pin(i2s_num, &pin_config);
    if (err != ESP_OK)
    {
        return err;
    }
```

```
        return i2s_zero_dma_buffer(i2s_num);
}
```

Since the peripheral is outputting, we set the data_out_num field of pin_config, just to be clear. Finally, we reset the DMA buffer and the I2S configuration is complete.

Having implemented all of the initialization functions, we can move onto app_main. First, we initialize the SPIFFS driver in init_hw and open the sound file by calling open_file:

```
void app_main(void)
{
    esp_err_t ret;

    ret = init_hw();
    if (ret != ESP_OK)
    {
        printf("err: %s\n", esp_err_to_name(ret));
        return;
    }

    wav_header_t header;
    ret = open_file(&header);
    if (ret != ESP_OK)
    {
        printf("err: %s\n", esp_err_to_name(ret));
        return;
    }
```

Then, we initialize the I2S peripheral with the sound metadata:

```
    ret = init_i2s(&header);
    if (ret != ESP_OK)
    {
        printf("err: %s\n", esp_err_to_name(ret));
        return;
    }
```

The initialization is complete, and we are ready to play the sound as follows:

```
    size_t bytes_written;
    size_t cnt;

    while (1)
    {
        cnt = fread(buff, 1, sizeof(buff), wav_fp);
        ret = i2s_write(i2s_num, (const void *)buff,
sizeof(buff), &bytes_written, portMAX_DELAY);
        if (ret != ESP_OK)
        {
            printf("err: %s\n", esp_err_to_name(ret));
            break;
        }
```

In a `while` loop, we read from the file into `buff`, and we use `i2s_write` to send the sound data to the I2S interface via the DMA buffer. When all of the data has been transferred, we can close the file and uninstall the I2S driver by using the `i2s_driver_uninstall` function:

```
        if (cnt < sizeof(buff))
        {
            break;
        }
    }

    fclose(wav_fp);
    i2s_driver_uninstall(i2s_num);
}
```

That is it! We can upload the application and enjoy the rooster sound.

In the next section, we will learn how to use a camera sensor with ESP[32].

Developing a camera application

It is not within the scope of this book to discuss image technologies in detail; however, as a piece of additional background knowledge, it would be beneficial for us to know about the basics to understand the capabilities of the hardware that we are using in this example. There are two main types of digital image sensors that are common in the market:

- **Charge-coupled device (CCD)**

- **Complementary metal-oxide semiconductor (CMOS)** sensors

CMOS sensors use a newer technology, and they have several important advantages over CCDs. They are low-cost, power-efficient, and have smaller components; therefore, they are more appropriate for battery-operated devices such as mobile phones or IoT devices.

In this example, we will use a CMOS image sensor, OV2640, from OmniVision. It provides a single-chip **Ultra Extended Graphics Array** (**UXGA**) (1600 x 1200 = 2 megapixels) camera and image processor in a small footprint package. It uses 900 μA on standby and consumes 140 mW power when active. The control interface is a serial interface, which is similar to I2C, and only requires two lines for the data and the clock. This interface is called the **Serial Camera Control Bus** (**SCCB**). The video port of OV2640 can be configured in 8-bit mode or 10-bit mode depending on the available resources on the host microcontroller.

To make life easier, Ai-Thinker has a camera devkit with ESP32 in its product portfolio, which is named Ai-Thinker ESP32-CAM. This is the devkit that we will employ in our example. It comes with an OV2640 sensor and a MicroSD slot integrated on it. You can view an image of ESP32-CAM in the following photograph:

Figure 4.8 – ESP32-CAM from Ai-Thinker with OV2640

ESP32-CAM is specialized for camera applications, so it is very convenient to experiment with it without any cabling hassle. We could also use our Az-Delivery ESP32 kit by attaching a camera module, but Ai-Thinker already has all of the necessary hardware out of the box. The only drawback is that it doesn't have a USB-UART chip onboard to program and monitor serially; therefore, we need to use our own USB-UART adapter to connect the board to our development machine. In this example, we will need the following components:

- Ai-Thinker ESP32-CAM
- A USB-UART adapter
- A MicroSD card (FAT32 formatted)

In the next section, we will learn how to prepare the development environment.

Preparing the development environment for ESP32-CAM

Unfortunately, at the time of writing this book, PlatformIO doesn't handle this board well, which means we require some extra steps to prepare the environment before developing with ESP32-CAM. Here are the steps:

1. First, create a new PlatformIO project with any ESP32 board type. Ai-Thinker ESP32-CAM is in the list of supported boards, but PlatformIO gives some errors when it is selected as the board. After creating a new project, we need to update the platformio.ini file, as follows:

```
[env:esp32cam]
platform = espressif32
board = esp32cam
framework = espidf
monitor_speed = 115200
board_build.partitions = partitions_singleapp.csv
```

2. Update CMakeList.txt in the project root folder for the camera driver library. We use an external library from Espressif to drive the camera sensors. However, I had to change it a bit due to some errors that I found while working with the ESP32-CAM devkit. The updated library is located at https://github.com/PacktPublishing/Internet-of-Things-with-ESP32/tree/main/common/esp32-camera:

```
cmake_minimum_required(VERSION 3.16.0)
list(APPEND EXTRA_COMPONENT_DIRS "../../common/esp32-camera")
include($ENV{IDF_PATH}/tools/cmake/project.cmake)
project(camera_example)
```

The highlighted command in the second line adds the library path as a component directory to the project.

3. Add a configuration file, called Kconfig.projbuild, under the src folder where main.c exists. It is for PlatformIO to update sdkconfig.h of ESP-IDF with camera configuration definitions such as pin numbers, supported camera sensors, and more. It is a relatively long file, so I can't show the content here. But you can download it from https://github.com/PacktPublishing/Internet-of-Things-with-ESP32/blob/main/ch4/camera_example/src/Kconfig.projbuild.

4. Activate the pio tool and run menuconfig:

```
$ source ~/.platformio/penv/bin/activate
(penv)$ pio run -t menuconfig
```

5. Update two keys here to be able to use a microSD card with the devkit. The first one is **Component config | ESP32 specific | Support for external SPI RAM | SPI RAM config | Type**, which you need to set to **Auto-detect**, as you can see in the following screenshot:

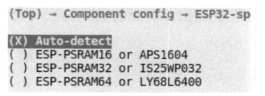

Figure 4.9 – Updating the SPI RAM chip type to Auto-detect

The second one is for long filename support by setting **Component config | FAT FS support | Long filename support**, as follows:

```
(Top) → Component config → FAT Filesystem support → Long filename support
                                                    Espressif IoT De
( ) No long filenames
(X) Long filename buffer in heap
( ) Long filename buffer on stack
```

Figure 4.10 – Long filename support

Now we are ready to press the compile button and can see that the project compiles without an error.

The next section describes how to program and monitor ESP32-CAM with an external USB-UART adapter.

Flashing and monitoring ESP32-CAM

As we discussed in the introductory part of this section, Ai-Thinker ESP32-CAM doesn't include any USB-UART chip on board. It is a trade-off between cost and functionality. Therefore, we need to use an adapter to connect it to our development PC. There are many adapters available on the market. I have a generic one with a CP2102 chip on it. An example is shown in the following photograph:

Figure 4.11 – The USB-UART adapter

Let's take a look at the steps to program and monitor the devkit:

1. First, make the following connections between the USB-UART adapter and ESP32-CAM:

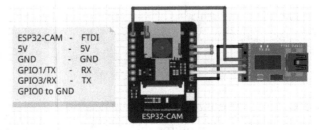

```
ESP32-CAM  -  FTDI
5V         -  5V
GND        -  GND
GPIO1/TX   -  RX
GPIO3/RX   -  TX
GPIO0 to GND
```

Figure 4.12 – Connecting to the USB-UART adapter – programming mode

> **Important note**
>
> ESP32-CAM needs to be powered by 5V. Most USB-UART adapters provide
> a 5V pin that you can use for this purpose. However, if you still encounter an
> error during flashing or normal operations, you might need to power your
> ESP32-CAM with an external 5V power source.

To be able to program ESP32-CAM, we need to keep GPIO0 low while powering
it. In fact, this is the programming mode of any ESP32 chip, but this process is
handled automatically in other devkits that have onboard USB-UART chips. When
we are done with flashing, we must free the GPIO0 pin to allow ESP32 to start the
application on it.

2. Clear the project, then recompile and flash ESP32-CAM with the following test
    code in `main.c`:

```c
#include <esp_system.h>
#include <nvs_flash.h>
#include "freertos/FreeRTOS.h"
#include "freertos/task.h"

#include "driver/sdmmc_host.h"
#include "driver/sdmmc_defs.h"
#include "sdmmc_cmd.h"
#include "esp_vfs_fat.h"

#include "esp_camera.h"

void app_main()
{
    while (1)
    {
        printf("hi!\n");
        vTaskDelay(2000 / portTICK_PERIOD_MS);
    }
}
```

3. Unplug the adapter, free the GPIO0 pin, and plug it again.

4. Then, start the PlatformIO serial monitor and view the messages coming from
    ESP32-CAM.

We have prepared our PlatformIO development environment and we have tested it with a simple print application by connecting ESP32-CAM via a USB-UART adapter. Next, we are going to implement the project.

Developing the project

The goal of this project is to develop a photo-trap device where we use a **Passive Infrared** (**PIR**) motion detection module together with ESP32-CAM. Whenever the PIR module detects a motion, ESP32-CAM takes a photo and saves it on the microSD memory card in its slot. The following figure of a Fritzing diagram shows the setup:

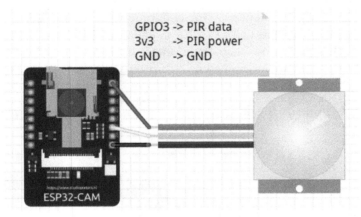

Figure 4.13 – Camera wiring example

We still need to power ESP32-CAM from its 5V pin, and we can monitor it if we connect the U0TXD (GPIO1) pin to the USB-UART adapter. We use GPIO3 (U0RXD) as the PIR module pin because all other pins are occupied by the SD card driver. If we didn't use an SD card on ESP32-CAM, then we could reassign those pins for other purposes. The power source warning still holds. If you see some erratic behavior after you power ESP32-CAM, it is better to look for an external power source. Now, let's continue with the application:

```
#include <esp_system.h>
#include <nvs_flash.h>
#include "freertos/FreeRTOS.h"
#include "freertos/task.h"

#include "driver/gpio.h"
#include "driver/sdmmc_host.h"
#include "driver/sdmmc_defs.h"
#include "sdmmc_cmd.h"
```

```
#include "esp_vfs_fat.h"


#include "esp_camera.h"


#define PIR_MOTION_PIN 3


static void pir_handler(void *arg);
static void take_pic(void *arg);
```

esp_camera.h is the header file where all ESP32-CAM-type definitions and function declarations are provided. We also need to include some more header files to drive the SD card. We have a macro definition for the PIR module pin. GPIO3 will provide interrupts to notify the application when a motion occurs. Then, we add the function prototype for the interrupt handler, named pir_handler, and another function prototype, take_pic, to take a picture to be called from the interrupt handler.

Let's examine how to initialize the hardware. init_hw is a bit lengthy, so we will discuss it in parts:

```
static esp_err_t init_hw(void)
{
    camera_config_t camera_config = {
        .pin_pwdn = CONFIG_PWDN,
        .pin_reset = CONFIG_RESET,
        .pin_xclk = CONFIG_XCLK,
        .pin_sscb_sda = CONFIG_SDA,
        .pin_sscb_scl = CONFIG_SCL,

        .pin_d7 = CONFIG_D7,
        .pin_d6 = CONFIG_D6,
        .pin_d5 = CONFIG_D5,
        .pin_d4 = CONFIG_D4,
        .pin_d3 = CONFIG_D3,
        .pin_d2 = CONFIG_D2,
        .pin_d1 = CONFIG_D1,
        .pin_d0 = CONFIG_D0,
        .pin_vsync = CONFIG_VSYNC,
        .pin_href = CONFIG_HREF,
```

```
    .pin_pclk = CONFIG_PCLK,

    .xclk_freq_hz = CONFIG_XCLK_FREQ,
    .ledc_timer = LEDC_TIMER_0,
    .ledc_channel = LEDC_CHANNEL_0,

    .pixel_format = PIXFORMAT_JPEG,
    .frame_size = FRAMESIZE_UXGA,

    .jpeg_quality = 12,
    .fb_count = 1};
```

In the camera_config variable, we use the pin configuration information coming from the PlatformIO Kconfig file that we had already added while configuring the development environment. PlatformIO reads that configuration file and adds all of the entries in it into sdkconfig.h as macro definitions to which we have access as CONFIG_* definitions. In terms of image format, we have the following options:

- PIXFORMAT_RGB565
- PIXFORMAT_RGB555
- PIXFORMAT_YUV422
- PIXFORMAT_GRAYSCALE
- PIXFORMAT_JPEG
- PIXFORMAT_RAW

The library supports some other formats but only those in the above list are available for this type of camera sensor. In our project, we choose PIXFORMAT_JPEG as the image format.

Then, we call the esp_camera_init function with camera_config to initialize the camera sensor:

```
esp_err_t err = esp_camera_init(&camera_config);
if (err != ESP_OK)
{
    return err;
}
```

If there is no error, we continue with mounting the SD card:

```
sdmmc_host_t host = SDMMC_HOST_DEFAULT();
sdmmc_slot_config_t slot_config = SDMMC_SLOT_CONFIG_
DEFAULT();
esp_vfs_fat_sdmmc_mount_config_t mount_config = {
    .format_if_mount_failed = false,
    .max_files = 3,
};
sdmmc_card_t *card;
err = esp_vfs_fat_sdmmc_mount("/sdcard", &host, &slot_
config, &mount_config, &card);
if (err != ESP_OK)
{
    return err;
}
```

Here, the `esp_vfs_fat_sdmmc_mount` function does the job. It needs an SD/MMC host, a slot configuration, and a mount configuration to mount the SD card.

Finally, we need to configure GPIO3 for motion interrupts, as follows:

```
gpio_config_t io_conf;
io_conf.mode = GPIO_MODE_INPUT;
io_conf.pin_bit_mask = (1ULL << PIR_MOTION_PIN);
io_conf.intr_type = GPIO_INTR_POSEDGE;
io_conf.pull_up_en = 1;
err = gpio_config(&io_conf);
if (err != ESP_OK)
{
    return err;
}
return gpio_isr_handler_add(PIR_MOTION_PIN, pir_handler,
NULL);
}
```

After completing the initialization, we can implement the `pir_handler` ISR, as follows:

```
static TickType_t next = 0;
const TickType_t period = 20000 / portTICK_PERIOD_MS;
```

```
static void IRAM_ATTR pir_handler(void *arg)
{
    TickType_t now = xTaskGetTickCountFromISR();

    if (now > next)
    {
        xTaskCreate(take_pic, "pic", configMINIMAL_STACK_SIZE *
5, NULL, 5, NULL);
    }
    next = now + period;
}
```

pir_handler creates a FreeRTOS task to call take_pic if there is a new motion after 20 seconds. Any motion in a 20-second time period will push the period forward without taking any picture.

Let's implement the function to take a picture next:

```
static void take_pic(void *arg)
{
    printf("Say cheese!\n");

    camera_fb_t *pic = esp_camera_fb_get();

    char pic_name[50];
    sprintf(pic_name, "/sdcard/pic_%li.jpg", pic->timestamp.
tv_sec);
    FILE *file = fopen(pic_name, "w");
    if (file == NULL)
    {
        printf("err: fopen failed\n");
    }
    else
    {
        fwrite(pic->buf, 1, pic->len, file);
        fclose(file);
    }
```

```
    vTaskDelete(NULL);
}
```

`take_pic` is the action part after a motion is detected. In the function, we call `esp_camera_fb_get` to get the frame buffer as a picture. The `camera_fb_t` structure contains image data along with other metadata such as the pixel format and timestamp.

All functions are completed except `app_main`, which follows next:

```
void app_main()
{
    esp_err_t err;
    err = init_hw();
    if (err != ESP_OK)
    {
        printf("err: %s\n", esp_err_to_name(err));
        return;
    }
}
```

In `app_main`, we only initialize the hardware, nothing more. The rest is handled by the PIR ISR handler, as we discussed earlier.

Now, we can test the application by flashing ESP32-CAM just like we did in the previous section. After flashing it successfully, we can return to this hardware setup and check whether it really takes a picture when a motion is detected.

> **Tip**
>
> If you don't want to unplug the USB-UART adapter, swap the PIR and UART pins, set GPIO0 to low, and plug the adapter again every time for the code-flash-test cycle, then you can prepare a simple setup on a breadboard with a toggle button, a 3-way switch, and hookup wires. Toggling the button keeps the GPIO0 pin low during flashing, and toggling again releases GPIO0 for normal operations. The 3-way switch is used to swap the PIR and UART connections.

In the next topic, we will discuss the power-saving modes of ESP32 and its ULP coprocessor.

Developing low-power applications

ESP32 allows us to develop low-power applications with its power management technology. This provides the following:

- Low-power clocks
- **Ultra-low power** (**ULP**) coprocessors
- **Real-time controller** (**RTC**) memory to be used in sleep modes
- Wake-up sources

By using these components on ESP32, we can develop highly efficient battery-powered IoT devices. There are five predefined power modes of ESP32:

- **Active**: All components of ESP32 are powered, with no power saving. In all examples up to this point, our devkit was in that mode.
- **Modem-sleep mode**: Here, Wi-Fi and Bluetooth are disabled, with no radio communication. For such **system-on-chip** (**SoC**) types, radio is on top in terms of power consumption. Therefore, when we turn the radio off, it makes quite a difference in saving power.
- **Light-sleep mode**: The high-speed clock and all dependent components stop. The cores and RAM are still powered but not available to use. Low-power features and the ULP processor are available. ESP32 preserves the application state, so it is easy and fast to wake it up. The current consumption is around 800 µA.
- **Deep-sleep mode**: In this state, ESP32 is fully in the low-power operation. The cores and RAM are off, so we have to use RTC memory for any data retention. The current consumption is around 6.5 µA.
- **Hibernation**: The ULP processor is also powered down and ESP32 doesn't have any computation capabilities in this mode. Only the RTC subsystem is available to wake the system up when an external event occurs.

Let's take a look at two examples where we put ESP32 in light-sleep mode and deep-sleep mode.

Waking up from light sleep

In this example, we will keep ESP32 in light-sleep mode. As wake-up sources, we will use a timer for periodic wake-up and a touch sensor for event-based wake-up. There will be no extra hardware component except a hookup wire for the touch sensor. We can simply code the application in `main.c`:

```c
#include "esp_sleep.h"
#include "driver/touch_pad.h"
#include "esp_timer.h"
#include <string.h>
#include <stdio.h>


#define SEC_MULTIPLIER 10000001
```

To access the ESP32 sleep functions, we include `esp_sleep.h` and the touchpad functions are declared in `driver/touch_pad.h`.

The hardware initialization function is given in the following code snippet:

```c
static void init_hw(void)
{
    touch_pad_init();
    touch_pad_set_fsm_mode(TOUCH_FSM_MODE_TIMER);
    touch_pad_set_voltage(TOUCH_HVOLT_2V7, TOUCH_LVOLT_0V5,
TOUCH_HVOLT_ATTEN_1V);

    touch_pad_config(TOUCH_PAD_NUM8, 0);
    touch_pad_filter_start(10);

    uint16_t val;
    touch_pad_read_filtered(TOUCH_PAD_NUM8, &val);
    touch_pad_set_thresh(TOUCH_PAD_NUM8, val * 0.2);
}
```

`init_hw` is only for touchpad initialization. We will use the `TOUCH_PAD_NUM8` channel as a wake-up source.

Next, we implement the `app_main` function:

```
void app_main(void)
{
    init_hw();
    int cnt = 0;

    while (1)
    {
        esp_sleep_enable_timer_wakeup(5 * SEC_MULTIPLIER);
        esp_sleep_enable_touchpad_wakeup();

        esp_light_sleep_start();
```

In a `while` loop, in `app_main`, first, we enable the timer and touchpad as wake-up sources, then we call `esp_light_sleep_start` to put ESP32 into light sleep. When ESP32 wakes up, it just starts from the next line to run the application, which is a `printf` statement where we print the cnt value:

```
        printf("cnt: %d\n", ++cnt);
        printf("active at (timer value): %lli\n", esp_timer_
get_time() / SEC_MULTIPLIER);
        printf("wakeup source: ");
```

We see that the cnt value is always preserved and incremented in each call of the `printf` statement.

We can use `esp_sleep_get_wakeup_cause` to understand what activated ESP32, as follows:

```
        switch (esp_sleep_get_wakeup_cause())
        {
        case ESP_SLEEP_WAKEUP_TIMER:
            printf("timer\n");
            break;
        case ESP_SLEEP_WAKEUP_TOUCHPAD:
        {
            touch_pad_t tp;
            touch_pad_get_wakeup_status(&tp);
            printf("touchpad (%d)\n", tp);
```

```
        break;
    }
    default:
        printf("err: no other configured\n");
        break;
    }
  }
}
```

That is it! We flash the devkit with the application and see how the light-sleep mode works. We can wake up the application by using the touchpad pin.

Let's continue with the deep-sleep example where we use the ULP coprocessor.

Using the ULP coprocessor in deep sleep

For further power saving, we can make use of deep-sleep mode. In this mode, the cores and RAM are powered off as well. We can configure ESP32 to wake up on external events or based on a schedule using a low-power timer. However, what if the criteria to wake up ESP32 is when the temperature or light level exceeds a certain threshold? In such cases, the ULP coprocessor comes in handy. In this example, we will use a photoresistor to approximate the ambient light level by using the ULP coprocessor, which runs a few lines of assembly code when ESP32 is in deep-sleep mode. If the light level is above the configured level, then ESP32 will be activated by the ULP coprocessor. The only hardware component in this application is a photoresistor module, such as the following:

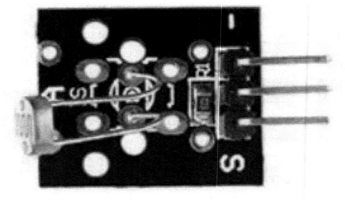

Figure 4.14 – A photoresistor module

The pin connections to the ESP32 devkit are shown in the following figure of a Fritzing diagram:

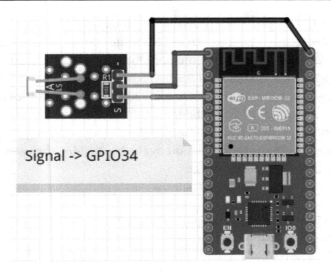

Figure 4.15 – A Fritzing sketch of the example

Before the application code, we need to make some preparations. Let's go over them step by step:

1. Create a project with the following the `platformio.ini` configuration file:

```
[env:az-delivery-devkit-v4]
platform = espressif32
board = az-delivery-devkit-v4
framework = espidf

monitor_speed = 115200
```

2. Next, provide some default configuration values in the `sdkconfig.defaults` file:

```
CONFIG_ESP32_ULP_COPROC_ENABLED=y
CONFIG_ESP32_ULP_COPROC_RESERVE_MEM=1024

CONFIG_BOOTLOADER_LOG_LEVEL_WARN=y
CONFIG_BOOTLOADER_LOG_LEVEL=2
CONFIG_LOG_DEFAULT_LEVEL_WARN=y
CONFIG_LOG_DEFAULT_LEVEL=2
CONFIG_BOOTLOADER_SKIP_VALIDATE_IN_DEEP_SLEEP=y
```

By default, the ULP coprocessor is disabled, and we need to enable it explicitly. CONFIG_ESP32_ULP_COPROC_ENABLED is the configuration option for this purpose. We also reserve some memory for the ULP coprocessor by setting CONFIG_ESP32_ULP_COPROC_RESERVE_MEM. The libraries in ESP-IDF print a lot of debugging information when the ESP32 is powered on. We set the log level in sdkconfig to get rid of this debugging information and have a clear output on the serial monitor. CONFIG_BOOTLOADER_SKIP_VALIDATE_IN_DEEP_SLEEP disables the application image validation by the bootloader after waking up from deep sleep to gain some performance.

> **Tip**
>
> If there is no sdkconfig in your project home, PlatformIO will create one by incorporating the settings in sdkconfig.defaults. You can also force PlatformIO to create a new sdkconfig by deleting the existing one, cleaning the project, and then recompiling it.

3. Add the assembly code, named adc.S, of the ULP coprocessor inside the ulp folder. In this code, we perform oversampling by reading from the ADC channel. Then, we compare the calculated ambient light value with the high threshold, and if it is above the threshold, we wake up ESP32. The assembly language is out of the scope of this book, so we will not discuss the source code. However, more information about ULP programming is available in the online documentation at https://docs.espressif.com/projects/esp-idf/en/latest/ esp32/api-guides/ulp.html. You can download the assembly code from the code repository of the book and include it in your project.

4. Finally, update src/CMakeLists.txt to tell ESP-IDF about the ULP application:

```
idf_component_register(SRCS "app_main.c"
                       INCLUDE_DIRS ""
                       REQUIRES soc nvs_flash ulp driver)

set(ulp_app_name ulp_main)
set(ulp_s_sources "../ulp/adc.S")
set(ulp_exp_dep_srcs "app_main.c")
ulp_embed_binary(${ulp_app_name} ${ulp_s_sources} ${ulp_exp_dep_srcs})
```

`ulp_embed_binary` is the directive that links the main application and the assembly code by specifying the paths and references.

After these steps, we will have a project folder structure that is similar to the following:

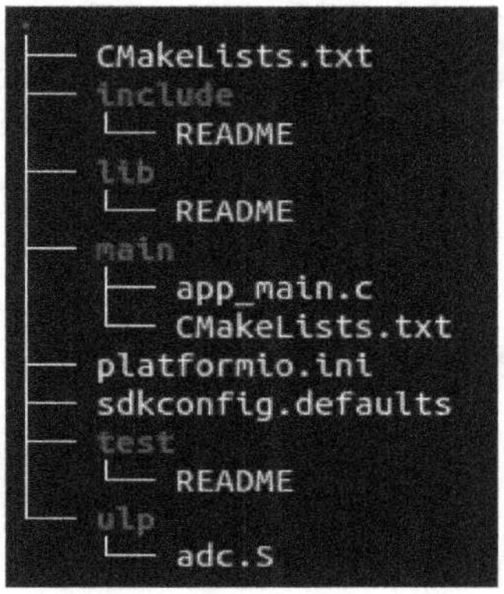

Figure 4.16 – The project files and folders before compilation

At this point, we compile the project to make PlatformIO generate all the necessary files and configurations for the project. There is one special header file, which is also generated when we compile, to be included in `app_main.c`, as we will see next. Now, we can continue with the project main application:

```c
#include <stdio.h>
#include <string.h>
#include "esp_sleep.h"
#include "driver/gpio.h"
#include "driver/rtc_io.h"
#include "driver/adc.h"


#include "esp32/ulp.h"
#include "ulp_main.h"


extern const uint8_t ulp_main_bin_start[] asm("_binary_ulp_
main_bin_start");
extern const uint8_t ulp_main_bin_end[]    asm("_binary_ulp_
main_bin_end");


static RTC_DATA_ATTR int cnt1 = 0;
static int cnt2 = 0;
```

`esp32/ulp.h` is the header file for the ULP functions. `ulp_main.h` is generated by ESP-IDF when we compile the project. It contains the global variables defined in the ULP assembly code. They are accessible to the main application when we include this header file. `ulp_main_bin_start` and `ulp_main_bin_end` mark the assembly code's beginning and end. We will use those variables to load the assembly application into the RTC memory. The next two variables, `cnt1` and `cnt2`, are to see the effect of `RTC_DATA_ATTR`. When ESP32 goes into a deep sleep, variables in the RAM cannot retain their values. The `RTC_DATA_ATTR` attribute commands the compiler to keep the target variable in the RTC memory so that the variable doesn't lose its value after a deep-sleep period.

In `init_hw`, we initialize the ADC peripheral and the ULP coprocessor, as follows:

```
static void init_hw()
{
    ulp_load_binary(0, ulp_main_bin_start,
                    (ulp_main_bin_end - ulp_main_bin_start) /
sizeof(uint32_t));

    adc1_config_channel_atten(ADC1_CHANNEL_6, ADC_ATTEN_DB_11);
    adc1_config_width(ADC_WIDTH_BIT_12);
    adc1_ulp_enable();
```

We first upload the ULP application into the RTC memory by using `ulp_load_binary`. Then, we configure the ADC1 peripheral at channel 6 (GPIO34) and enable it for the ULP coprocessor to access. Next, we continue with the ULP initialization:

```
    ulp_high_thr = 2000;

    ulp_set_wakeup_period(0, 20000);

    rtc_gpio_isolate(GPIO_NUM_12);
    rtc_gpio_isolate(GPIO_NUM_15);
    esp_deep_sleep_disable_rom_logging();
}
```

`ulp_high_thr` is a global variable defined in the assembly code. Any variable that has the `ulp_` appendix is defined in the assembly. We have access to them by including `ulp_main.h`. We initialize `ulp_high_thr` with `2000` so that when the ULP application takes a reading from the photoresistor module of over `2000`, it will wake ESP32 up. `ulp_set_wakeup_period` is the function to set the ULP timer timeout value. With the help of this timer, the ULP coprocessor will run its code every 20 ms to take a measurement. The rest of the initialization is about disabling any unnecessary features and components.

Let's continue with `app_main`:

```
void app_main()
{
    if (esp_sleep_get_wakeup_cause() != ESP_SLEEP_WAKEUP_ULP)
    {
        printf("Powered\n");
        init_hw();
    }
    else
    {
        printf("Wakeup (%d - %d)\n", ++cnt1, ++cnt2);
    }
```

In `app_main`, we first check whether the wake-up reason is ULP or not. If not, it means ESP32 has gone through a power-up reset and we call `init_hw` to initialize ULP and ADC. If ESP32 has woken up by ULP, we print the `cnt1` and `cnt2` values on the serial monitor. Next, we just run the ULP application:

```
    ulp_run(&ulp_entry - RTC_SLOW_MEM);
    esp_sleep_enable_ulp_wakeup();
    esp_deep_sleep_start();
}
```

The ULP application starts at the `entry` symbol of the assembly code. This symbol is global and accessible via the `ulp_entry` variable. We enable ULP wake-up and go into a deep sleep. ULP will be in charge after that point.

When we run the application, we can see that `cnt1` keeps its value since we have defined it in the RTC memory, which stays powered during the deep-sleep periods.

Selecting a power mode for ESP32 is a trade-off between the power requirements and responsiveness of a product. When we develop, say, a battery-powered sensor device, we can put ESP32 in deep-sleep or hibernation mode to save the battery. However, if the project is about continuous monitoring of a motor system to detect the position or any failures, then we need to always keep ESP32 in active mode, or maybe modem-sleep mode if we don't require radio communication, and power ESP32 accordingly.

This was the last topic of this chapter. In the next chapter, we will develop a complete project to practice what we have learned so far.

Summary

In this chapter, we have learned a lot about the advanced features of ESP32 to develop professional, real-world IoT devices. UART is a prominent protocol that provides robust communication between different MCUs without a need for a common clock, as long as they are configured with the same UART parameters. We have learned how to develop multimedia applications. ESP32 supports the I2S protocol to let us develop audio applications. We have discussed common camera sensor technologies and developed a photo-trap device by using an ESP32-CAM devkit.

Finally, a great feature of ESP32, the power management subsystem, was the topic in the last section. If you want to design a battery-operated IoT device, you will definitely need to know about the power modes of ESP32. ESP32 incorporates a ULP coprocessor that can be used to take ambient measurements even if ESP32 is in deep-sleep mode.

We are going to develop a full project in the next chapter. The output of the project will be a multisensor device that we can use in any indoor location. We will list all of the required features first, then select hardware components corresponding to those features. After discussing the firmware architecture, we will develop the code to have a multisensor with the required features.

Questions

Let's test our knowledge with the following questions of this chapter:

1. For a UART connection given as *9600, 8N1*, which information is not provided?

    a) Baudrate

    b) Parity

    c) The start bit

    d) The stop bit

2. Which one is not true when we compare UART with other serial protocols such as I2C or SPI?

    a) UART is an asynchronous protocol, while others are not.

    b) UART doesn't need a common clock.

    c) UART is peer-to-peer, while others support multiple devices on the same bus.

    d) UART has two different lines for transmit and receive, while others use a single line for data.

3. Which is not true as an I2C and I2S comparison?

    a) I2S is specifically for sound, while I2C is a generic protocol.

    b) They need the same number of pin connections.

    c) I2S uses a channel select signal.

    d) They both have a master clock.

4. In which modes does ESP32 RAM keep existing data without any loss (that is, full RAM retention)?

    a) Modem sleep and light sleep

    b) Light sleep and deep sleep

    c) Deep sleep and hibernation

    d) Hibernation and modem sleep

5. In a battery-operated ESP32 project, you need to know the ambient light level, but only in some cases will you need to take action. What would be the best solution?

    a) Light-sleep; take measurements from time to time.

    b) Light-sleep; use interrupts.

    c) Deep-sleep; periodic wake-up.

    d) Deep-sleep; employ the ULP coprocessor.

5
Practice – Multisensor for Your Room

Practice is the key to attaining a new skill, and this especially applies to developers. We have covered many topics in the first four chapters. Starting from using ESP32 **general-purpose input/output (GPIO)** pins, we have learned how to communicate with sensor devices, how to drive different display types, and—finally—advanced features of ESP32, such as **ultra-low power (ULP)** and power management to develop outstanding **Internet of Things (IoT)** products. There are endless numbers of sensors and actuators, but the communication methods and techniques for them are limited. As long as we have some degree of proficiency with those methods, we are good to go in many IoT projects. This chapter is a great opportunity to practice what we have learned so far by combining several sensors into a single device—a multisensor.

In this chapter, we will cover the following topics:

- Feature list of the multisensor
- Solution architecture
- Implementation

Technical requirements

The source code of the project is located at this link:

`https://github.com/PacktPublishing/Internet-of-Things-with-ESP32/tree/main/ch5`

We will use the same libraries of the device drivers as in the previous chapters. You can find the drivers here: `https://github.com/PacktPublishing/Internet-of-Things-with-ESP32/tree/main/common`.

The hardware components of the project are listed as follows:

- An ESP32 **development kit** (**devkit**)
- A BME280 sensor module
- A TSL2561 sensor module
- A **passive infrared** (**PIR**) motion detector
- A rotary encoder
- An active buzzer
- An **organic light-emitting diode** (**OLED**) display

Check out the following video to see the code in action: `https://bit.ly/3wmQjPj`

Feature list of the multisensor

Most IoT projects start with a request coming from a business. The product manager in the project then tries to provide a list of features by analyzing the market, competitors, and requirements from the business to fulfill the business goals. Let's assume our product manager comes up with the following feature list for the multisensor:

- The device can measure temperature, humidity, pressure, and ambient light level.
- It has a display to show readings from the sensors. The display shows only one reading at a time.
- Users can switch between sensors by using a rotary encoder.
- A sound warning is generated for high and low temperature values.
- The device sleeps to decrease energy usage when there is no-one around and wakes up when someone is detected.

As we now know the features, we can propose a solution for the project next.

Solution architecture

Based on the feature list, we will have the following subsystems:

- **Sensor subsystem**: This contains sensors and provides sensor readings. We will use BME280 and TSL2561 hardware modules in this subsystem and will read from them in a software module.

- **User interaction subsystem**: This contains a rotary encoder to get input from the user and employs an OLED display to output readings. For sound warnings, this subsystem drives a buzzer.

- **Power management subsystem**: In this subsystem, we will have a PIR module to detect surrounding motion. If no motion is detected for a while, then it will put the device into light-sleep mode. The rotary encoder will also provide input to this subsystem since if the user is using the rotary encoder, the device should be in an active mode of operation.

The following diagram shows the execution of the overall solution:

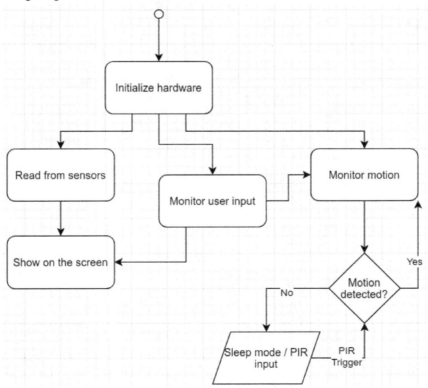

Figure 5.1 – Solution flowchart

After the hardware initialization, all subsystems start to monitor their corresponding sensors. The sensor subsystem will read from the BME280 and TSL2561 modules, the user interaction subsystem will monitor the rotary encoder for user input, and the power management subsystem will monitor motion by using the PIR detector and incoming data from the user interaction subsystem. The PIR detector also provides a trigger to exit from sleep mode.

Next, we will implement this solution.

Implementation

Let's discuss the hardware first. The following *Fritzing* diagram shows the connections between ESP32 and other hardware components:

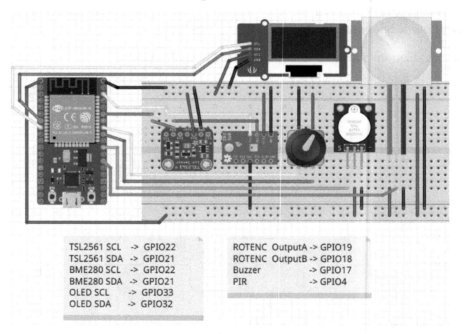

TSL2561 SCL	->	GPIO22
TSL2561 SDA	->	GPIO21
BME280 SCL	->	GPIO22
BME280 SDA	->	GPIO21
OLED SCL	->	GPIO33
OLED SDA	->	GPIO32

ROTENC OutputA	->	GPIO19
ROTENC OutputB	->	GPIO18
Buzzer	->	GPIO17
PIR	->	GPIO4

Figure 5.2 – Fritzing diagram of the project

The interesting point here is the **Inter-Integrated Circuit (I²C)** connections. I²C is a bus, so we can connect multiple devices on the same bus, as long as they have different bus addresses. Therefore, we connect BME280 and TSL2561 to the same pins of ESP32, GPIO21 and GPIO22. The OLED screen is also an I²C device, but its driver uses the second I²C channel of ESP32, so it is a good idea to connect the OLED screen to other GPIO pins to avoid any configuration conflicts.

Before delving into the code, we need to update the configuration files. Let's start with `platformio.ini`, as follows:

```
[env:az-delivery-devkit-v4]
platform = espressif32
board = az-delivery-devkit-v4
framework = espidf


monitor_speed = 115200
lib_extra_dirs =
    ../../common/esp-idf-lib/components
    ../../common/components
```

PlatformIO generates the first part of the `platformio.ini` file for us when we create the project. We add the second part for `monitor_speed` and `lib_extra_dirs` to specify the path for the external libraries in the project.

Then, we create `Kconfig.projbuild` in the project root for additional `sdkconfig` parameters to be incorporated into the final `sdkconfig.h` file. Here is the content of `Kconfig.projbuild`:

```
menu "Misc"

config I2CDEV_TIMEOUT
    int "I2C timeout"
    default "100000"
    help
        I2C device timeout

config I2C_FREQ_HZ
    int "I2C bus frequency"
    default "400000"
    help
        I2C bus frequency, default 400kHz

endmenu
```

This configuration has two entries for the I²C library: I2CDEV_TIMEOUT and I2C_FREQ_HZ, located under the Misc menu. The generated sdkconfig.h file will have these two new definitions when we compile the project. They are needed by the drivers of BME280 and TSL2561. We can also see this menu when we run menuconfig, as follows:

```
$ source $HOME/.platformio/penv/bin/activate
(penv)$ pio run -t menuconfig
```

These definitions are located under the Misc category, as illustrated in the following screenshot:

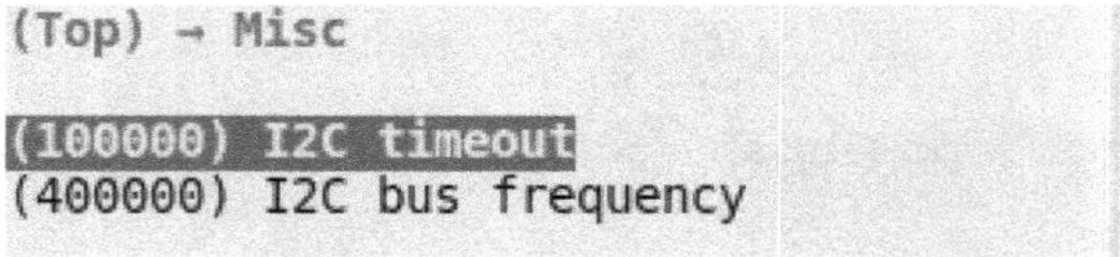

```
(Top) → Misc

(100000) I2C timeout
(400000) I2C bus frequency
```

Figure 5.3 – Misc menu in menuconfig

With these configurations ready, we can continue with the code. First, we copy the rotary encoder driver into the project lib folder, which you can find in the GitHub repository. Actually, it is quite possible to keep the driver under the ../../common/components folder to avoid having to copy it every time it is needed, but I modified it a bit to make it compatible with the project.

The application will have different source code files for the subsystems to make the program modular. Here are the files in our multisensor application:

```
$ ls -1 *.{c*,h}
common.h
main.cpp
pmsub.cpp
pmsub.h
sesub.cpp
sesub.h
uisub.cpp
uisub.h
```

common.h defines shared structures between modules. main.cpp is the main application where app_main exists, and all modules are integrated in order to compose the multisensor application. The other files contain the subsystems' implementations. pmsub.h and pmsub.cpp are for the power management subsystem, sesub.h and sesub.cpp are for the sensor subsystem, and uisub.h and uisub.cpp are for the user interaction subsystem. Let's start with the sensor subsystem.

Sensor subsystem

The sensor subsystem is responsible for providing ambient measurements in the solution. It initializes BME280 and TSL2561 and then starts to acquire readings periodically. sesub.h shows its interface, as follows:

```
#ifndef sesub_h_
#define sesub_h_

#include "common.h"

typedef void (*sensor_reading_f)(sensor_reading_t);
typedef void (*temp_alarm_f)(void);

typedef struct
{
    int sensor_sda;
    int sensor_scl;

    float temp_high;
    float temp_low;

    sensor_reading_f new_sensor_reading;
    temp_alarm_f temp_alarm;
} sesub_config_t;

extern "C"
{
    void sesub_init(sesub_config_t);
    void sesub_start(void);
}

#endif
```

The sensor subsystem has two functions in its interface. The first one is `sesub_init`, to initialize the subsystem. It takes a parameter of `sesub_config_t`, where we can provide I²C pins, high and low temperatures for the alarm, and two callback functions to be called for new readings and alarm cases. The second function is provided to start ambient readings. The source code file `sesub.cpp` contains the following code:

```
#include <freertos/FreeRTOS.h>
#include <freertos/task.h>
#include <freertos/semphr.h>
#include <tsl2561.h>
#include <bmp280.h>
#include <esp_err.h>
#include <string.h>


#include "sesub.h"


static ts12561_t light_sensor;
static bmp280_t temp_sensor;
static sesub_config_t config;


static void read_ambient(void *arg);
```

We start with including the necessary header files and global variable definitions. Next, we implement `sesub_init`, which is called by client code for the sensor subsystem initialization. The code for this is shown in the following snippet:

```
void sesub_init(sesub_config_t c)
{
    config = c;

    i2cdev_init();

    memset(&light_sensor, 0, sizeof(ts12561_t));
    light_sensor.i2c_dev.timeout_ticks = 0xffff / portTICK_
PERIOD_MS;

    ts12561_init_desc(&light_sensor, TSL2561_I2C_ADDR_FLOAT, 0,
(gpio_num_t)c.sensor_sda, (gpio_num_t)c.sensor_scl);
    ts12561_init(&light_sensor);
```

```
    memset(&temp_sensor, 0, sizeof(bmp280_t));
    temp_sensor.i2c_dev.timeout_ticks = 0xffff / portTICK_
PERIOD_MS;

    bmp280_params_t params;
    bmp280_init_default_params(&params);

    bmp280_init_desc(&temp_sensor, BMP280_I2C_ADDRESS_0, 0,
(gpio_num_t)c.sensor_sda, (gpio_num_t)c.sensor_scl);
    bmp280_init(&temp_sensor, &params);
}
```

light_sensor and temp_sensor share the same I²C pins as provided with the configuration parameter, thus we pass the same pin numbers as parameters to their corresponding initialization functions.

sesub_start is another interface function of the sensor subsystem and is shown in the following code snippet:

```
void sesub_start(void) {
    xTaskCreate(read_ambient, "read", 5 * configMINIMAL_STACK_
SIZE, NULL, 5, NULL);
}
```

sesub_start simply creates a FreeRTOS task to get readings from the sensors and read_ambient is the function called in the task for this purpose, as illustrated in the following code snippet:

```
static void read_ambient(void *arg)
{
    float pressure, temperature, humidity;
    uint32_t lux;

    while (1)
    {
        vTaskDelay(10000 / portTICK_PERIOD_MS);
        ESP_ERROR_CHECK(bmp280_read_float(&temp_sensor,
&temperature, &pressure, &humidity));
        ESP_ERROR_CHECK(tsl2561_read_lux(&light_sensor, &lux));
```

```
        if (temperature > config.temp_high || temperature <
config.temp_low)
        {
            if (config.temp_alarm)
            {
                config.temp_alarm();
            }
        }
        if (config.new_sensor_reading)
        {
            sensor_reading_t reading = {(int)temperature, (int)
humidity, (int)(pressure / 1000), (int)lux};
            config.new_sensor_reading(reading);
        }
    }
}
```

read_ambient reads from BME280 and TSL2561 and checks whether the temperature value is between the limits. If so it is calls the alarm callback function as provided in the configuration. Next, it shares the ambient measurements by using the new_sensor_reading callback function.

User interaction subsystem

This subsystem provides **input/output (I/O)** to the user. The rotary encoder, the OLED screen, and the buzzer are all in this subsystem. Here is the header file, uisub.h, listing its functionality:

```
#ifndef uisub_h_
#define uisub_h_

#include "common.h"

typedef void (*rotenc_changed_f)(void);

typedef struct
{
    int buzzer_pin;
```

```
    int rotenc_clk_pin;
    int rotenc_dt_pin;
    rotenc_changed_f rotenc_changed;

    int oled_sda;
    int oled_scl;
} uisub_config_t;

extern "C"
{
    void uisub_init(uisub_config_t);
    void uisub_sleep(void);
    void uisub_resume(void);
    void uisub_beep(int);
    void uisub_show(sensor_reading_t);
}

#endif
```

uisub_init is the function that initializes the subsystem with the given configuration. The configuration structure contains all GPIO pins information for the buzzer, the rotary encoder, and the OLED display. It also has a callback function to let the other components know about the rotary encoder position change. uisub_show is called to display recent sensor readings. This function receives sensor readings as a parameter and shows them according to the rotary encoder position. To generate a beep sound, this subsystem provides the uisub_beep function to the system with a parameter for the beep count. uisub_sleep and uisub_resume are the functions to be called before sleep and after wakeup, respectively. The former turns the OLED screen off to preserve energy, and the latter restores the latest view when the multisensor wakes up. Unfortunately, the source code is a bit lengthy, so it is not possible to list it here. However, you can easily check it out on the GitHub repository, in uisub.cpp.

Power management subsystem

The multisensor will light-sleep when there is no surrounding motion. For this, a PIR detector is included in this subsystem. When motion occurs, the subsystem keeps the device up and running, and if nothing is detected for a while it then puts the device into light-sleep mode. The following code snippet shows the content of the pmsub.h header file:

```c
#ifndef pmsub_h_
#define pmsub_h_

typedef void (*before_sleep_f)(void);
typedef void (*after_wakeup_f)(void);


typedef struct
{
    int pir_pin;

    before_sleep_f before_sleep;
    after_wakeup_f after_wakeup;
} pmsub_config_t;

extern "C"
{
    void pmsub_init(pmsub_config_t);
    void pmsub_update(bool from_isr);
    void pmsub_start(void);
}

#endif
```

The functionality provided by the power management subsystem is relatively simple. pmsub_init initializes the subsystem hardware and configures the wakeup trigger as a signal from the PIR detector. pmsub_start checks if the sleep-time threshold has been reached since the last motion. If so, it starts light-sleep mode. This function also runs the before_sleep and after_wakeup callback functions so that other parts of the system are informed about those events. The final function of this subsystem is pmsub_update, which pushes the next sleep to a later point in time. Other components of the solution can use this function to support the power management subsystem with information on a motion, such as a rotary encoder position change. Again, you can find the full implementation in the GitHub repository.

Main application

All subsystems are integrated in the main.cpp file to form the main application. Let's go through it, as follows:

```
#include "uisub.h"
#include "pmsub.h"
#include "sesub.h"

#define SENSOR_BUS_SDA 21
#define SENSOR_BUS_SCL 22
#define OLED_SDA 32
#define OLED_SCL 33
#define BUZZER_PIN 17
#define PIR_MOTION_PIN 4
#define ROTENC_CLK_PIN 19
#define ROTENC_DT_PIN 18
```

We start with including the header files and defining pin macros, as usual. What is different this time is that we have managed to hide all low-level implementation details in the subsystem implementations. Therefore, it is enough for us to only include their header files and nothing else. Next, we implement the callback functions for the subsystems, as follows:

```
static void update_power_man(void)
{
    pmsub_update(false);
}
```

```
static void alarm(void)
{
    uisub_beep(3);
}
```

update_power_man is the function to be run by the user interaction subsystem when the rotary encoder has a new position. Inside it, we call pmsub_update to let the power management subsystem update its internals. alarm is another connecting function, for the sensor subsystem to be called in case of an alarm, and it calls uisub_beep to make a sound warning.

We continue with implementing the initialization function of our application, as follows:

```
static void init_subsystems(void)
{
    uisub_config_t ui_cfg = {
        .buzzer_pin = BUZZER_PIN,
        .rotenc_clk_pin = ROTENC_CLK_PIN,
        .rotenc_dt_pin = ROTENC_DT_PIN,
        .rotenc_changed = update_power_man,
        .oled_sda = OLED_SDA,
        .oled_scl = OLED_SCL,
    };
    uisub_init(ui_cfg);
```

init_subsystems is the most notable function here, where we initialize and integrate all components. We start with the user interaction subsystem initialization by calling uisub_init with the configuration. The configuration variable specifies the pins of the subsystem devices and the rotenc_changed callback function is set to update_power_man. Next, we initialize the other subsystems as illustrated in the following code snippet:

```
    sesub_config_t se_cfg = {
        .sensor_sda = SENSOR_BUS_SDA,
        .sensor_scl = SENSOR_BUS_SCL,
        .temp_high = 30,
        .temp_low = 10,
        .new_sensor_reading = uisub_show,
        .temp_alarm = alarm,
    };
```

```
    sesub_init(se_cfg);

    pmsub_config_t pm_cfg = {
        .pir_pin = PIR_MOTION_PIN,
        .before_sleep = uisub_sleep,
        .after_wakeup = uisub_resume,
    };
    pmsub_init(pm_cfg);
}
```

Similarly, we call `sesub_init` and `pmsub_init` to initialize the other two subsystems—the sensor and power management subsystems—respectively. They are all integrated by means of the callbacks.

The initialization is done. Let's implement the application entry point, `app_main`, as follows:

```
extern "C" void app_main(void)
{
    init_subsystems();

    uisub_beep(2);

    sesub_start();
    pmsub_start();
}
```

In the `app_main` function, we only need to call `init_subsystems` and start the sensor and power subsystems. We have a very short and clean application since we have abstracted the subsystems well.

This is the end of our sample project. We are ready to compile it and flash ESP32 with the firmware to see how it works.

We can improve this project by adding more features. For example, you can try integrating a **thin-film transistor (TFT)** screen instead of an OLED to show interesting graphics to the user, or you can add a different alarm pattern such as two short beeps and a long stop. Another feature could be to include an LED in the project as a visual alarm indicator in addition to the buzzer. Practice is the key to learning, and this project has plenty of scope for you to practice. Enjoy it!

Summary

The most important aspect of such projects is to gain hands-on experience, and this chapter has provided a good opportunity to do so. We started with listing the features and designed a solution to implement those features. The key element in any software design is to have a clean interface between components. We defined the subsystems clearly and, as a result of this, it became a straightforward task to implement the main application.

This was the final chapter in the first part of this book. With the next chapter, we are going to discover the wireless connectivity capabilities of ESP32.

Section 2: Local Network Communication

An IoT solution generally requires several IoT devices to cooperate in the same local network and share data to accomplish a task. ESP32 has two built-in communication technologies for this purpose: Wi-Fi and Bluetooth.

This part of the book comprises the following chapters:

- *Chapter 6, A Good Old Friend – Wi-Fi*

- *Chapter 7, Security First!*

- *Chapter 8, I Can Speak BLE*

- *Chapter 9, Practice – Making Your Home Smart*

6
A Good Old Friend – Wi-Fi

Wi-Fi (of the **IEEE 802.11** family of standards) is the most prominent wireless standard in the industry, so Espressif has integrated this technology into all of its products – ESP32 is no exception. In this chapter, we will learn how to use ESP32 in a Wi-Fi environment by connecting it to a local Wi-Fi network. After connecting to local Wi-Fi, a huge world of IoT opens that lets ESP32 communicate with servers and other connected devices. ESP-IDF provides all the software support needed to develop **Transmission Control Protocol/Internet Protocol (TCP/IP)** applications.

This chapter contains practical examples of client/server solutions over TCP/IP. We will discuss how to implement **Hypertext Transfer Protocol (HTTP)** server and client applications on ESP32 as well as examples of other application layer protocols, such as **Multicast Domain Name System (mDNS)** and **Simple Network Time Protocol (SNTP)**, which can be needed in some real-world scenarios. In the *Further reading* section, you can find more resources to learn about the basics of modern networking and the TCP/IP family of protocols if you are not familiar.

In this chapter, we're going to cover the following topics:

- Using Wi-Fi in station and access point modes
- Using lwIP – a TCP/IP stack for embedded devices

Technical requirements

As hardware, we need an ESP32 devkit, an OLED display, and a DHT11 sensor in this chapter. We will also need a mobile phone or any other device with Wi-Fi capability for when we test the examples. The examples in the chapter are located in the GitHub repository here: `https://github.com/PacktPublishing/Internet-of-Things-with-ESP32/tree/main/ch6`.

There are several third-party applications and command-line tools that we need to use in the examples. On *nix machines, use these:

- **avahi-browse**: This is for mDNS service browsing. You can read the manual at this link: `https://linux.die.net/man/1/avahi-browse`.
- **nc**: The netcat utility provides a wide range of functionality regarding TCP and UDP protocols. The manual page is here: `https://linux.die.net/man/1/nc`.

For Windows machines, use these:

- **Bonjour browser for Windows**: This is one of the options on Windows platforms for mDNS service discovery. The download page is here: `https://hobbyistsoftware.com/bonjourbrowser`.
- **Ncat**: Ncat is another implementation of netcat from the Nmap project. Here is the download page: `https://nmap.org/ncat/`.

Check out the following video to see the code in action: `https://bit.ly/2TM53Ko`

Using Wi-Fi

Nodes in a Wi-Fi network form a star topology, which means a central hub exists and other nodes connect to the central hub to communicate within the Wi-Fi network or with the outside world if the central hub is connected to a router or is itself a router. Therefore, we see two different modes of operation in a Wi-Fi network:

- Station (**STA**) mode
- Access point (**AP**) mode

We can configure ESP32 in both modes. In STA mode, ESP32 can connect to an access point and join a Wi-Fi network as a node. When it is in AP mode, other Wi-Fi-capable devices, such as mobile phones, can connect to the Wi-Fi network that ESP32 starts as the access point. The following figure shows both cases with two different Wi-Fi networks:

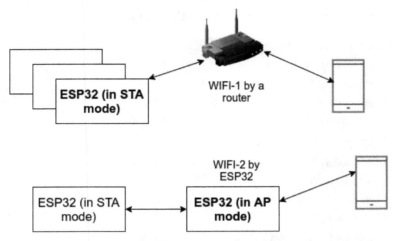

Figure 6.1 – ESP32 in STA mode and AP mode

Let's start with an example of STA mode.

STA mode

In this example, we will configure ESP32 in STA mode to connect to a local Wi-Fi network and send a GET request to a URL. After receiving the resource pointed to by the URL, it will print the content on the serial console.

As we always do, we first create a PlatformIO project and edit the platformio.ini file:

```
[env:az-delivery-devkit-v4]
platform = espressif32
board = az-delivery-devkit-v4
framework = espidf

monitor_speed = 115200
build_flags =
    -DWIFI_SSID=${sysenv.WIFI_SSID}
    -DWIFI_PASS=${sysenv.WIFI_PASS}
```

There are two environment variables to be passed to the application, WIFI_SSID and WIFI_PASS. We could specify them in the application as well, but it would be a wrong decision from the security standpoint since we keep our code in a code repository visible to everyone.

With the configuration ready, we can move on to the application:

```
#include "freertos/FreeRTOS.h"
#include "freertos/task.h"
#include "freertos/event_groups.h"
#include "esp_system.h"
#include "esp_wifi.h"
#include "esp_event.h"
#include "esp_log.h"
#include "nvs_flash.h"
#include "lwip/err.h"
#include "lwip/sys.h"
#include "esp_http_client.h"

static EventGroupHandle_t wifi_events;
#define WIFI_CONNECTED_BIT BIT0
#define WIFI_FAIL_BIT BIT1

#define MAX_RETRY 10
static int retry_cnt = 0;

static const char *TAG = "wifi_app";

static void request_page(void *);
static esp_err_t handle_http_event(esp_http_client_event_t *);
static void handle_wifi_connection(void *, esp_event_base_t,
int32_t, void *);
```

We start by including numerous header files to access the functions and definitions in them. Then we define a global variable, wifi_events, to pass Wi-Fi event information between different parts of the application. We have some function prototypes that we will discuss one by one later.

Let's see how we initialize ESP32 Wi-Fi. init_wifi manages the whole Wi-Fi connection process as follows:

```
static void init_wifi(void)
{
    if (nvs_flash_init() != ESP_OK)
```

```
    {
        nvs_flash_erase();
        nvs_flash_init();
    }
```

We first initialize the nvs partition. The nvs partition is used by the Wi-Fi library. Then, we create an event group and register an event handling function to act on Wi-Fi events, as shown in the following code snippet:

```
    wifi_events = xEventGroupCreate();
    esp_event_loop_create_default();
    esp_event_handler_register(WIFI_EVENT, ESP_EVENT_ANY_ID,
  &handle_wifi_connection, NULL);
    esp_event_handler_register(IP_EVENT, IP_EVENT_STA_GOT_IP,
  &handle_wifi_connection, NULL);
```

wifi_events is the global variable to notify init_wifi about changes after we start the Wi-Fi connection process. Next, we create an event loop to monitor changes and register the handle_wifi_connection function in the default event loop to handle WIFI_EVENT and IP_EVENT. Now, we are ready to start the connection process:

```
    wifi_config_t wifi_config = {
        .sta = {
            .ssid = WIFI_SSID,
            .password = WIFI_PASS,
            .threshold.authmode = WIFI_AUTH_WPA2_PSK,
            .pmf_cfg = {
                .capable = true,
                .required = false},
        },
    };

    esp_netif_init();
    esp_netif_create_default_wifi_sta();
    wifi_init_config_t cfg = WIFI_INIT_CONFIG_DEFAULT();
    esp_wifi_init(&cfg);
    esp_wifi_set_mode(WIFI_MODE_STA);
    esp_wifi_set_config(ESP_IF_WIFI_STA, &wifi_config);
    esp_wifi_start();
```

We define a variable, `wifi_config`, to hold the credentials. We will need it before starting the Wi-Fi connection. We then initialize the network interface and Wi-Fi with the default configuration. We set the Wi-Fi mode to `WIFI_MODE_STA` and specify the credentials by calling `esp_wifi_set_config`. As the final step of the process, we simply call `esp_wifi_start`. Then, we wait for a success or fail event on `xEventGroupWaitBits`:

```
    EventBits_t bits = xEventGroupWaitBits(wifi_events, WIFI_
CONNECTED_BIT | WIFI_FAIL_BIT, pdFALSE, pdFALSE, portMAX_
DELAY);

    if (bits & WIFI_CONNECTED_BIT)
    {
        xTaskCreate(request_page, "http_req", 5 *
configMINIMAL_STACK_SIZE, NULL, 5, NULL);
    }
    else
    {
        ESP_LOGE(TAG, "failed");
    }
}
```

When either of the two bits of the `wifi_events` variable is set, `xEventGroupWaitBits` returns and we check which bit is set. If it is the success bit, we create a FreeRTOS task to send an HTTP GET request to a URL.

Let's see what happens in the `handle_wifi_connection` function, which we have registered in the default event loop:

```
static void handle_wifi_connection(void *arg, esp_event_base_t
event_base, int32_t event_id, void *event_data)
{
    if (event_base == WIFI_EVENT && event_id == WIFI_EVENT_STA_
START)
    {
        esp_wifi_connect();
    }
```

`handle_wifi_connection` is the registered function to be called for Wi-Fi and IP events. When the event is `WIFI_EVENT_STA_START`, we call `esp_wifi_connect` to connect to the Wi-Fi network. Another event that we handle is the STA-disconnected event. This is how we deal with it:

```
    else if (event_base == WIFI_EVENT && event_id == WIFI_
EVENT_STA_DISCONNECTED)
    {
        if (retry_cnt++ < MAX_RETRY)
        {
            esp_wifi_connect();
            ESP_LOGI(TAG, "wifi connect retry: %d", retry_cnt);
        }
        else
        {
            xEventGroupSetBits(wifi_events, WIFI_FAIL_BIT);
        }
    }
```

If the event is `WIFI_EVENT_STA_DISCONNECTED`, it means that our previous attempt to connect failed. We retry the connection until the count reaches `MAX_RETRY`. If the connection still fails after `MAX_RETRY`, we just give up by setting the fail bit of `wifi_events`.

If the connection attempt succeeds, the `IP_EVENT_STA_GOT_IP` event happens after a while. We handle it as follows:

```
    else if (event_base == IP_EVENT && event_id == IP_EVENT_
STA_GOT_IP)
    {
        ip_event_got_ip_t *event = (ip_event_got_ip_t *)event_
data;
        ESP_LOGI(TAG, "ip: %d.%d.%d.%d", IP2STR(&event->ip_
info.ip));
        retry_cnt = 0;
        xEventGroupSetBits(wifi_events, WIFI_CONNECTED_BIT);
    }
}
```

We set the success bit of the global `wifi_events` variable to let the `init_wifi` function know about this change, which eventually creates a FreeRTOS task to send an HTTP GET request to the specified URL. The task function is `request_page`, which we define in the following code snippet:

```
static void request_page(void *arg)
{
    esp_http_client_config_t config = {
        .url = "https://raw.githubusercontent.com/espressif/
esp-idf/master/examples/get-started/blink/main/blink.c",
        .event_handler = handle_http_event,
    };
    esp_http_client_handle_t client = esp_http_client_
init(&config);

    if (esp_http_client_perform(client) != ESP_OK)
    {
        ESP_LOGE(TAG, "http request failed");
    }
    esp_http_client_cleanup(client);

    vTaskDelete(NULL);
}
```

We start the function by defining an HTTP configuration variable, `config`. It contains the URL info and a handler for HTTP events. We don't need to specify the HTTP method in `config` since the default is HTTP GET. Then we create an HTTP client with that configuration and call `esp_http_client_perform` with `client` as the parameter. To close the HTTP session, we simply call `esp_http_client_cleanup`.

Next, we implement the `handle_http_event` function to handle the HTTP events:

```
static esp_err_t handle_http_event(esp_http_client_event_t
*http_event)
{
    switch (http_event->event_id)
    {
    case HTTP_EVENT_ON_DATA:
        printf("%.*s\n", http_event->data_len, (char *)http_
event->data);
```

```
        break;
    default:
        break;
    }
    return ESP_OK;
}
```

There are several HTTP events in a single session, such as on-connected, header-sent, and header-received. In this function, we only handle HTTP_EVENT_ON_DATA to show the data returned from the server.

Finally, we write app_main to complete the application:

```
void app_main(void)
{
    init_wifi();
}
```

The only thing to do in app_main is to call init_wifi to start the whole process.

We compile and upload the application from the command line as follows:

```
$ source ~/.platformio/penv/bin/activate
(penv)$ export WIFI_SSID='\"<your-wifi-ssid>\"'
(penv)$ export WIFI_PASS='\"<your-wifi-password>\"'
(penv)$ pio run
(penv)$ pio run -t erase
(penv)$ pio run -t upload
```

After activating the virtual environment, we define the environment variables to be used as the Wi-Fi credentials. Then we run pio run to compile the application with these credentials and generate the binary.

> **Tip**
> On *nix systems, we use export to set environment variables. If the development environment is a Windows machine, then the set command does the job.

Before uploading the application, we want to make sure the flash of ESP32 is clear because the Wi-Fi library uses the nvs partition of the flash and this partition must be clear to operate properly. After erasing the entire flash, we can upload the application and see the output on the serial monitor, which is some simple example code from Espressif hosted on GitHub as we provided in the config variable.

> **Important Note**
>
> If your ESP32 devkit doesn't connect to your Wi-Fi network although the credentials are correct, it is highly likely there is a problem with the nvs partition. To fix the problem, erase the entire flash again and upload the application.

The next example is about how to start ESP32 in AP mode.

AP mode

Let's say we want our ESP32 device to operate in any Wi-Fi network without prior knowledge of credentials. In this case, we need to somehow pass the credentials to the ESP32 device. One method is to start the device in AP mode and run a web server to provide a form that collects the local Wi-Fi credentials from the user. Let's prepare the project with the following steps:

1. Create a PlatformIO project with this platformio.ini:

    ```
    [env:az-delivery-devkit-v4]
    platform = espressif32
    board = az-delivery-devkit-v4
    framework = espidf

    monitor_speed = 115200
    ```

2. Edit sdkconfig to update the HTTP request header length since the default buffer length as provided in sdkconfig is not enough. We first activate the Python virtual environment and then start menuconfig as follows:

    ```
    $ source ~/.platformio/penv/bin/activate
    (penv)$ pio run -t menuconfig
    ```

3. Set the HTTP request header length to 2048 under Component config/HTTP Server:

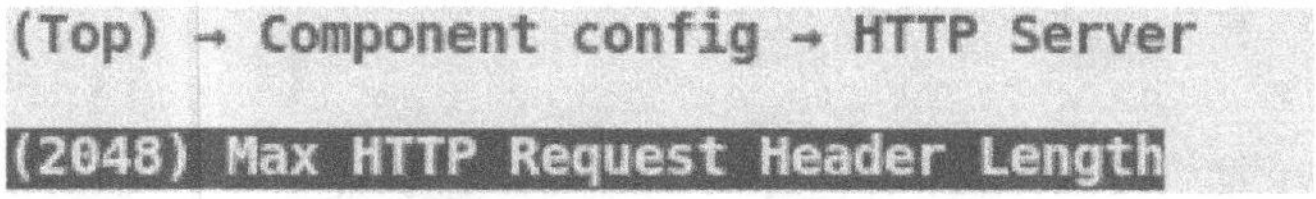

```
(Top) → Component config → HTTP Server

(2048) Max HTTP Request Header Length
```

Figure 6.2 – Configuring the HTTP header length

Now, we can continue with the code:

```c
#include "freertos/FreeRTOS.h"
#include "freertos/task.h"
#include "esp_system.h"
#include "esp_wifi.h"
#include "esp_event.h"
#include "esp_log.h"
#include "nvs_flash.h"
#include "lwip/err.h"
#include "lwip/sys.h"
#include "esp_http_server.h"
#include <string.h>

#define WIFI_SSID "esp32_ap1"
#define WIFI_PWD "A_pwd_is_needed_here"
#define WIFI_CHANNEL 11
#define MAX_CONN_CNT 1

static const char *TAG = "ap-app";
```

We first include the relevant header files. Then we define some macros for the access point service. The Wi-Fi SSID will be esp32_ap1 when we start ESP32 in AP mode:

```c
static const char *HTML_FORM =
"<html><form action=\"/\" method=\"post\">"
"<label for=\"ssid\">Local SSID:</label><br>"
"<input type=\"text\" id=\"ssid\" name=\"ssid\"><br>"
"<label for=\"pwd\">Password:</label><br>"
"<input type=\"text\" id=\"pwd\" name=\"pwd\"><br>"
"<input type=\"submit\" value=\"Submit\">"
"</form></html>";
```

```
static void start_webserver(void);
static esp_err_t handle_http_get(httpd_req_t *req);
static esp_err_t handle_http_post(httpd_req_t *req);
static void handle_wifi_events(void *, esp_event_base_t,
int32_t, void *);
```

HTML_FORM contains the HTML code of the web form where we collect the local Wi-Fi credentials. The web server will publish this form. We will discuss the function prototypes later.

Let's look at the init_wifi function next:

```
static void init_wifi(void)
{
    if (nvs_flash_init() != ESP_OK)
    {
        nvs_flash_erase();
        nvs_flash_init();
    }

    esp_event_loop_create_default();
    esp_event_handler_register(WIFI_EVENT, ESP_EVENT_ANY_ID,
&handle_wifi_events, NULL);
```

init_wifi manages the whole process. We first initialize the nvs partition as we did in the STA mode example. Then we create an event loop to monitor the Wi-Fi events and register handle_wifi_events for this purpose. The next step is to start the Wi-Fi access point. This is how we do that:

```
    esp_netif_init();
    esp_netif_create_default_wifi_ap();
    wifi_init_config_t cfg = WIFI_INIT_CONFIG_DEFAULT();
    esp_wifi_init(&cfg);

    wifi_config_t wifi_config = {
        .ap = {
            .ssid = WIFI_SSID,
            .ssid_len = strlen(WIFI_SSID),
            .channel = WIFI_CHANNEL,
```

```
                  .password = WIFI_PWD,
                  .max_connection = MAX_CONN_CNT,
                  .authmode = WIFI_AUTH_WPA_WPA2_PSK},
      };
      esp_wifi_set_mode(WIFI_MODE_AP);
      esp_wifi_set_config(ESP_IF_WIFI_AP, &wifi_config);
      esp_wifi_start();


      start_webserver();
}
```

We initialize the network interface and Wi-Fi module with the default configuration. We define a variable, wifi_config, to hold the access point configuration. This variable is passed to esp_wifi_set_config before starting the Wi-Fi. We start the Wi-Fi and call start_webserver, which makes our device ready to be connected to from another device, such as a mobile phone.

We handle the Wi-Fi events in the following function:

```
static void handle_wifi_events(void *arg, esp_event_base_t
event_base, int32_t event_id, void *event_data)
{
    if (event_id == WIFI_EVENT_AP_STACONNECTED)
    {
        ESP_LOGI(TAG, "a station connected");
    }
}
```

In the handle_wifi_events function, we do nothing but print a log message saying a device is connected to the ESP32 access point.

Let's see how we start a web server:

```
static void start_webserver(void)
{
    httpd_uri_t uri_get = {
        .uri = "/",
        .method = HTTP_GET,
        .handler = handle_http_get,
```

```
        .user_ctx = NULL};

    httpd_uri_t uri_post = {
        .uri = "/",
        .method = HTTP_POST,
        .handler = handle_http_post,
        .user_ctx = NULL};

    httpd_config_t config = HTTPD_DEFAULT_CONFIG();
    httpd_handle_t server = NULL;
    if (httpd_start(&server, &config) == ESP_OK)
    {
        httpd_register_uri_handler(server, &uri_get);
        httpd_register_uri_handler(server, &uri_post);
    }
}
```

Starting a web server is quite easy. We simply call `httpd_start` and register functions for GET and POST requests. Then, we implement the handler functions as follows:

```
static esp_err_t handle_http_get(httpd_req_t *req)
{
    return httpd_resp_send(req, HTML_FORM, HTTPD_RESP_USE_
STRLEN);
}
```

When a client sends a GET request, we reply with HTML_FORM in the handle_http_get function. The other HTTP handler is the POST request handler, which is given in the following code snippet:

```
static esp_err_t handle_http_post(httpd_req_t *req)
{
    char content[100];
    if (httpd_req_recv(req, content, req->content_len) <= 0)
    {
        return ESP_FAIL;
    }
    ESP_LOGI(TAG, "%.*s", req->content_len, content);
```

```
    return httpd_resp_send(req, "received", HTTPD_RESP_USE_
STRLEN);
}
```

The user fills in the form with the local Wi-Fi network credentials and presses the **Submit** button on the form. This causes a POST request on the ESP32 side. In the handle_http_post function, we receive the credentials by calling httpd_req_recv. At that point, we can parse the data in the content array to find the SSID and password, and start ESP32 in STA mode to connect to the local Wi-Fi network as we did in the previous example.

We complete the application by adding the app_main function:

```
void app_main(void)
{
    init_wifi();
}
```

In app_main, we only call init_wifi to trigger the whole process. Now, it is time to flash ESP32 and test it.

When ESP32 reboots, it starts an access point with the name esp32_ap1 as follows:

Figure 6.3 – ESP32 access point

We connect it by entering the password as A_pwd_is_needed_here:

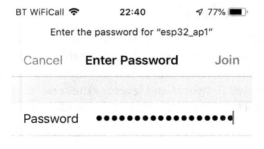

Figure 6.4 – Entering the AP password

When we open a web browser and enter the ESP32 IP address, we see the form:

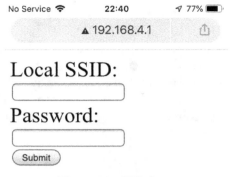

Figure 6.5 – Web form

We enter the local SSID and the password, then submit the form. The web server running on ESP32 returns a response as follows:

received

Figure 6.6 – Response from the web server

That is it. We have started the ESP32 in AP mode and have run a web server on it to get the local Wi-Fi credentials. We can use this method to provision our ESP32 device on any Wi-Fi network by switching to STA mode and using the credentials provided by the user.

In the next section, we are going to discuss the ESP32 TCP/IP stack and see an example of starting a UDP server to deliver temperature and humidity data over a local network.

Developing with lwIP

lightweight IP (lwIP) is an open source TCP/IP stack for embedded systems and ESP-IDF has imported it into the framework. The idea behind lwIP is to create a small-footprint TCP/IP protocol suite that resource-constrained embedded systems can use to connect to IP-based networks and leverage the services in a network. lwIP is one of the most popular TCP/IP stacks targeting embedded systems on the market.

Basically, the ESP-IDF port supports the following APIs of lwIP:

- **Berkeley Software Distribution (BSD)** sockets API for TCP and UDP connections
- **Dynamic Host Configuration Protocol (DHCP)** for dynamic IP addressing
- **Simple Network Time Protocol (SNTP)** as a time protocol
- **Multicast Domain Name System (mDNS)** for host name resolution and service information
- **Internet Control Message Protocol (ICMP)** for network monitoring and diagnostics

Actually, we have already used some of these behind the scenes in our previous examples. In the STA mode example, we can ICMP ping the ESP32 after it gets a dynamic IP from the DHCP server of the local Wi-Fi router. In the AP mode example, ESP32 provides dynamic IPs to station devices by using the DHCP server API of lwIP. Espressif has good documentation about the ESP-IDF port of lwIP here: `https://docs.espressif.com/projects/esp-idf/en/latest/esp32/api-guides/lwip.html`.

Let's see some other services that we haven't touched on yet. The next example shows how to develop a sensor service on ESP32 that employs mDNS as its underlying protocol.

Sensor service over mDNS

In this example, we will develop a sensor UDP service on the local network. ESP32 will connect to the Wi-Fi network and advertise its service over **multicast DNS (mDNS)**. When a client connects and asks for data, it will reply with a UDP datagram. As the sensor, we will use a DHT11 connected to GPIO17 of an ESP32.

Let's create a `PlatformIO` project with the following `platformio.ini`:

```
[env:az-delivery-devkit-v4]
platform = espressif32
board = az-delivery-devkit-v4
framework = espidf

monitor_speed = 115200
lib_extra_dirs =
    ../../common/esp-idf-lib/components
build_flags =
    -DWIFI_SSID=${sysenv.WIFI_SSID}
    -DWIFI_PASS=${sysenv.WIFI_PASS}
```

In platformio.ini, we specify the local Wi-Fi credentials as environment variables.

I have refactored the Wi-Fi STA mode connection code as a separate library in the project's lib folder. You can download it from the GitHub repository here: https://github.com/PacktPublishing/Internet-of-Things-with-ESP32/tree/main/ch6/udp_temp_service/lib/wifi_connect. The following shows the library files:

```
$ ls -R lib/
lib/:
README   wifi_connect

lib/wifi_connect:
wifi_connect.c  wifi_connect.h
```

It is enough for us to see wifi_connect.h to understand how to use it in the main application:

```
#ifndef wifi_connect_h_
#define wifi_connect_h_

typedef void (*on_connected_f)(void);
typedef void (*on_failed_f)(void);

typedef struct {
    on_connected_f on_connected;
    on_failed_f on_failed;
} connect_wifi_params_t;

void connect_wifi(connect_wifi_params_t);

#endif
```

There is only one function in this library, connect_wifi, which takes a parameter to pass callback functions for Wi-Fi connected and failed events.

Let's develop the application in main.c:

```
#include "wifi_connect.h"
#include "esp_log.h"
```

```
#include "freertos/FreeRTOS.h"
#include "freertos/task.h"
#include "dht.h"
#include "hal/gpio_types.h"
#include "mdns.h"

#include "lwip/err.h"
#include "lwip/sockets.h"
#include "lwip/sys.h"

#define DHT11_PIN GPIO_NUM_17
#define SVC_PORT 1111

static const char *TAG = "sensor_app";

static int16_t temperature;
static int16_t humidity;
```

We include the necessary header files, then define the DHT11 pin and the service port number, SVC_PORT. It is the UDP port number for the sensor service where clients connect and query temperature and humidity.

The function to start the mDNS service follows next:

```
static void start_mdns(void)
{
    mdns_init();
    mdns_hostname_set("esp32_sensor");
    mdns_instance_name_set("esp32 with dht11");

    mdns_txt_item_t serviceTxtData[4] = {
        {"temperature", "y"},
        {"humidity", "y"},
        {"pressure", "n"},
        {"light", "n"},
    };

    mdns_service_add("ESP32-Sensor", "_sensor", "_udp", SVC_
```

```
PORT, serviceTxtData, 4);
}
```

In the `start_mdns` function, we first initialize the library and then set the host name as `esp32_sensor`, which will be listed in the network as `esp32_sensor.local`. We can ping `esp32_sensor.local` and get replies from it if everything goes well. We also add a service with the name of `ESP32-Sensor`. In its service description, we specify which data can be queried from this service. For this sensor, clients can query temperature and humidity.

Next, we will see the service implementation:

```
static void start_udp_server(void)
{
    char data_buffer[64];
    struct sockaddr_in server_addr = {
        .sin_family = AF_INET,
        .sin_port = htons(SVC_PORT),
        .sin_addr = {
            .s_addr = htonl(INADDR_ANY)}};
```

The `start_udp_server` function implements the service. Although it seems a bit lengthy, the logic is very simple. We first define the server socket address with the port `SVC_PORT`. Then, we start a `while` loop to create and manage a UDP socket as follows:

```
while (1)
{
    int sock = socket(AF_INET, SOCK_DGRAM, IPPROTO_IP);
    if (bind(sock, (struct sockaddr *)&server_addr,
sizeof(server_addr)) < 0)
    {
        ESP_LOGE(TAG, "bind failed");
    }
```

After creating a UDP `socket`, we bind it (using `bind`) to the server address. There are two `while` loops. The outer one is to keep the service up and running in case of any errors. We define another `while` loop if the `bind` function is successful:

```
else
{
    while (1)
```

```
                {
                    struct sockaddr_storage client_addr;
                    socklen_t socklen = sizeof(client_addr);
                    int len = recvfrom(sock, data_buffer,
                                    sizeof(data_buffer) - 1, 0,
                                    (struct sockaddr *)&client_
    addr,
                                    &socklen);
```

The inner loop listens for clients. The `recvfrom` function waits for a request from a client. When it receives a request, we check whether it is a temperature or humidity query:

```
    if (len < 0)
    {
        ESP_LOGE(TAG, "recvfrom failed");
        break;
    }
    data_buffer[len] = 0;

    if (!strcmp(data_buffer, "temperature"))
    {
        sprintf(data_buffer, "%d", temperature);
    }
    else if (!strcmp(data_buffer, "humidity"))
    {
        sprintf(data_buffer, "%d", humidity);
    }
    else
    {
        sprintf(data_buffer, "err");
    }
```

Then, we arrange a reply accordingly and send the reply by calling the `sendto` function:

```
    len = strlen(data_buffer);

    if (sendto(sock, data_buffer, len, 0,
            (struct sockaddr *)&client_addr,
```

```
                              sizeof(client_addr)) < 0)
                {
                    ESP_LOGE(TAG, "sendto failed");
                    break;
                }
            }
        }
    }
```

We handle all of the requests and reply to them in the inner loop. Nonetheless, if any of the function calls fail, the loop breaks and we get into the scope of the outer loop, as follows:

```
        if (sock != -1)
        {
            shutdown(sock, 0);
            close(sock);
        }

        vTaskDelay(1000);
    }
}
```

If no function fails in the inner loop, this part of the code will not be executed. However, as a safeguard, we close the socket to handle the fail case and let the outer loop create another socket.

The rest is straightforward. We only need to start the service when the Wi-Fi is connected. The following function does this job:

```
static void start_sensor_service(void *arg)
{
    start_mdns();
    start_udp_server();

    vTaskDelete(NULL);
}
```

start_sensor_service runs as a FreeRTOS task. It calls the functions that we have implemented before to start the mDNS service and UDP server, and then just deletes itself from the FreeRTOS task list.

Next, we implement a callback function for the Wi-Fi connected event:

```
static void wifi_connected_cb(void)
{
    ESP_LOGI(TAG, "wifi connected");
    xTaskCreate(start_sensor_service, "svc", 5 * configMINIMAL_
STACK_SIZE, NULL, 5, NULL);
}
```

wifi_connected_cb is the callback function to be called when the local Wi-Fi is connected. It creates the FreeRTOS task with start_sensor_service. We also need another callback function for the failure case:

```
static void wifi_failed_cb(void)
{
    ESP_LOGE(TAG, "wifi failed");
}
```

In wifi_failed_cb, we print a log message on the serial monitor so that we can understand if the WiFi connection attempt has failed.

We have another FreeRTOS task function, read_dht11, which reads temperature and humidity from DHT11 and stores values in the corresponding global variables regularly:

```
static void read_dht11(void *arg)
{
    while (1)
    {
        vTaskDelay(2000 / portTICK_RATE_MS);
        dht_read_data(DHT_TYPE_DHT11, DHT11_PIN, &humidity,
&temperature);
        humidity /= 10;
        temperature /= 10;
    }
}
```

Finally, in app_main, we simply call connect_wifi from the project library and create the DHT11 task, as follows:

```
void app_main()
{
```

```
    connect_wifi_params_t p = {
        .on_connected = wifi_connected_cb,
        .on_failed = wifi_failed_cb};
    connect_wifi(p);
    xTaskCreate(read_dht11, "temp", 3 * configMINIMAL_STACK_
SIZE, NULL, 5, NULL);
}
```

The application is complete. We can compile, upload, and test it:

```
$ source ~/.platformio/penv/bin/activate
(penv)$ export WIFI_SSID='\"<your_wifi_ssid>\"'
(penv)$ export WIFI_PASS='\"<your_wifi_passwd>\"'
(penv)$ pio run
(penv)$ pio run -t erase
(penv)$ pio run -t upload
```

After uploading the application, we should have our ESP32 sensor up and running. Let's try to ping the sensor:

```
(penv)$ ping esp32_sensor.local
PING esp32_sensor.local (192.168.1.82) 56(84) bytes of data.
64 bytes from espressif (192.168.1.82): icmp_seq=1 ttl=255
time=512 ms
64 bytes from espressif (192.168.1.82): icmp_seq=2 ttl=255
time=80.9 ms
64 bytes from espressif (192.168.1.82): icmp_seq=3 ttl=255
time=456 ms
```

It seems alright. We can list all mDNS services in the network to see whether our sensor is in there:

```
(penv)$ avahi-browse -a
+ wlp2s0 IPv6 HP OfficeJet [9CE993] _uscans._tcp          local
+ wlp2s0 IPv4 ESP32-Sensor _sensor._udp          local
```

Yes, we have it. We can see the details of the sensor service as follows:

```
(penv)$ avahi-browse _sensor._udp -rt
+ wlp2s0 IPv4 ESP32-Sensor _sensor._udp          local
= wlp2s0 IPv4 ESP32-Sensor _sensor._udp          local
   hostname = [esp32_sensor.local]
   address = [192.168.1.82]
   port = [1111]
   txt = ["temperature=y" "humidity=y" "pressure=n" "light=n"]
```

The server name, the IP address and port, and the services provided by the server are all listed when we query the sensor. As we see in the output, the server shares temperature and humidity values, but it doesn't have data about pressure or light.

Finally, we ask for *temperature* and *humidity*. It replies with the latest ambient readings. On the other hand, when we ask for *light*, it returns `err` as the response since it doesn't provide that service:

```
(penv)$ echo -n "temperature" | nc -4u -w1 esp32_sensor.local
1111
23
(penv)$ echo -n "humidity" | nc -4u -w1 esp32_sensor.local 1111
54
(penv)$ echo -n "light" | nc -4u -w1 esp32_sensor.local 1111
err
```

Great! We have a network sensor that we can query from any device on the network.

In the next example, we will see how to develop a digital clock application that gets date/time information from an SNTP server.

Digital clock with SNTP

SNTP is a time synchronization protocol for network devices. The underlying transport layer protocol is UDP. A client requests the universal time from the configured SNTP server and updates its internal time accordingly. We will develop a digital clock in this example. ESP32 will query an SNTP server for the universal time and after receiving the time information, it will show it on an OLED display in the hour-minute-second format.

The hardware setup is simple: we only use an OLED display as an I²C device by connecting the GND, 3v3, SDA, and SCL pins. SDA and SCL will be connected to GPIO21 and GPIO22, respectively.

After the hardware setup, let's create a new project in the following steps:

1. Create a `PlatformIO` project and edit the configuration file, `platformio.ini`:

```
[env:az-delivery-devkit-v4]
platform = espressif32
board = az-delivery-devkit-v4
framework = espidf

monitor_speed = 115200
lib_extra_dirs =
    ../../common/components
    ../../common/esp-idf-lib/components
build_flags =
    -DWIFI_SSID=${sysenv.WIFI_SSID}
    -DWIFI_PASS=${sysenv.WIFI_PASS}
```

2. Copy the `wifi_connect` library from the project repository here: https://github.com/PacktPublishing/Internet-of-Things-with-ESP32/tree/main/ch6/sntp_clock_ex/lib/wifi_connect.

3. Rename the application source file to `main.cpp` to compile with the C++ compiler.

We're ready to develop the application in `main.cpp` as follows:

```
#include <stdio.h>
#include <string.h>
#include <time.h>
#include <sys/time.h>

#include <freertos/FreeRTOS.h>
#include <freertos/task.h>

#include "esp_log.h"
#include "esp_sntp.h"

#include "ssd1306.h"
#include "wifi_connect.h"
```

```
#define TAG "sntp_ex"

#define OLED_CLK 22
#define OLED_SDA 21

extern "C" void app_main(void);
```

We include the necessary header files. Two of them are important for our purposes.
time.h contains the standard C library time functions, such as for getting time
information, converting into different time zones, and formatting as strings. The other
header file, esp_sntp.h, provides SNTP connection and communication functionality.

We then define the OLED I²C pins and declare app_main as extern "C", which
commands the C++ compiler not to mangle the name. Let's jump into app_main to
follow the application flow:

```
void app_main()
{
    init_hw();
    connect_wifi_params_t p = {
        .on_connected = wifi_conn_cb,
        .on_failed = wifi_failed_cb};
    connect_wifi(p);
}
```

In app_main, we first initialize the hardware by calling init_hw and then connect
to the local Wi-Fi. connect_wifi takes a parameter that denotes the success and fail
callbacks of the application. Then, we implement the init_hw function:

```
static void init_hw(void)
{
    ssd1306_128x64_i2c_initEx(OLED_CLK, OLED_SDA, 0);
}
```

init_hw calls only the OLED initialization function with I²C pins. We don't have any
other external devices to be initialized in this application.

The Wi-Fi callbacks of our application are as follows:

```
void wifi_conn_cb(void)
{
    init_sntp();
    xTaskCreate(sync_time, "sync", 8192, NULL, 5, NULL);
}


void wifi_failed_cb(void)
{
    ESP_LOGE(TAG, "wifi failed");
}
```

wifi_conn_cb and wifi_failed_cb are the callback functions that let the application know about the result of the Wi-Fi connection attempt. If the connection fails, we simply print an error message on the serial console. If it succeeds, we start with the SNTP operations. We first need to configure the SNTP API and then create a task to synchronize the time. Let's look at the init_sntp function next:

```
static void init_sntp(void)
{
    sntp_setservername(0, "pool.ntp.org");
    sntp_init();
}
```

In init_sntp, we use the SNTP library functions from esp_sntp.h. Now, sntp_setservername sets the SNTP server as pool.ntp.org and sntp_init starts the synchronization process. We need to poll the status of the synchronization process in a task as follows:

```
static void sync_time(void *arg)
{
    ssd1306_clearScreen();
    ssd1306_setFixedFont(ssd1306xled_font8x16);
    ssd1306_printFixed(0, 32, "Running sync...", STYLE_NORMAL);
```

`sync_time` is a FreeRTOS task function where we complete the synchronization. The task is created when Wi-Fi is connected. We first inform the end user about the status by printing a message on the OLED display. Then, we try to synchronize the time with the configured time server:

```
    int retry = 0;
    const int retry_count = 10;


    while (sntp_get_sync_status() == SNTP_SYNC_STATUS_RESET &&
++retry < retry_count)
    {
        vTaskDelay(2000 / portTICK_PERIOD_MS);
    }
    if (retry == retry_count)
    {
        ssd1306_clearScreen();
        ssd1306_printFixed(0, 32, "Sync failed.", STYLE_
NORMAL);
        vTaskDelete(NULL);
        return;
    }
```

In a `while` loop, we poll the status. `sntp_get_sync_status` returns `SNTP_SYNC_STATUS_COMPLETED` when the process is successful. If the synchronization fails, we again inform the end user with a message and exit the task. If the synchronization succeeds, we start another task, `show_time`, which will display the time on the OLED screen:

```
    xTaskCreate(show_time, "show_time", 8192, NULL, 5, NULL);
    vTaskDelete(NULL);
}
```

Let's see how we implement the `show_time` function:

```
static void show_time(void *arg)
{
    time_t now = 0;
    struct tm timeinfo;
    memset((void *)&timeinfo, 0, sizeof(timeinfo));
```

```
char buf[64];

ssd1306_clearScreen();
ssd1306_setFixedFont(ssd1306xled_font8x16);
```

We start with declaring variables and setting up the OLED display. In show_time, we use the definitions from the standard C time library, time.h. Next comes a while loop where we update the OLED display every second:

```
while (1)
{
    vTaskDelay(1000 / portTICK_PERIOD_MS);
    time(&now);
    localtime_r(&now, &timeinfo);
    strftime(buf, sizeof(buf), "%a", &timeinfo);
    ssd1306_printFixed(0, 0, buf, STYLE_NORMAL);
    strftime(buf, sizeof(buf), "%H:%M:%S", &timeinfo);
    ssd1306_printFixed(0, 32, buf, STYLE_BOLD);
}
}
```

To update the time on the display, we first get the time in seconds by calling the time function. localtime_r converts now to timeinfo, a more useful format to show year, month, day, time, and so on. We print two bits of information on the display. In the first row, the day name will be printed in a short format, for example, *Mon*, *Tue*, and so on. We use strftime for this purpose. In the second row, we print time of day in the %H:%M:%S format. The strftime format string is explained here: https://man7.org/linux/man-pages/man3/strftime.3.html.

The application is ready and we can test it by flashing the compiled firmware onto our ESP32 devkit.

SNTP is the easiest solution when we need date/time information in our ESP32 projects. After synchronization, ESP32 performs timekeeping by using its timers. Timekeeping is still available, even if ESP32 is in deep-sleep mode, with the help of the RTC timer. The RTC timer is already enabled for this purpose in the default sdkconfig settings, which is defined in **Component config/ESP32-specific/Timers used for gettimeofday function**.

Before closing the chapter, let's talk a bit about the new Wi-Fi standard, **Wi-Fi 6 (IEEE 802.11ax)**. The main purpose of Wi-Fi 6 is to improve efficiency and increase the throughput of the network. The modulation technology behind Wi-Fi 6 is **Orthogonal Frequency-Division Multiple Access (OFDMA)**, which is the same modulation technique as in cellular communication. Another important improvement is **Target Wake Time (TWT)**, to decrease the energy consumption of nodes in a network. STA devices can negotiate their access times to the network with the AP, so they can sleep for a long period of time before any radio communication happens. This technology substantially improves the battery life of IoT devices on a network. Espressif recently (in April 2021) announced a new SoC, ESP32-C6, which supports Wi-Fi 6. Unlike the previous chip variants with Xtensa CPUs, ESP32-C6 has a single-core, 32-bit RISC-V microcontroller in it. There is a nice review of it on Hackaday here: `https://hackaday.com/2021/04/11/new-part-day-espressif-esp32-c6/`.

In the next chapter, we will discuss the security features of ESP32.

Summary

One reason why ESP32 is so popular is its superior connectivity features. Wi-Fi, as the most common wireless protocol in the world, is integrated in ESP32 to help developers create outstanding products. In this chapter, we have learned a lot about how we can utilize ESP32's Wi-Fi functionality in our projects. On top of Wi-Fi, ESP32 supports almost any kind of TCP/IP application with its advanced framework, ESP-IDF. The lwIP stack is adopted in the framework. It enables us to connect to servers on the internet and communicate with other connected devices, which is at the heart of IoT.

The next chapter is devoted to the security features of ESP32. It would be a serious mistake to launch an IoT product on the market without well-planned, well-designed, and well-tested security. ESP32 provides all the hardware support necessary for this. We will discuss how to leverage ESP32 to develop secure IoT applications in the next chapter.

Questions

Here are some questions to revise what we have learned in this chapter:

1. If you want to run a simple web server, in which operation mode of Wi-Fi should you configure ESP32?

    a. STA or AP

    b. Only AP

    c. HTTP

    d. HTTPS

2. If ESP32 doesn't connect to the local Wi-Fi, which of these wouldn't be the reason why?

    a. Wi-Fi credentials

    b. ESP32 memory partitions

    c. Web URL

    d. Wi-Fi authentication mode

3. Which protocol would you think of enabling on ESP32 if you wanted to expose services on a local Wi-Fi network?

    a. SNTP

    b. MQTT

    c. mDNS

    d. TCP/IP

4. Which protocol available in lwIP would be the first choice to check whether an ESP32 device is up and running on the local network?

    a. SNTP

    b. mDNS

    c. DHCP

    d. ICMP

5. If you need to log all sensor readings with date/time information, which protocol would you need to use in your application?

    a. SNTP

    b. mDNS

    c. DHCP

    d. ICMP

Further reading

- *Networking Fundamentals, Gordon Davies, Packt Publishing* (https://www.packtpub.com/product/networking-fundamentals/9781838643508): *Chapter 4, Understanding Wireless Networking,* explains all the basics of Wi-Fi starting from the physical layer, including the network topology. TCP/IP protocols are discussed in *Chapter 10, Understanding TCP/IP.*

- *Hands-On Network Programming with C, Lewis Van Winkle, Packt Publishing* (https://www.packtpub.com/product/hands-on-network-programming-with-c/9781789349863): I strongly recommend this book if you want to learn more about network programming. Sockets are discussed in *Chapter 2, Getting to Grips with Socket APIs.* Application layer protocols, such as HTTP, are explained in *Section 2* of the book. *Chapter 14, Web Programming for the Internet of Things,* is dedicated to IoT connectivity, which is discussed in broad terms to give you the overall picture.

7

Security First!

Any internet-facing solution must be designed with security-first in mind, otherwise it is vulnerable to cyber-attacks. This especially applies to IoT products since they are usually introduced in batches to the market and delivered to end users who often don't have any basic understanding of IoT security.

When it comes to security, *ESP32* provides a good level of hardware support for developers with its cryptography subsystem. *ESP-IDF* also integrates industry-standard encryption libraries and provides a good abstraction when a custom security solution is needed. In this chapter, we will discuss the essentials of the ESP32 platform when developing production-grade IoT devices and see examples of secure communication protocols to understand how to utilize them in our projects. This chapter requires some background knowledge to follow the examples easily. If you don't feel comfortable with the security fundamentals, you can find some resources to help you in the *Further reading* section at the end of the chapter.

In this chapter, we're going to cover the following topics:

- Secure boot and **over-the-air** (**OTA**) updates
- Securing communication with TLS/DTLS
- Integrating with secure elements

Technical requirements

As to hardware, we will continue with our ESP32 devkit. A new module, *OPTIGA™ Trust X Shield2Go Security*, is needed while discussing secure elements. For more information, you can check out the product website at this link: `https://www.infineon.com/cms/en/product/evaluation-boards/s2go-security-optiga-x/`.

On the software side, we are going to use the industry-standard `openssl` tool to generate certificates and run web servers. You can find the binaries here: `https://wiki.openssl.org/index.php/Binaries`.

The examples in the chapter are in the GitHub repository here: `https://github.com/PacktPublishing/Internet-of-Things-with-ESP32/tree/main/ch7`.

Check out the following video to see the code in action: `https://bit.ly/3hoUplJ`

Secure boot and over-the-air (OTA) updates

Basically, secure boot is the way we make sure our devices run only our firmware and prevent third parties from tampering with our devices. Before delving into secure boot, let's talk about the boot process of ESP32.

The boot process has three stages:

1. **First-stage bootloader**: This happens upon reset. ESP32 has two processors, named **PRO CPU (cpu0)** and **APP CPU (cpu1)**. PRO CPU runs and does all hardware initialization. We don't have any control at this stage. After initialization, control is passed to the second stage bootloader.

2. **Second-stage bootloader**: The main responsibility of the second-stage bootloader is to find and load the application. It reads the partition table, checks factory and OTA partitions, and based on the OTA info, it loads the correct partition as the application. It also controls flash encryption, secure boot, and OTA updates. The source code is provided along with ESP-IDF, so we can modify this bootloader according to our needs.

3. **Application startup**: At this stage, the application starts to run. Both processors start their FreeRTOS schedulers. PRO CPU then runs the main task and the `app_main` function in this task.

ESP-IDF provides two different secure boot schemes for different revisions of ESP32. *Secure boot v1* is for the initial versions of ESP32, and *secure boot v2* is supported from ESP32 Rev3 and in ESP-S2 series chips. Unfortunately, the previous revisions of ESP32 have some vulnerabilities. The good news is that it requires physical access to the device, and an attacker would need to know a specific type of attack, called voltage fault injection, to bypass secure boot and flash encryption. Otherwise, ESP32 is resilient to remote attacks as long as the right security measures are taken at production.

Let's see how these secure boot schemes work.

Secure boot v1

The technique recommended by *Espressif* to secure devices in the field is to configure the devices with the following:

- Secure boot
- Flash encryption

Secure boot creates a chain of trust, from boot to the application firmware, by authenticating the running software at each step. The whole process may sound a bit confusing, but in simple terms it works as follows:

1. Authenticate the bootloader by using the symmetric key (AES-256) in eFuses Block2: ESP32 has 1,024-bit **One-Time Programmable (OTP)** memory to keep system settings and secrets. This OTP is composed of four blocks of eFuses. The secure boot key is kept in block 2. After enabling secure boot, it is not possible to read the key using software due to the read/write protection. ESP32 verifies the bootloader image by using the secure boot key.

2. Authenticate the application by using the asymmetric key pair generated by the **Elliptic Curve Digital Signature Algorithm (ECDSA)**: Each application is signed by the private part of a key pair and the bootloader has the public key. Before loading the application in the memory, the bootloader verifies the signature by using the public key it has.

For more information about secure boot v1, the official documentation is a perfect resource at this link: `https://docs.espressif.com/projects/esp-idf/en/latest/esp32/security/secure-boot-v1.html`.

The second layer of protection is flash encryption. The flash encryption key (AES-256) is stored in eFuses Block1. Again, the key is not accessible using software. When flash encryption is enabled, ESP32 encrypts the bootloader, partition table, and application partition. The *Espressif* documentation explains all the details about flash encryption here: `https://docs.espressif.com/projects/esp-idf/en/latest/esp32/security/flash-encryption.html`.

Secure boot v2

Secure boot v2 is available for ESP32 Rev3 and ESP-S2 series chips. The main difference from secure boot v1 is that bootloader authentication is also done by asymmetric key signature verification, using **Rivest–Shamir–Adleman-Probabilistic Signature Scheme (RSA-PSS)**. This time, eFuses Block2 keeps the SHA-256 of the public key, which is embedded in the bootloader. ESP32 first validates the public key of the bootloader and then verifies the signature of the bootloader by using this public key. After the bootloader is authenticated, control is passed to the bootloader to continue with the application authentication. If any signatures in these steps don't match, ESP32 simply won't run the application. The advantage of this scheme is that there is no private key on ESP32; therefore, it is literally impossible to run any malicious code on the device if the private key is kept in a secure location. For more information about how to enable secure boot v2, you can refer to the official documentation here: `https://docs.espressif.com/projects/esp-idf/en/latest/esp32/security/secure-boot-v2.html`.

> **Important note**
> Secure boot and flash encryption are not reversible. Therefore, only apply them to production devices.

There are several key points to remember before going to mass production:

- We must ensure the authenticity of the firmware; that is, the firmware running on our ESP32 device must be our firmware. The way to do that is to enable secure boot. The critical issues here are the generation of cryptographic keys and the security of private keys. We want to keep the private keys private, and we should only share the public keys with third parties, such as production and assembly factories.

- Secure boot guarantees authenticity, but it doesn't encrypt firmware, which means that it is flashed as plaintext. Anyone can read the firmware and use it somewhere else. Moreover, if we have to embed some sensitive data in it, the implications of this vulnerability can reach beyond the device itself. Flash encryption is used to prevent attacks. However, firmware is still open to exploitation at the assembly factory if we share the application firmware. Therefore, it might be a good idea to use two different firmware binaries: the first one for the assembly factory that validates the hardware and the second one being the real application, where we flash it in a trusted factory area with flash encryption.

In the examples of this chapter, we won't enable secure boot or flash encryption on our devkits but will do a secure OTA update over HTTPS.

Updating OTA

One security best practice is that we need to set a mechanism to update firmware of devices in the field. If we find a vulnerability after installation, calling all devices back would be quite costly for both the client and us, not to mention the service downtime. Instead, the devices can check an online server to see whether there is new firmware or not and then download and activate any updates. In this example, this will be our goal. Before starting, let's briefly see what we need to do:

- We need a secure web server. It will serve the firmware binaries. The tool that we can use is `openssl` for both generating a private/public key pair and starting a secure web server with this key pair.
- The flash will have two OTA partitions to keep the active firmware and room for a new firmware while downloading from the web server.
- In the OTA update logic, we need to compare the versions of the active firmware and the firmware on the server. When they have the same version, it means that there is no new firmware, and no firmware update will happen. If the version numbers are different, we download the new firmware and reboot ESP32 to run it.

Having this overview, let's start a new PlatformIO project and configure it as in the following steps:

1. We create the project and edit `platformio.ini`:

```
[env:az-delivery-devkit-v4]
platform = espressif32
board = az-delivery-devkit-v4
framework = espidf

monitor_speed = 115200
board_build.embed_txtfiles =
    server/ca_cert.pem

build_flags =
    -DWIFI_SSID=${sysenv.WIFI_SSID}
    -DWIFI_PASS=${sysenv.WIFI_PASS}
    -DAPP_OTA_URL=${sysenv.APP_OTA_URL}

board_build.partitions = with_ota_parts.csv
```

We will later create a self-signed certificate, named `ca_cert.pem`, and embed it in the output hex file of the application. We will also define the partition table with room for a new firmware. These settings are all defined in `platformio.ini`.

2. We update `src/CMakeLists.txt` with the certificate path as well:

```
FILE(GLOB_RECURSE app_sources ${CMAKE_SOURCE_DIR}/
src/*.*)
idf_component_register(SRCS ${app_sources})
target_add_binary_data(${COMPONENT_TARGET} "../server/
ca_cert.pem" TEXT)
```

3. We define the environment variables for the local Wi-Fi and server URL:

```
$ source ~/.platformio/penv/bin/activate
(penv)$ export WIFI_SSID='\"<your_wifi_ssid>\"'
(penv)$ export WIFI_PASS='\"<your_wifi_pass>\"'
(penv)$ export APP_OTA_URL='\"https://<server_ip>:1111/
firmware.bin\"'
```

We can use our development PC as a server. It will publish `firmware.bin` over port `1111`.

4. We will provide a partition definition file, `with_ota_parts.csv`, for ESP-IDF. There will be two OTA partitions to download a new firmware:

```
# Name, Type, Subtyp, Ofs, Size, Flags
nvs, data, nvs, , 0x4000,
otadata, data, ota, , 0x2000,
phy_init, data, phy, , 0x1000,
factory, app, factory,, 1M,
ota_0, app, ota_0, , 1M,
ota_1, app, ota_1, , 1M,
```

When there is a `data/ota` partition, the bootloader uses that partition to determine which `ota_[0-1]` contains the active application. The other OTA partition will be used to download a new firmware. `app/factory` is not used in OTA applications.

5. We generate a public-private key pair for the HTTPS server. The firmware will use the public key to establish a secure connection:

```
(penv)$ mkdir server && cd server
(penv)$ openssl req -x509 -newkey rsa:2048 -keyout ca_
key.pem -out ca_cert.pem -days 365 -nodes
```

We use the industry-standard `openssl` tool to generate the key pair. The preceding command generates a self-signed certificate to be used with the HTTPS server. When we run the command, it collects some information for the certificate. The important entry is the **Common Name (CN)** field. We need to enter the local IP of the development PC where we are going to run the HTTPS server.

6. We create a version file, `version.txt`, to distinguish between firmware versions. The filename is important since ESP-IDF looks for the file to set the firmware version. The version number will be used in the OTA update logic to check whether an update is published on the server by comparing with the existing version number:

```
$ cat version.txt
0.0.1
```

We are free to choose any version numbering scheme. Major-minor-build is good for our purposes. The crucial point is that we need to update this file and clear the project every time before building it to set a new version number in the new firmware. Otherwise, ESP-IDF will use the previous version number.

7. We place the wifi_connect library under the lib folder. The source code is available in the GitHub repository here: https://github.com/ PacktPublishing/Internet-of-Things-with-ESP32/tree/main/ ch7/ota_update_ex/lib/wifi_connect.

8. By the end, we should have the following files in place:

```
$ ls -R
.:
CMakeLists.txt  include  lib  platformio.ini  sdkconfig
server  src  test  version.txt  with_ota_parts.csv

./lib:
README  wifi_connect

./lib/wifi_connect:
wifi_connect.c  wifi_connect.h

./server:
ca_cert.pem  ca_key.pem

./src:
CMakeLists.txt  main.c
```

We are ready to continue with the code. Let's open main.c to edit:

```
#include "freertos/FreeRTOS.h"
#include "freertos/task.h"
#include "esp_system.h"
#include "esp_event.h"
#include "esp_log.h"
#include "esp_ota_ops.h"
#include "esp_http_client.h"
#include "esp_https_ota.h"
#include "string.h"
```

```
#include "nvs.h"
#include "nvs_flash.h"
#include "esp_wifi.h"

#include "wifi_connect.h"

static const char *TAG = "ota_test";
extern const uint8_t server_cert_pem_start[] asm("_binary_ca_
cert_pem_start");
extern const uint8_t server_cert_pem_end[] asm("_binary_ca_
cert_pem_end");

void exit_ota(const char *mess)
{
    printf("> exiting: %s\n", mess);
    vTaskDelay(1000 / portTICK_PERIOD_MS);
    vTaskDelete(NULL);
}
```

We include the necessary header files and extern define two global variables, marking the start and end addresses of the server certificate that is embedded in the firmware binary. The certificate is needed for secure connection to the HTTPS server. exit_ota is a simple helper function to be used before exiting the OTA process.

We implement the OTA update in the following function:

```
void start_ota(void *arg)
{
    esp_http_client_config_t config = {
        .url = APP_OTA_URL,
        .cert_pem = (char *)server_cert_pem_start,
    };
    esp_https_ota_config_t ota_config = {
        .http_config = &config,
    };

    esp_https_ota_handle_t https_ota_handle = NULL;
```

```
    if (esp_https_ota_begin(&ota_config, &https_ota_handle) !=
ESP_OK)
    {
        exit_ota("esp_https_ota_begin failed");
        return;
    }
```

We start by defining the HTTP client configuration to connect to the secure server. It takes the firmware URL as APP_OTA_URL and the address of the embedded certificate. Then we start the process by calling esp_https_ota_begin. Next, we check whether a new firmware exists on the server by comparing the existing version of the running firmware and the version of the image on the server, as follows:

```
    esp_app_desc_t new_app;
    if (esp_https_ota_get_img_desc(https_ota_handle, &new_app)
!= ESP_OK)
    {
        exit_ota("esp_https_ota_get_img_desc failed");
        return;
    }

    const esp_partition_t *current_partition = esp_ota_get_
running_partition();
    esp_app_desc_t existing_app;
    esp_ota_get_partition_description(current_partition,
&existing_app);

    ESP_LOGI(TAG, "existing version: '%s'", existing_app.
version);
    ESP_LOGI(TAG, "target version: '%s'", new_app.version);

    if (memcmp(new_app.version, existing_app.version,
sizeof(new_app.version)) == 0)
    {
        exit_ota("no update");
        return;
    }
```

We use the `esp_https_ota_get_img_desc` function to retrieve the application description from the OTA server. The application description contains the version information. We compare it with the existing image version. If they are the same, we simply exit the process. Otherwise, we start the OTA process next:

```
    ESP_LOGI(TAG, "updating...");
    while (esp_https_ota_perform(https_ota_handle) == ESP_ERR_
HTTPS_OTA_IN_PROGRESS)
        ;

    if (esp_https_ota_is_complete_data_received(https_ota_
handle) != true)
    {
        exit_ota("download failed");
        return;
    }

    if (esp_https_ota_finish(https_ota_handle) == ESP_OK)
    {
        ESP_LOGI(TAG, "rebooting..");
        vTaskDelay(1000 / portTICK_PERIOD_MS);
        esp_restart();
    }

    exit_ota("ota failed");
}
```

The hero here is the `esp_https_ota_perform` function. It downloads the firmware from the server in chunks. If the download is successful, we call `esp_https_ota_finish` to complete the process and reboot ESP32 to let the bootloader load the new firmware. If something fails at any point, we exit the process by giving an error message.

We implement the Wi-Fi callback functions, as follows:

```
void wifi_conn_cb(void)
{
    xTaskCreate(&start_ota, "ota", 8192, NULL, 5, NULL);
}
```

```
void wifi_failed_cb(void)
{
    ESP_LOGE(TAG, "wifi failed");
}
```

The `wifi_conn_cb` callback function is the one to be executed when ESP32 connects to the local Wi-Fi network. It starts a FreeRTOS task with the `start_ota` function that we have implemented before.

We complete the application by implementing the `app_main` function:

```
void app_main(void)
{
    ESP_LOGI(TAG, "this is 0.0.1");
    connect_wifi_params_t p = {
        .on_connected = wifi_conn_cb,
        .on_failed = wifi_failed_cb};
    connect_wifi(p);

    esp_wifi_set_ps(WIFI_PS_NONE);
}
```

The `app_main` function calls `connect_wifi` with the callbacks. `esp_wifi_set_ps` is used to disable power-save options of Wi-Fi for an efficient OTA firmware update.

We have completed the application and it is time for testing:

```
(penv)$ pio run -t clean
(penv)$ pio run
(penv)$ pio run -t erase
(penv)$ pio run -t upload
```

We flash the first firmware over the USB port. With this initial firmware, our devkit is ready for OTA updates. The next step for testing is to start the HTTPS server. We can use the `openssl` tool for this purpose:

1. In another shell, run the following commands to start the server:

    ```
    $ cd server
    $ openssl s_server -WWW -key ca_key.pem -cert ca_cert.pem
    -port 1111
    ```

2. Now we should have our secure firmware server up and running. To verify it, we can use `openssl` again. We also need to check whether the firewall blocks port `1111` and add an exception if necessary:

```
$ openssl s_client -connect localhost:1111
CONNECTED(00000003)
```

3. Compile another version of the firmware and copy it to the `server` folder:

```
(penv)$ pio run -t clean
(penv)$ echo "0.0.2" > version.txt
(penv)$ pio run
(penv)$ cp ./.pio/build/az-delivery-devkit-v4/firmware.
bin server/
```

4. To see if the devkit downloads the new firmware, press the reset button and see the messages in the serial monitor. We can also observe that, after the reboot, the application checks the server again for any new firmware, but it aborts the process since the version numbers match this time.

> **Tip**
>
> If you encounter any problem with the `openssl` web server, any other secure web server should work. There is also a simple Python example that you can help yourself to here: `https://gist.github.com/dergachev/7028596`.

In the next section, we are going to see an example of securing network communication by using TLS.

Securing communication with TLS/DTLS

Basically, **Transport Layer Security** (TLS) is used to encrypt data transmitted over any open network, including the internet, to keep communication between two parties secure. TLS uses both asymmetric keys and symmetric keys to secure a connection. When a client application tries to connect to a server, a process called a TLS handshake happens. During a TLS handshake, the following happens:

1. Supported cipher suites (encryption algorithms) are exchanged between the parties and one is agreed upon for further communication.

2. The server is authenticated on the client side by checking its certificate to see whether the certificate is issued by a **Certificate Authority** (**CA**). This step is important since the client needs to know whether the server is legitimate. A CA is an authority that approves/disapproves the authenticity of a certificate.

3. A symmetric key is generated for the session communication in a secure way. Both parties use the same symmetric key to encrypt/decrypt messages between them.

When the TLS handshake is successful, the parties can communicate over any secure application layer protocols, such as HTTPS, secure-MQTT, or **websockets over TLS** (**WSS**). The latest version of TLS, TLS v1.3, is published here: `https://tools.ietf.org/html/rfc8446`.

When it comes to datagram protocols, such as UDP, the **Datagram Transport Layer Security** (**DTLS**) protocol provides communication security. It works in a similar way to TLS. On top of DTLS, for example, we can run **Constrained Application Protocol** (**CoAP**) to exchange UDP messages between wireless sensor nodes.

Let's see an example of how we employ TLS in an application. In this example, we will send an HTTP `GET` request to an online REST API HTTPS server and read the response from it. The approach to do that is as follows:

- We need a secure server to connect. It is `https://reqbin.com` in the example. It is an online REST and SOAP API testing tool that provides different endpoints for testing purposes. We will send a request to the GET JSON endpoint located at `/echo/get/json`.

- We need the server's certificate on ESP32 for a TLS connection. We will download it manually by using `openssl` and embed it in the firmware.

- In the firmware, we will open a TLS connection to the server by using its certificate. Then we will send a `GET` request to the GET JSON endpoint over the TLS connection. The server is expected to reply with sample JSON data. We will print it on the serial monitor and close the connection.

Let's configure a project with the following steps:

1. Create a PlatformIO project with the following `platformio.ini`:

```
[env:az-delivery-devkit-v4]
platform = espressif32
board = az-delivery-devkit-v4
framework = espidf
```

```
monitor_speed = 115200
build_flags =
    -DWIFI_SSID=${sysenv.WIFI_SSID}
    -DWIFI_PASS=${sysenv.WIFI_PASS}
board_build.embed_txtfiles = server/server_cert.pem
```

We will retrieve the server certificate in a later step.

2. Update `src/CMakeLists.txt` with the certificate path:

```
FILE(GLOB_RECURSE app_sources ${CMAKE_SOURCE_DIR}/
src/*.*)
idf_component_register(SRCS ${app_sources})
target_add_binary_data(${COMPONENT_TARGET} "../server/
server_cert.pem" TEXT)
```

3. Create a folder, named `server`, to keep the server certificate. We will download this certificate from the server in the next step and use it later in the application to communicate with the server:

```
$ mkdir server && cd server
```

4. Use `openssl` to download the server certificate. However, the output has some more information, so we need to edit the output file, `server_cert.pem`, to save only the server's certificate. When we open the file, we see there are two certificates in there. The second certificate is the one that we should keep in the file:

```
$ openssl s_client -showcerts -connect reqbin.com:443 < /
dev/null > server_cert.pem
$ vi server_cert.pem
```

5. Copy the `wifi_connect` library under the `lib` folder. Here is the link for the library: `https://github.com/PacktPublishing/Internet-of-Things-with-ESP32/tree/main/ch7/tls_ex/lib/wifi_connect`.

After copying the library, we should have the following directory tree in the project:

```
$ ls -R
.:
CMakeLists.txt  include  lib  platformio.ini  sdkconfig
server  src  test
./lib:
README  wifi_connect
```

```
./lib/wifi_connect:
wifi_connect.c  wifi_connect.h

./server:
server_cert.pem

./src:
CMakeLists.txt  main.c
```

With the project configured, we can continue with the code in main.c:

```
#include <string.h>
#include <stdlib.h>
#include "freertos/FreeRTOS.h"
#include "freertos/task.h"
#include "esp_wifi.h"
#include "esp_log.h"
#include "esp_system.h"
#include "esp_tls.h"
#include "wifi_connect.h"
#include "private_include/esp_tls_mbedtls.h"

static const char *TAG = "tls_ex";

static const char REQUEST[] = "GET /echo/get/json HTTP/1.1\r\n"
                              "Host: reqbin.com\r\n"
                              "User-Agent: esp32\r\n"
                              "Accept: */*\r\n"
                              "\r\n";

extern const uint8_t server_root_cert_pem_start[] asm("_binary_
server_cert_pem_start");
extern const uint8_t server_root_cert_pem_end[] asm("_binary_
server_cert_pem_end");
```

After including the necessary header files, we define the HTTP request that we are going to send when the server is connected. `server_root_cert_pem_start` and `server_root_cert_pem_end` mark the beginning and end of the server certificate embedded in the firmware.

The `do_https_get` function does the job. It connects to the server, sends the request, and gets the response as follows:

```c
static void do_https_get(void *arg)
{
    char buf[512];
    int ret, len;

    esp_tls_cfg_t cfg = {
        .cacert_buf = server_root_cert_pem_start,
        .cacert_bytes = server_root_cert_pem_end - server_root_
cert_pem_start,
    };

    struct esp_tls *tls = esp_tls_conn_http_new("https://
reqbin.com", &cfg);
    if (tls == NULL)
    {
        ESP_LOGE(TAG, "esp_tls_conn_http_new failed");
        vTaskDelete(NULL);
        return;
    }

    ret = esp_mbedtls_write(tls, REQUEST, strlen(REQUEST));
```

We start by creating a TLS connection by calling `esp_tls_conn_http_new`. Then we call `esp_mbedtls_write` to send REQUEST. The ESP-IDF API function for this is `esp_tls_conn_write`, according to the documentation, but it seems that the ESP-IDF version that comes with PlatformIO has some bugs. Therefore, we need to make a direct call to the underlying `esp_mbedtls_write` function. If the write operation is successful, we create a `while` loop to read the response as in the following code snippet:

```
if (ret > 0)
{
    while (1)
    {
        len = sizeof(buf) - 1;
        ret = esp_mbedtls_read(tls, (char *)buf, len);
        if (ret > 0)
        {
            buf[ret] = 0;
            ESP_LOGI(TAG, "%s", buf);
        }
        else
        {
            break;
        }
    }
}
```

After sending the request, we can read the response by calling `esp_mbedtls_read`. We read the response into the buffer until there is nothing left from the server response bytes. Before exiting the function, we need to close the TLS connection, as follows:

```
esp_tls_conn_delete(tls);
vTaskDelete(NULL);
}
```

The `esp_tls_conn_delete` function frees all resources allocated by the TLS library.

> **Important note**
> **mbedTLS** is the default TLS library supported by ESP-IDF. Another option that we can choose as the TLS library is **wolfSSL**.

The rest is straightforward. In the rest of the code, we simply connect to the local Wi-Fi and start a FreeRTOS task with do_https_get when ESP32 connects:

```
void wifi_conn_cb(void)
{
    xTaskCreate(&do_https_get, "https", 8192, NULL, 5, NULL);
}

void wifi_failed_cb(void)
{
    ESP_LOGE(TAG, "wifi failed");
}

void app_main(void)
{
    connect_wifi_params_t p = {
        .on_connected = wifi_conn_cb,
        .on_failed = wifi_failed_cb};
    connect_wifi(p);
}
```

We're done. Now it is time to test the application:

```
$ source ~/.platformio/penv/bin/activate
(penv)$ export WIFI_SSID='\"<local_wifi_ssid>\"'
(penv)$ export WIFI_PASS='\"<local_wifi_password>\"'
(penv)$ pio run && pio run -t upload
(penv)$ pio device monitor
```

We can see the whole HTTP response of the REST API server in the serial output of EPS32 when we connect to the serial monitor. This response includes JSON data as a part of the REST API reply:

```
{"success":"true"}
```

In the next section, we are going to investigate how secure elements work with ESP32.

Integrating with secure elements

When we want private keys in a device totally isolated from any kind of access, we can use secure elements. Let's say that in our project we have a requirement for **IEEE 802.1AR-Secure Device Identity** compliance. The standard says each device in the network should have a **unique device identifier (DevID)** that is cryptographically bound to the device to manage its whole life cycle. The clauses in the standard pretty much define the capabilities of a secure element, which protects private keys from any type of external access and provides an interface for cryptographic operations. In such a use case, a secure element can generate a private/public key pair and store the private key in its vault (secure, non-volatile memory) to prevent any access from outside, including the application code running on the host MCU. All cryptographic functions are provided by the secure element so that a host **System-on-Chip (SoC)**, such as ESP32, can query it via the cryptographic API of the secure element, which means the host application doesn't need to know about the private key for secure operations.

Espressif already has such a module, **ESP32-WROOM-32SE** (the SE at the end stands for **secure element**), which integrates *Microchip's* **ATECC608A cryptoauth** chip within it. When we need a secure element in our project, we can use that module easily without any design and porting issues since Espressif provides it out of the box.

In this example, however, our devkit doesn't have an ESP32-WROOM-32SE module on it, so we will integrate an Optiga TrustX Security Shield2Go. You can see an image of an Optiga TrustX Security Shield2Go here:

Figure 7.1 – Optiga TrustX Security Shield2Go

In its datasheet (which you can find here: `https://www.infineon.com/cms/en/product/evaluation-boards/s2go-security-optiga-x/`), it is described as follows:

> *With built-in tamper-proof NVM for secure storage and Symmetric/ Asymmetric crypto engine to support ECC 256, AES-128 and SHA-256.*

This means that it uses the **Elliptic-Curve Cryptography** (ECC) algorithm for asymmetric encryption, **Advanced Encryption Standard** (AES) as the symmetric block cipher, and the **SHA-256 Cryptographic Hash Algorithm** for generating signatures. With these capabilities, Optiga TrustX provides a modern cryptographic engine with secure, non-volatile memory to support IoT applications. If you want to learn more about the use cases, Infineon provides great guidance in the *OPTIGA™ Trust X1 Solution Reference Manual*, which is listed in the *Further reading* section.

Optiga also provides a software library and good documentation in its GitHub repository here: `https://github.com/Infineon/optiga-trust-x`. The library defines a clear API for developers. We only interact with the library at the **Platform Abstraction Layer** (PAL) level and the application level. Luckily, there exists a reference implementation for ESP32 in the GitHub repository that we can adapt for our purposes.

Here is what we will do in this example:

- We will connect to Optiga TrustX over I²C and read the certificate in its first public key slot. It can store up to four private and four public keys in its secure memory, and they are accessible only by its API over I²C.

- We will integrate mbedTLS and Optiga TrustX by overriding the mbedTLS interface functions. mbedTLS, with its default configuration, uses the ESP32 cryptographic features, but we can redirect the calls to Optiga TrustX by updating the mbedTLS API functions.

- We will use mbedTLS to connect to a secure web server and send data over a secured channel. We will start the web server on our development PCs by running `openssl` from the command line.

The connection between the Optiga TrustX module and ESP32 is simple. Since the secure element is an I²C device, we connect the SDA and SCL pins of the module to GPIO21 and GPIO22 of ESP32, respectively. One extra pin is RST and we connect it to GPIO23. After attaching GND and 3.3 V, we are ready to drive Optiga TrustX.

Let's create a project and configure it as follows:

1. Edit `platformio.ini` first:

```
[env:az-delivery-devkit-v4]
platform = espressif32
board = az-delivery-devkit-v4
framework = espidf

monitor_speed = 115200
```

```
board_build.embed_txtfiles =
    src/dummy_private_key.pem
    src/test_ca_list.pem

build_flags =
    -DPAL_OS_HAS_EVENT_INIT
    -DWIFI_SSID=${sysenv.WIFI_SSID}
    -DWIFI_PASS=${sysenv.WIFI_PASS}
    -DWEB_SERVER=${sysenv.TEST_WEB_SERVER}
```

ESP-IDF has mbedTLS in its components list as an implementation of the TLS protocol to develop secure applications. Therefore, we need to integrate mbedTLS and the Optiga TrustX library at the PAL level and use the mbedTLS API in the application. `src/dummy_private_key.pem` is needed by mbedTLS only for configuration purposes. Optiga TrustX will handle all operations where the private key is needed. `src/test_ca_list.pem` is the list of CA certificates needed to create a chain of trust. The same list will be used by the test web server as well. `PAL_OS_HAS_EVENT_INIT` is a macro definition that is required by the Optiga TrustX library for the ESP32 platform integration. Finally, we will use our development PC as the test web server and `sysenv.TEST_WEB_SERVER` is the local IP of our PC.

2. Update `src/CMakeLists.txt` with the security keys:

```
FILE(GLOB_RECURSE app_sources ${CMAKE_SOURCE_DIR}/
src/*.*)

idf_component_register(SRCS ${app_sources})

target_add_binary_data(${COMPONENT_TARGET} "../src/dummy_
private_key.pem" TEXT)

target_add_binary_data(${COMPONENT_TARGET} "../src/test_
ca_list.pem" TEXT)
```

3. The next step is to include the `wifi_connect` and `optiga` libraries in the application. I had to refactor the `optiga` library that comes with PlatformIO to make it compatible with ESP-IDF. You can directly copy the libraries from the GitHub repository here: `https://github.com/PacktPublishing/Internet-of-Things-with-ESP32/tree/main/ch7/optiga_ex/lib/optiga`.

4. To test the application, we will run a test web server. The server also needs a certificate, a private key, and the CA certificates for the application. They are in the same GitHub repository under the `server` folder.

5. The `optiga` library needs a `menuconfig` section for its parameters. It is provided in `src/Kconfig.projbuild`.

When we have all the required files in place, we should have the following directory structure:

```
$ ls -R .
.:
CMakeLists.txt   include   lib   platformio.ini   sdkconfig   server
src

./lib:
optiga   README   wifi_connect

./lib/optiga:
include   src

./lib/optiga/include:
<optiga header files>

./lib/optiga/src:
<optiga source files>

./lib/wifi_connect:
wifi_connect.c   wifi_connect.h

./server:
OPTIGA_Trust_X_InfineonTestServer_EndEntity_Key.pem   OPTIGA_
Trust_X_InfineonTestServer_EndEntity.pem   OPTIGA_Trust_X_
trusted_CAs.pem

./src:
CMakeLists.txt   dummy_private_key.pem   Kconfig.projbuild
main.c   test_ca_list.pem
```

Having all supporting files in place, we can continue with the application in `main.c`:

```c
#include <string.h>
#include <stdlib.h>
#include "freertos/FreeRTOS.h"
#include "freertos/task.h"
#include "freertos/event_groups.h"
#include "esp_log.h"
#include "esp_system.h"

#include "mbedtls/platform.h"
#include "mbedtls/net.h"
#include "mbedtls/esp_debug.h"
#include "mbedtls/ssl.h"
#include "mbedtls/entropy.h"
#include "mbedtls/ctr_drbg.h"
#include "mbedtls/error.h"
#include "mbedtls/certs.h"
#include "mbedtls/base64.h"

#include "optiga/optiga_util.h"
#include "optiga/pal/pal_os_event.h"
#include "optiga/ifx_i2c/ifx_i2c_config.h"
#include "wifi_connect.h"
#include "driver/gpio.h"
```

We first include a bunch of header files. `optiga/*` headers define all structures and functions to communicate with the Optiga TrustX module. Next comes the macros and the global variables of the application:

```c
#define CERT_LENGTH 512
#define WEB_COMMONNAME "Infineon Test Server End Entity
Certificate"
#define WEB_PORT "50000"

static const char *TAG = "optiga_ex";
```

```
static const char *REQUEST = ">> Super important data from the
client |";
```

The WEB_PORT macro defines the server port that we will connect to and REQUEST is
the data that we will send to the server after a successful TLS connection. We continue
to define more global variables, as follows:

```
optiga_comms_t optiga_comms = {(void *)&ifx_i2c_context_0,
NULL, NULL, OPTIGA_COMMS_SUCCESS};

extern const uint8_t server_root_cert_pem_start[] asm("_binary_
test_ca_list_pem_start");
extern const uint8_t server_root_cert_pem_end[] asm("_binary_
test_ca_list_pem_end");

extern const uint8_t my_key_pem_start[] asm("_binary_dummy_
private_key_pem_start");
extern const uint8_t my_key_pem_end[] asm("_binary_dummy_
private_key_pem_end");

uint8_t my_cert[CERT_LENGTH];
uint16_t my_cert_len = CERT_LENGTH;
```

The optiga_comms structure holds the I²C connection data to the Optiga TrustX
module. Then we define the start and end of the embedded cryptographic files. my_cert
is the byte array in which we will download the device certificate from the Optiga TrustX
module.

The initialization function comes next:

```
static void init_hw(void)
{
    uint8_t err_code;

    gpio_set_direction(CONFIG_PAL_I2C_MASTER_RESET, GPIO_MODE_
OUTPUT);
    pal_os_event_init();
    err_code = optiga_util_open_application(&optiga_comms);
    ESP_ERROR_CHECK(err_code);
```

`pal_os_event_init` is a platform-specific Optiga function to handle any event in the `optiga` library. Basically, it creates a FreeRTOS task and monitors whether there are any registered functions to run. Then, `optiga_util_open_application` initializes the I²C channel and starts the application in the secure element. Next, we read the certificate from the secure element:

```
    err_code = optiga_util_read_data(CONFIG_OPTIGA_TRUST_X_
CERT_SLOT, 0x09, my_cert, &my_cert_len);
    ESP_ERROR_CHECK(err_code);
```

We use `optiga_util_read_data` to read the certificate into `my_cert` from one of the four certificate slots in the secure element. The slot address is configured in `sdkconfig`. At the end of the initialization, we configure the current limit of the secure element, as follows:

```
    uint8_t curlim = 0x0e;
    err_code = optiga_util_write_data(eCURRENT_LIMITATION,
OPTIGA_UTIL_WRITE_ONLY, 0, &curlim, 1);
    ESP_ERROR_CHECK(err_code);
}
```

We increase the current limit of the secure element for better performance by calling `optiga_util_write_data` with the `eCURRENT_LIMITATION` enumeration. In low-power applications, we can set this value to the minimum.

Next, we define some supporting functions in the application:

```
static void exit_task(const char *mesg)
{
    if (mesg)
    {
        ESP_LOGI(TAG, "%s", mesg);
    }
    vTaskDelete(NULL);
}


static void free_mbedtls(mbedtls_ssl_context *ssl, mbedtls_net_
context *server_fd, int ret)
{
    char buf[128];
    mbedtls_ssl_session_reset(ssl);
```

```
mbedtls_net_free(server_fd);

if (ret != 0)
{
    mbedtls_strerror(ret, buf, sizeof(buf) - 1);
    ESP_LOGE(TAG, "Last error was: -0x%x - %s", -ret, buf);
}
}
```

exit_task and free_mbedtls are two supporting functions that we use before exiting the TLS connection or in the case of an error. In free_mbedtls, we call mbedtls_ssl_session_reset to close the session and then mbedtls_net_free to close the underlying socket. There are many mbedTLS functions that we use in this application. It is not possible to discuss them one by one but if you would like to learn more, the online API documentation is a good resource here: https://tls.mbed. org/api/. I recommend keeping the online documentation open while reading the application code next.

> **Tip**
>
> **Secure Sockets Layer (SSL)** is the predecessor protocol to TLS, and SSL and TLS can be used interchangeably on many occasions. The mbedTLS documentation calls a secure connection as an SSL session. Similarly, a TLS certificate is also commonly referred to as an SSL certificate.

In the following function, we connect to the secure server and send data by using the mbedTLS functions:

```
static void connect_server_task(void *args)
{
    int ret = 0;

    mbedtls_entropy_context entropy;
    mbedtls_ctr_drbg_context ctr_drbg;
    mbedtls_ssl_context ssl;
    mbedtls_x509_crt cacert;
    mbedtls_x509_crt mycert;
    mbedtls_pk_context mykey;
    mbedtls_ssl_config conf;
```

```
    mbedtls_net_context server_fd;


    mbedtls_ssl_init(&ssl);
    mbedtls_x509_crt_init(&cacert);
    mbedtls_x509_crt_init(&mycert);
    mbedtls_pk_init(&mykey);
    mbedtls_ctr_drbg_init(&ctr_drbg);
    mbedtls_ssl_config_init(&conf);
    mbedtls_entropy_init(&entropy);
    mbedtls_ctr_drbg_seed(&ctr_drbg, mbedtls_entropy_func,
&entropy, NULL, 0);
```

There is a long list of mbedTLS initialization code before actually starting communication with the server. What we initialize is as follows:

- Entropy source for randomness (mbedtls_entropy_context)

- Random number generation subsystem (mbedtls_ctr_drbg_context)

- CA certificates and the device certificate (mbedtls_x509_crt)

- TCP socket for the server communication (mbedtls_net_context)

- TLS configuration and context structures to keep the connection status (mbedtls_ssl_context)

Key parsing comes next:

```
if (mbedtls_x509_crt_parse(&cacert, server_root_cert_pem_
start,server_root_cert_pem_end - server_root_cert_pem_start) <
0)
    {
        exit_task("mbedtls_x509_crt_parse/root cert failed");
        return;
    }


    if (mbedtls_x509_crt_parse_der(&mycert, my_cert, my_cert_
len) < 0)
    {
        exit_task("mbedtls_x509_crt_parse/local cert failed");
        return;
    }
```

```
    mbedtls_pk_parse_key(&mykey, (const unsigned char *)my_key_
pem_start,my_key_pem_end - my_key_pem_start, NULL, 0);
```

We parse the keys into the mbedTLS variables, which will be used by mbedTLS during the server handshake and communication. The return value of mbedtls_pk_parse_key in the last line is not important since the secure element will handle cryptographic operations where the private key is needed. mycert contains the public part of the asymmetric key pair. After this, we initialize the communication infrastructure by using the mbedTLS library functions:

```
    mbedtls_ssl_set_hostname(&ssl, WEB_COMMONNAME);
    mbedtls_ssl_config_defaults(&conf, MBEDTLS_SSL_IS_CLIENT,
MBEDTLS_SSL_TRANSPORT_STREAM, MBEDTLS_SSL_PRESET_DEFAULT);
    mbedtls_ssl_conf_authmode(&conf, MBEDTLS_SSL_VERIFY_
REQUIRED);
    mbedtls_ssl_conf_ca_chain(&conf, &cacert, NULL);
    mbedtls_ssl_conf_rng(&conf, mbedtls_ctr_drbg_random, &ctr_
drbg);
    mbedtls_ssl_conf_own_cert(&conf, &mycert, &mykey);
    mbedtls_ssl_setup(&ssl, &conf);

    mbedtls_net_init(&server_fd);
```

There are several things to do to set up a successful connection to the secure server. The important one here is that we configure mbedTLS to check the server certificate by calling the mbedtls_ssl_conf_authmode function. During the TLS handshake, the server certificate will be verified. To complete the initialization process, we call mbedtls_ssl_setup to initialize the secure layer and mbedtls_net_init to initialize the underlying BSD socket. Now, we are ready to try a connection:

```
    if ((ret = mbedtls_net_connect(&server_fd, WEB_SERVER, WEB_
PORT, MBEDTLS_NET_PROTO_TCP)) != 0)
    {
        exit_task("mbedtls_net_connect failed");
        free_mbedtls(&ssl, &server_fd, ret);
        return;
    }

    mbedtls_ssl_set_bio(&ssl, &server_fd, mbedtls_net_send,
```

```
mbedtls_net_recv, NULL);


    while ((ret = mbedtls_ssl_handshake(&ssl)) != 0)
    {
        if (ret != MBEDTLS_ERR_SSL_WANT_READ && ret != MBEDTLS_
ERR_SSL_WANT_WRITE)
        {
            exit_task("mbedtls_ssl_handshake failed");
            free_mbedtls(&ssl, &server_fd, ret);
            return;
        }
    }
```

We connect to the server by calling mbedtls_net_connect. If the TCP connection is successful, we call mbedtls_ssl_handshake to start the TLS handshake. When the TLS handshake finishes, we need to check the result, as follows:

```
    if ((ret = mbedtls_ssl_get_verify_result(&ssl)) != 0)
    {
        exit_task("mbedtls_ssl_get_verify_result failed");
        free_mbedtls(&ssl, &server_fd, ret);
        return;
    }


    while ((ret = mbedtls_ssl_write(&ssl, (const unsigned char
*)REQUEST, strlen(REQUEST))) <= 0)
    {
        if (ret != MBEDTLS_ERR_SSL_WANT_READ && ret != MBEDTLS_
ERR_SSL_WANT_WRITE)
        {
            exit_task("mbedtls_ssl_write failed");
            free_mbedtls(&ssl, &server_fd, ret);
            return;
        }
    }
```

The `mbedtls_ssl_get_verify_result` function is used to check whether the server certificate is valid. If the server certificate passes the verification process, we send `REQUEST` over the secure channel by calling `mbedtls_ssl_write`. Finally, we call `mbedtls_ssl_close_notify` to let the server know about the session end and close the connection as in the following code snippet:

```
mbedtls_ssl_close_notify(&ssl);
free_mbedtls(&ssl, &server_fd, 0);
exit_task(NULL);
}
```

Now, it is time to implement the Wi-Fi connection callbacks and `app_main`:

```
static void wifi_conn_cb(void)
{
    xTaskCreate(&connect_server_task, "connect_server_task",
8192, NULL, 5, NULL);
}

static void wifi_failed_cb(void)
{
    ESP_LOGE(TAG, "wifi failed");
}

void app_main(void)
{
    init_hw();

    connect_wifi_params_t p = {
        .on_connected = wifi_conn_cb,
        .on_failed = wifi_failed_cb};
    connect_wifi(p);
}
```

In `app_main`, we simply call `init_hw` and `connect_wifi`. When the local Wi-Fi is connected, `connect_server_task` is scheduled to run by FreeRTOS.

The last crucial topic here is how we can integrate the mbedTLS library with any secure element. The ESP32 port of mbedTLS talks to the cryptographic accelerator of ESP32, not to the Optiga TrustX module.

mbedTLS provides a list of functions for third-party integrations and controls them using a configuration header. ESP-IDF uses this configuration to implement the integration. What we should normally do in a real project is to remove the ESP32 port of mbedTLS from ESP-IDF and replace it with our own port for the Optiga module. Since I cannot list the whole ported code here, we will divert only the entropy calls to the Optiga module when the random number generator needs a seed. The mbedTLS API function for this is mbedtls_hardware_poll, which is enabled by defining the MBEDTLS_ENTROPY_HARDWARE_ALT macro in the mbedTLS configuration header. The configuration header file is mbedtls/config.h. Let's first implement our version in lib/optiga/src/trustx_random.c:

```c
#if !defined(MBEDTLS_CONFIG_FILE)
#include "mbedtls/config.h"
#else
#include MBEDTLS_CONFIG_FILE
#endif

#include <sys/types.h>
#include <stdlib.h>
#include <stdio.h>
#include "optiga/optiga_crypt.h"
#include "mbedtls/entropy_poll.h"
#include "mbedtls/esp_config.h"
#include "esp_log.h"
```

We first include the necessary header files to access the functions in them. Then we continue with the function definition, as follows:

```c
#if defined(MBEDTLS_ENTROPY_HARDWARE_ALT)

int mbedtls_hardware_poll( void *data, unsigned char *output,
size_t len, size_t *olen )
{
    ESP_LOGI("optiga", "in mbedtls_hardware_poll");
    optiga_lib_status_t status = OPTIGA_LIB_ERROR;
```

```
    status = optiga_crypt_random(eTRNG, output, len);
    if ( status != OPTIGA_LIB_SUCCESS)
    {
      *olen = 0;
       return 1;
    }

      *olen = len;
      return 0;
}
#endif
```

In mbedtls_hardware_poll, we call optiga_crypt_random from the optiga library to get an array of random bytes. Next, we need to divert the ESP-IDF implementation that is in $HOME/.platformio/packages/framework-espidf/components/mbedtls/port/esp_hardware.c:

```
#if !defined(MBEDTLS_CONFIG_FILE)
#include "mbedtls/config.h"
#else
#include MBEDTLS_CONFIG_FILE
#endif

#include <sys/types.h>
#include <stdlib.h>
#include <stdio.h>
#include <esp_system.h>
#include <esp_log.h>

#include "mbedtls/entropy_poll.h"

#ifndef MBEDTLS_ENTROPY_HARDWARE_ALT
#error "MBEDTLS_ENTROPY_HARDWARE_ALT should always be set in ESP-IDF"
#endif

extern int mbedtls_hardware_poll(void *data, unsigned char *output, size_t len, size_t *olen);
```

We have replaced the implementation of the function with the `extern` definition, so the compiler uses our version of `mbedtls_hardware_poll`.

That's it. Now we can compile the application:

```
$ source ~/.platformio/penv/bin/activate
(penv)$ export WIFI_SSID='\"<wifi_ssid>\"'
(penv)$ export WIFI_PASS='\"<wifi_pwd>\"'
(penv)$ export TEST_WEB_SERVER='\"<pc_local_ip>\"'
(penv)$ pio run && pio run -t upload
```

We need a secure web server to test our application. `openssl` is a very handy tool for such tests. We can start the server as follows:

```
$ cd server
$ openssl s_server -tls1_2 -cipher ECDHE-ECDSA-AES128-
CCM8 -accept 50000 -cert OPTIGA_Trust_X_InfineonTestServer_
EndEntity.pem -key OPTIGA_Trust_X_InfineonTestServer_EndEntity_
Key.pem -CAfile OPTIGA_Trust_X_trusted_CAs.pem -debug -state
```

If everything goes well, ESP32 should connect to the web server, complete the TLS handshake, verify the certificate, then send `REQUEST`, which will be printed on the server side.

This was the last example of this very important chapter.

In the next chapter, we are going to learn about the **Bluetooth Low Energy** (**BLE**) features of ESP32 by example.

Summary

Cyber security is an important aspect of any IoT project, and it is always a good idea to apply security best practices while designing and developing IoT products. For ESP32, it means enabling **secure boot** and **flash encryption** before rolling out a new product in the field. The application firmware also needs to support **OTA updates** for new versions to patch any security vulnerabilities. **TLS/DTLS** protocols can be employed at the application level to secure communication with remote servers or any other computing devices. In this chapter, we have learned some techniques to secure our IoT devices.

Nonetheless, it is hard to say we can have 100% secure devices even if we think we have taken all precautions. It is always good practice to look for any possible vulnerabilities after installation in the field and set up an infrastructure to monitor the health of installed devices when necessary.

We will continue with another connectivity feature of ESP32 in the next chapter. As we mentioned earlier, ESP32 also supports BLE technology as a wireless connectivity option. We will see how BLE works and develop several interesting examples to practice with it.

Questions

Let's practice what we have learned in this chapter by answering the following questions:

1. Which of these is not a security best practice before installing an ESP32 device in the field?

   A. Starting a secure web server on ESP32

   B. Ensuring there are no GPIO pins or JTAG ports exposed

   C. Enabling secure boot

   D. Flash encryption

2. Which of these would not be desirable if you want to restrict access to the private part of an asymmetric key pair?

   A. Integrating with a Microchip ATECC608A

   B. Integrating with an Optiga TrustX

   C. Using an ESP32-WROOM-32SE

   D. Embedding the key in the encrypted flash

3. Which feature of application firmware is important after installing devices in the field in terms of patching discovered vulnerabilities?

   A. Secure boot

   B. Flash encryption

   C. TLS communication

   D. OTA updates

4. Which of these events doesn't happen during a TLS handshake?

   A. Exchanging supported cipher suites

   B. Secure data exchange

   C. Certificate authentication

   D. Symmetric key generation

5. If a secure OTA update fails, which of these can't be the reason why?

A. Server authentication failure

B. Difference in version file content

C. Bootloader failure

D. Wrong partition definition file

Further reading

- *Practical Internet of Things Security - Second Edition, Brian Russell, Drew Van Duren, Packt Publishing* (`https://www.packtpub.com/product/practical-internet-of-things-security-second-edition/9781788625821`): This book covers all security considerations for IoT products. *Chapter 6, Cryptographic Fundamentals for IoT Security Engineering*, explains the fundamentals of cryptography, such as random number generation, symmetric and asymmetric encryption, digital signatures, hashes, and ciphersuites.

- *OPTIGA Trust X1 – Solution Reference Manual*: It is freely available at this link: `https://github.com/Infineon/Assets/raw/master/PDFs/OPTIGA_Trust_X_SolutionReferenceManual_v1.35.pdf`. This document lists the major use cases of secure elements. It also documents external API functions and the I²C binary protocol used to communicate with secure elements, which is implemented by the library that we imported in the last section of this chapter.

8
I Can Speak BLE

Bluetooth is a short-range wireless standard for portable equipment applications. It was originally designed as a wireless alternative to serial communication protocols such as RS-232, to provide communication between two devices. Bluetooth specifications are developed by the Bluetooth **Special Interest Group** (**SIG**) with thousands of members worldwide. Starting from the Bluetooth 4.0 core specification, the Bluetooth SIG especially targets IoT applications to support device developers with modern features such as low energy, mesh networking, and location services.

The current standard specifies two radio versions, Bluetooth Classic (BR/EDR) and **Bluetooth Low Energy** (**BLE**). ESP32 supports both of them by design. In this chapter, we will discuss BLE features of ESP32 with practical examples and learn how to use BLE in real-life scenarios. BLE is a huge subject to discuss in detail in a single chapter, so I have provided a reference book in the *Further reading* section if you want to learn more about any BLE-related concepts mentioned in the examples of this chapter.

The main topics that we'll cover in this chapter are the following:

- BLE basics
- Developing a simple BLE beacon
- Developing a GATT server as an ambient temperature peripheral
- Setting up a BLE Mesh network with ESP32

Technical requirements

In all examples, we only use a single devkit. In the BLE Mesh networking example, however, you can add more nodes in the network by flashing several devkits with different firmware where you can try different BLE parameters.

On the software side, we will use the **nRF Connect** and **nRF Mesh** mobile applications from Nordic Semiconductor. The applications are freely available for both Android and iOS platforms.

You can find the example code in the GitHub repository here: `https://github.com/PacktPublishing/Internet-of-Things-with-ESP32/tree/main/ch8`.

Check out the following video to see the code in action: `https://bit.ly/3jUqGTj`

Understanding BLE basics

The fastest track to understand how BLE works is to look at its architecture diagram:

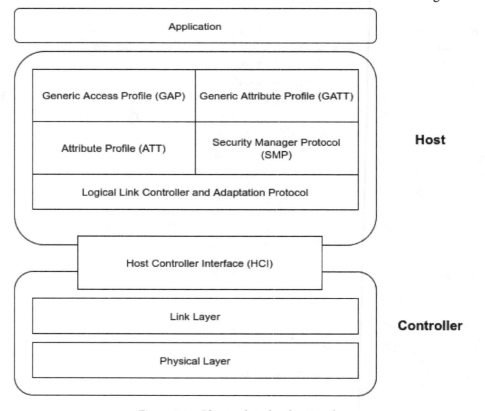

Figure 8.1 – Bluetooth technology stack

The architecture contains two major sections – **Controller** and **Host**. The controller section manages the radio and the host section implements the stack providing an interface for applications. Therefore, it is possible to design a device with an application processor and a Bluetooth network co-processor separately or to use a single **system-on-chip** (**SoC**) having the Bluetooth radio embedded in it. ESP32 falls into the second category.

On the host side, ESP32 uses **Bluedroid** as the default Bluetooth host. The Bluedroid stack is an open source implementation of the Bluetooth standard for Android devices imported into ESP-IDF. Let's have a quick look at the host-level functionality that we need while developing applications.

The Generic Access Profile

Generic Access Profile (**GAP**) defines the discovery and connection services of the stack. A BLE device can operate in *connectionless* mode (broadcasting or scanning BLE advertisements) or *connection-oriented* mode. GAP specifies four different roles in those modes. Roles in connectionless mode are as follows:

- **Broadcaster** to send out BLE advertisements, for example, a beacon
- **Observer** to scan broadcasted BLE advertisements

Roles in connection-oriented mode are as follows:

- **Peripheral** to deliver data, for example, a sensor device
- **Central** to request data, for example, a mobile phone

In connectionless mode, data goes in one direction only, from broadcaster to observer. In connection-oriented mode, the data flow is bidirectional.

The Attribute Profile

An attribute is the building block of BLE. All features of a BLE device are described as a list of attributes. Each attribute has the following fields:

- **Handle**: The unique identifier of the attribute
- **Type**: The data type of the attribute
- **Value**: The value of the attribute
- **Permissions**: Read/write permissions for the **Value** field

The attribute profile also defines two roles: server and client. A server exposes data or a request interface for clients. A BLE device can implement both roles at the same time, depending on the device's functionality.

The Generic Attribute Profile

Generic Attribute Profile (GATT) defines the logical interface to clients by introducing **Services** and **Characteristics**. A service contains one or more characteristics. For example, the my-light-sensor service can contain the following characteristics:

- A lux characteristic

- A location characteristic

- A battery-status characteristic

The services and the characteristics are described as attributes in a BLE application. We will learn more about how to define a service in an example later.

The Security Manager Protocol

Security Manager Protocol (SMP) manages all pairing, authentication, and key generation operations.

After having this introduction to the BLE standard, we can work on practical examples to see how we can develop BLE applications on ESP32.

Developing a BLE beacon

A BLE beacon is a device that transmits its unique identifier as a BLE advertisement so that a mobile application reacts when the phone detects the beacon. This technique is especially useful when proximity sensing is required, for example, tracking applications or in museums to show more information about an object.

One implementation of this technique is **iBeacon**, which is developed by Apple. An iBeacon frame in a BLE advertisement contains three data fields related to the application:

- 16 bytes of UUID: The globally unique identifier of the application. All devices share this UUID.

- Major (2 bytes): The application-specific major identifier to group iBeacon devices into regions.

- Minor (2 bytes): The application-specific minor identifier to group iBeacon devices into locations in a given region.

For more information about how iBeacon works, you can refer to this document: `https://developer.apple.com/ibeacon/Getting-Started-with-iBeacon.pdf`.

An iBeacon frame also contains the TX power value of the device, which is measured from a 1-meter distance during the calibration process. The mobile application estimates the distance to the iBeacon device by comparing this value and its received signal strength while iBeacon is in use in the field.

With this knowledge, we are ready to develop our own iBeacon device as follows:

1. After creating a PlatformIO project, we start `menuconfig` to enable the Bluetooth component and Bluedroid:

```
$ source ~/.platformio/penv/bin/activate
(penv)$ pio run -t menuconfig
```

2. The command opens the `menuconfig` interface and we navigate to **Bluetooth Host** to select **Bluedroid**:

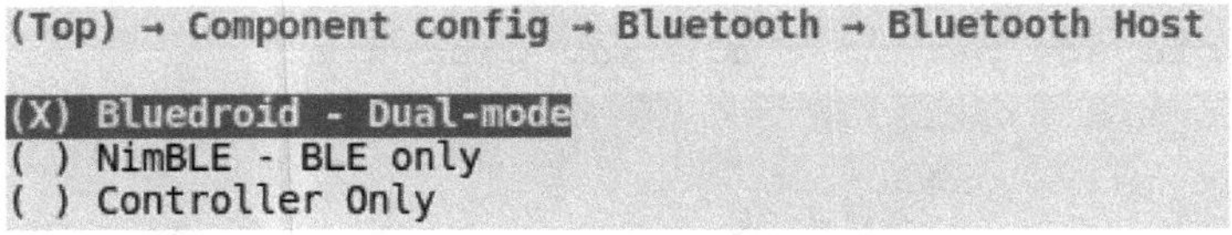

```
(Top) → Component config → Bluetooth → Bluetooth Host

(X) Bluedroid - Dual-mode
( ) NimBLE - BLE only
( ) Controller Only
```

Figure 8.2 – Bluedroid in menuconfig

3. We add a local library in the `lib` folder by downloading it from the GitHub repo here: `https://github.com/PacktPublishing/Internet-of-Things-with-ESP32/tree/main/ch8/beacon_ex/lib/ibeacon`. This library hides the iBeacon implementation details. Now, we have the following files in our project folder:

```
(penv)$ ls -R
.:
CMakeLists.txt  include  lib  platformio.ini  sdkconfig
src   test

./lib:
ibeacon   README

./lib/ibeacon:
esp_ibeacon_api.c   esp_ibeacon_api.h
```

```
./src:
CMakeLists.txt    main.c
```

We have configured the project and we can continue with the code in `main.c`:

```c
#include "nvs_flash.h"
#include "esp_bt.h"
#include "esp_gap_ble_api.h"
#include "esp_bt_main.h"
#include "esp_bt_defs.h"
#include "esp_ibeacon_api.h"
#include "esp_log.h"
#include "freertos/FreeRTOS.h"

static const char *TAG = "ibeacon";

static esp_ble_adv_params_t ble_adv_params = {
    .adv_int_min = 0x20,
    .adv_int_max = 0x40,
    .adv_type = ADV_TYPE_NONCONN_IND,
    .own_addr_type = BLE_ADDR_TYPE_PUBLIC,
    .channel_map = ADV_CHNL_ALL,
    .adv_filter_policy = ADV_FILTER_ALLOW_SCAN_ANY_CON_ANY,
};
```

We first include the necessary header files and define the advertisement parameters in a variable, `ble_adv_params`. It contains the following:

- Minimum and maximum advertisement intervals. The BLE stack provides randomness between these minimum and maximum values.

- Advertisement type, which is non-connectable, non-scannable, undirected advertising for iBeacon. Any mobile device can detect the advertisements, but cannot connect to our iBeacon.

- The device address type, which is specified as public.

- BLE channels to advertise. BLE defines three advertisement channels and our device will use them all.

- A filter policy for connection and scan requests.

Next, we implement the GAP event handler:

```
static void ble_gap_event_handler(esp_gap_ble_cb_event_t event,
esp_ble_gap_cb_param_t *param)
{
    switch (event)
    {
    case ESP_GAP_BLE_ADV_DATA_RAW_SET_COMPLETE_EVT:
        esp_ble_gap_start_advertising(&ble_adv_params);
        break;

    case ESP_GAP_BLE_ADV_START_COMPLETE_EVT:
        if (param->adv_start_cmpl.status != ESP_BT_STATUS_
SUCCESS)
        {
            ESP_LOGE(TAG, "advertisement failed");
        }
        break;

    default:
        break;
    }
}
```

During initialization, we will register ble_gap_event_handler to handle GAP events. There are many events defined in GAP but we are only interested in when the advertisement data is set and after starting the advertisement. After setting advertisement data, we start the advertisement by calling esp_ble_gap_start_advertising and check the result in the ESP_GAP_BLE_ADV_START_COMPLETE_EVT event.

We implement the initialization function as follows:

```
void init(void)
{
    nvs_flash_init();
```

```
    esp_bt_controller_mem_release(ESP_BT_MODE_CLASSIC_BT);

    esp_bt_controller_config_t bt_cfg = BT_CONTROLLER_INIT_
CONFIG_DEFAULT();
    esp_bt_controller_init(&bt_cfg);
    esp_bt_controller_enable(ESP_BT_MODE_BLE);

    esp_bluedroid_init();
    esp_bluedroid_enable();

    esp_ble_gap_register_callback(ble_gap_event_handler);
}
```

The `init` function has three main responsibilities:

- Initializing the Bluetooth controller in BLE mode
- Initializing the host stack, Bluedroid
- Initializing GAP by setting the GAP event handler and the device name

We continue with `app_main` next:

```
void app_main(void)
{
    init();

    esp_ble_ibeacon_t ibeacon_adv_data;
    esp_init_ibeacon_data(&ibeacon_adv_data);
    esp_ble_gap_config_adv_data_raw((uint8_t *)&ibeacon_adv_
data, sizeof(ibeacon_adv_data));
}
```

After getting the BLE component ready, we only define the iBeacon advertisement data and pass it to `esp_ble_gap_config_adv_data_raw`, which triggers GAP to start the iBeacon advertisement.

Our application is ready to test. We flash the devkit with this application and run nRF Connect on any mobile device to see if our ESP32 iBeacon is detected:

Figure 8.3 – ESP32 iBeacon in nRF Connect

We can see our ESP32 iBeacon listed in the nRF Connect application. nRF Connect also shows the latest **Received Signal Strength Indicator** (**RSSI**) value and advertisement interval of the ESP32 iBeacon.

In the next section, we will see how to use the GATT API in order to deliver data to other BLE peers.

Developing a GATT server

When we want to share sensor data with client applications, we need more than a simple beacon. In this example, we will develop a Bluetooth temperature sensor that we can connect to and receive temperature readings by using a mobile application, such as nRF Connect. One interesting feature is that the sensor will be able to push data to the client application when a new reading is available.

The hardware preparation is easy. We will only use a DHT11 connected to GPIO17 of ESP32. After the hardware setup, we configure a new project:

1. Let's start with a new PlatformIO project with the following `platformio.ini`:

```
[env:az-delivery-devkit-v4]
platform = espressif32
board = az-delivery-devkit-v4
framework = espidf

monitor_speed = 115200
lib_extra_dirs =
        ../../common/esp-idf-lib/components
```

`esp-idf-lib` contains the driver for DHT11. The source code is located here: `https://github.com/PacktPublishing/Internet-of-Things-with-ESP32/tree/main/common/esp-idf-lib`.

2. Then we need to add two files, `app.h` and `app.c`, into the project, which are located here: `https://github.com/PacktPublishing/Internet-of-Things-with-ESP32/tree/main/ch8/gatt_server_ex/src`. These files hide some BLE-related implementation details so that our main application is clear and easy to understand. After saving these files in the `src` directory, we need to configure ESP-IDF to enable Bluedroid by running `menuconfig`:

```
$ source ~/.platformio/penv/bin/activate
(penv)$  pio run -t menuconfig
```

3. We navigate to **Bluetooth Host** and select **Bluedroid**:

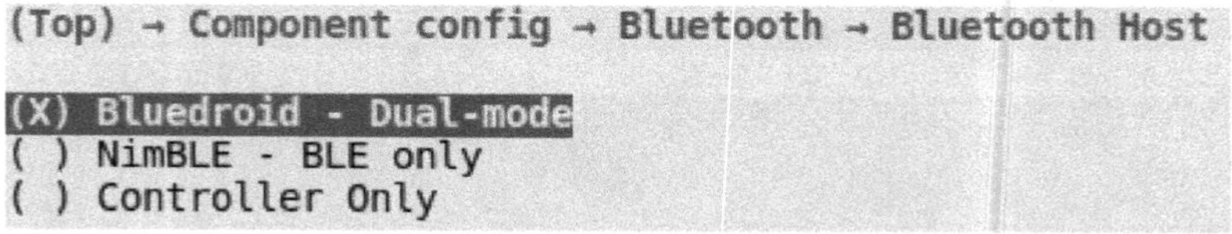

```
(Top) → Component config → Bluetooth → Bluetooth Host

(X) Bluedroid - Dual-mode
( ) NimBLE - BLE only
( ) Controller Only
```

Figure 8.4 – Bluedroid enabled

That is it. We are ready to continue with the application in `main.c`:

```
#include <string.h>
#include "freertos/FreeRTOS.h"
#include "freertos/task.h"
#include "freertos/event_groups.h"
#include "esp_system.h"
#include "esp_log.h"
#include "nvs_flash.h"
#include "esp_bt.h"

#include "esp_gap_ble_api.h"
#include "esp_gatts_api.h"
#include "esp_bt_defs.h"
#include "esp_bt_main.h"
#include "esp_gatt_common_api.h"

#include "sdkconfig.h"
```

```
#include "app.h"
#include "dht.h"

#define TAG "app"
#define SENSOR_NAME "ESP32-DHT11"
#define DHT11_PIN 17
```

We first include the necessary header files and the application macros. One of the macros defines the name of our Bluetooth sensor.

Next, we declare the global variables:

```
static int16_t temp, hum;

static esp_attr_value_t sensor_data = {
    .attr_max_len = (uint16_t)sizeof(temp),
    .attr_len = (uint16_t)sizeof(temp),
    .attr_value = (uint8_t *)(&temp),
};
```

temp and hum are the variables to hold DHT11 readings. sensor_data is the way we pass a temperature reading to the BLE API to be processed inside.

Let's jump into the app_main function to see how it all starts:

```
void app_main(void)
{
    init_service_def();

    esp_err_t ret = nvs_flash_init();
    if (ret == ESP_ERR_NVS_NO_FREE_PAGES || ret == ESP_ERR_NVS_
NEW_VERSION_FOUND)
    {
        ESP_ERROR_CHECK(nvs_flash_erase());
        ESP_ERROR_CHECK(nvs_flash_init());
    }
    esp_bt_controller_mem_release(ESP_BT_MODE_CLASSIC_BT);

    esp_bt_controller_config_t bt_cfg = BT_CONTROLLER_INIT_
CONFIG_DEFAULT();
```

```
    esp_bt_controller_init(&bt_cfg);
    esp_bt_controller_enable(ESP_BT_MODE_BLE);
    esp_bluedroid_init();
    esp_bluedroid_enable();
    esp_ble_gap_set_device_name(SENSOR_NAME);
```

The `init_service_def` function is defined in `app.c` to initialize some BLE-related global variables. We then initialize the `nvs` partition of the flash and enable the BT controller in the BLE mode of operation. We also initialize Bluedroid, the BLE host.

We complete the implementation of the `app_main` function as follows:

```
    esp_ble_gap_register_callback(gap_handler);
    esp_ble_gatts_register_callback(gatt_handler);
    esp_ble_gatts_app_register(0);

    xTaskCreate(read_temp_task, "temp", configMINIMAL_STACK_
SIZE * 3, NULL, 5, NULL);
}
```

We register the callback functions `gap_handler` and `gatt_handler` to handle GAP and GATT events respectively. The BLE application is registered by calling `esp_ble_gatts_app_register`, which triggers the first event in the GATT layer of BLE. Then we simply start a FreeRTOS task to read from DHT11 periodically. Let's see which events we handle in `gatt_handler`:

```
static void gatt_handler(esp_gatts_cb_event_t event, esp_gatt_
if_t gatts_if, esp_ble_gatts_cb_param_t *param)
{
    switch (event)
    {
    case ESP_GATTS_REG_EVT:
        esp_ble_gatts_create_service(gatts_if, &service_def.
service_id, GATT_HANDLE_COUNT);
        break;
```

gatt_handler is a lengthy function so we will discuss the GATT events handled in it one by one. The first event is ESP_GATTS_REG_EVT, which happens after the BLE application is registered in app_main. When this event happens, we create the BLE **service** to be seen by BLE clients. service_def is a variable declared in app.h. It holds all the descriptive information about our BLE service. Next, we handle the ESP_GATTS_ CREATE_EVT event:

```
    case ESP_GATTS_CREATE_EVT:
        service_def.service_handle = param->create.service_
handle;
        esp_ble_gatts_start_service(service_def.service_handle);
        esp_ble_gatts_add_char(service_def.service_handle,
                            &service_def.char_uuid,
                            ESP_GATT_PERM_READ | ESP_GATT_
PERM_WRITE,
                            ESP_GATT_CHAR_PROP_BIT_READ |
ESP_GATT_CHAR_PROP_BIT_NOTIFY,
                            &sensor_data, NULL);
```

ESP_GATTS_CREATE_EVT happens after creating the service in the previous event. We start the service here and add a **characteristic** in it to serve sensor_data. We configure the characteristic as **read** and **notify**. **Read** means the client can read the value and **notify** means the client can configure the characteristic to deliver value changes without the need for an explicit read request. When the notify bit is set by the client, then all temperature changes will be delivered automatically.

When the characteristic is added, the ESP_GATTS_ADD_CHAR_EVT event happens. We handle is as in the following code snippet:

```
    case ESP_GATTS_ADD_CHAR_EVT:
    {
        service_def.char_handle = param->add_char.attr_handle;
        esp_ble_gatts_add_char_descr(service_def.service_handle,
&service_def.descr_uuid, ESP_GATT_PERM_READ | ESP_GATT_PERM_
WRITE, NULL, NULL);
        break;
    }
```

In this event, we add a **characteristic descriptor** for the characteristic that we have added in the previous step. This descriptor provides the interface for the client to enable or disable the notifications. When the client writes a value of `0x00` to the descriptor, the characteristic's notify bit is reset. For any non-zero values, the notify bit is set.

Adding the characteristic descriptor causes the `ESP_GATTS_ADD_CHAR_DESCR_EVT` event to be fired, and we handle it as follows:

```
case ESP_GATTS_ADD_CHAR_DESCR_EVT:
    service_def.descr_handle = param->add_char_descr.attr_
handle;
    esp_ble_gap_config_adv_data(&adv_data);
    break;
```

This is the last step of setting up the BLE service. Having the service ready, we can call `esp_ble_gap_config_adv_data`, which configures the advertisement data and triggers an event in the GAP layer. Next, we will discuss the GATT events when a client connects:

```
case ESP_GATTS_CONNECT_EVT:
{
    update_conn_params(param->connect.remote_bda);
    service_def.gatts_if = gatts_if;
    service_def.client_write_conn = param->write.conn_id;
    break;
}
```

`ESP_GATTS_CONNECT_EVT` is the first event when a client connects. We update the connection parameters by calling `update_conn_params`, which is implemented in `app.c`. Then we store the communication handles in `service_def` to use them later when we need to send BLE messages.

The `ESP_GATTS_READ_EVT` event happens for a read request. We handle it as follows:

```
case ESP_GATTS_READ_EVT:
{
    esp_gatt_rsp_t rsp;
    memset(&rsp, 0, sizeof(esp_gatt_rsp_t));
    rsp.attr_value.handle = param->read.handle;
    rsp.attr_value.len = sensor_data.attr_len;
    memcpy(rsp.attr_value.value, sensor_data.attr_value,
```

```
sensor_data.attr_len);
        esp_ble_gatts_send_response(gatts_if, param->read.conn_
id, param->read.trans_id, ESP_GATT_OK, &rsp);
        break;
    }
```

When a read request comes from the client, we reply to it with the current temperature value by calling esp_ble_gatts_send_response.

For a write request, the ESP_GATTS_WRITE_EVT event happens. The following code snippet shows how we handle it:

```
    case ESP_GATTS_WRITE_EVT:
    {
        if (service_def.descr_handle == param->write.handle)
        {
            uint16_t descr_value = param->write.value[1] << 8 |
param->write.value[0];
            if (descr_value != 0x0000)
            {
                ESP_LOGI(TAG, "notify enable");
                esp_ble_gatts_send_indicate(gatts_if, param-
>write.conn_id, service_def.char_handle, sensor_data.attr_len,
sensor_data.attr_value, false);
            }
            else
            {
                ESP_LOGI(TAG, "notify disable");
            }
            esp_ble_gatts_send_response(gatts_if, param->write.
conn_id, param->write.trans_id, ESP_GATT_OK, NULL);
        }
        else
        {
            esp_ble_gatts_send_response(gatts_if, param->write.
conn_id, param->write.trans_id, ESP_GATT_WRITE_NOT_PERMIT,
NULL);
        }
```

```
        break;
    }
```

When a write request is received from the client, we first check whether it is for the descriptor. If so, and the write value is non-zero, then we immediately return the current value of `sensor_data` by calling `esp_ble_gatts_send_indicate`. This function sends data if the notify bit of the corresponding characteristic is set.

Finally, the `ESP_GATTS_DISCONNECT_EVT` event happens when the client disconnects:

```
case ESP_GATTS_DISCONNECT_EVT:
    service_def.gatts_if = 0;
    esp_ble_gap_start_advertising(&adv_params);
    break;

default:
    break;
    }
}
```

In this event handling code, we simply start advertising to wait for another connection. There are several other GATT events that we don't need to handle in this example, but you can read the ESP-IDF documentation (https://docs.espressif.com/projects/esp-idf/en/latest/esp32/api-reference/bluetooth/esp_gatts.html) to see what they are for. Let's move on to the `gap_handler` callback function:

```
static void gap_handler(esp_gap_ble_cb_event_t event, esp_ble_
gap_cb_param_t *param)
{
    switch (event)
    {
    case ESP_GAP_BLE_ADV_DATA_SET_COMPLETE_EVT:
        esp_ble_gap_start_advertising(&adv_params);
        break;
    default:
        break;
    }
}
```

`gap_handler` is very brief; we only look for the `ESP_GAP_BLE_ADV_DATA_SET_COMPLETE_EVT` event to start advertising. The others are not necessary for us. Next, we define a function to read the ambient temperature:

```
static void read_temp_task(void *arg)
{
    while (1)
    {
        vTaskDelay(2000 / portTICK_PERIOD_MS);
        if (dht_read_data(DHT_TYPE_DHT11, (gpio_num_t)DHT11_PIN, &hum, &temp) == ESP_OK)
        {
            temp /= 10;
            ESP_LOGI(TAG, "temp: %d", temp);
            if (service_def.gatts_if > 0)
            {
                esp_ble_gatts_send_indicate(service_def.gatts_if, service_def.client_write_conn, service_def.char_handle, sensor_data.attr_len, sensor_data.attr_value, false);
            }
        }
        else
        {
            ESP_LOGE(TAG, "DHT11 read failed");
        }
    }
}
```

`read_temp_task` is the function that is started from `app_main` as a FreeRTOS task. In it, we update the global `temp` variable and call `esp_ble_gatts_send_indicate` to let the connected client know about the change. If the notify bit of the characteristic is set, this function sends a BLE message with the new temperature value.

The application is now completed. Let's test it to see how it works:

1. After flashing the firmware, we can open nRF Connect on a mobile device to list all Bluetooth devices around.

2. Our device is listed in nRF Connect. Let's tap on the **Connect** button:

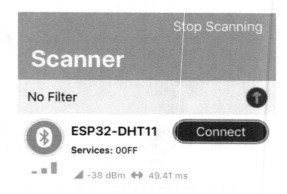

Figure 8.5 – nRF Connect listing ESP32-DHT11

3. Under the **Services** tab, we see our service with the UUID of `00FF`. Below it, the characteristic is listed. It doesn't have any name; it is only listed as unknown since it is a custom definition. As we see in the screenshot, the characteristic properties are **Read** and **Notify** as we have configured in the application. After that, the characteristic descriptor is displayed with the name of **Client Characteristic Configuration**, which has a predefined UUID of `2902` in the BLE standard:

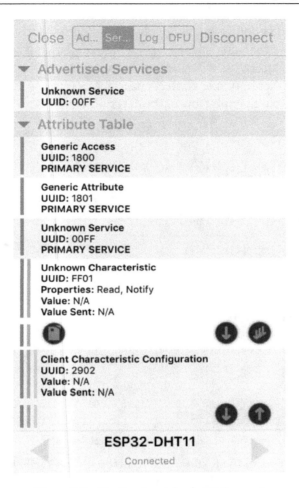

Figure 8.6 – The Services tab of nRF Connect

4. To enable or disable the notification, we have two options. Either we can use the up arrow of the descriptor to enter a value or we tap on the down-arrows button of the characteristic to toggle the notification. Let's try toggling first:

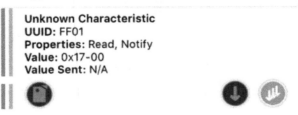

Figure 8.7 – Notification toggle

5. When we enable the notification, temperature readings start to come. We see that the value of the characteristic is `0x17`, which corresponds to 23°C ambient temperature. If we tap on the down-arrows button again, it will disable the notification. The other option to control notifications is to use the descriptor directly. When we tap the up-arrow of the descriptor, it pops up the following dialog:

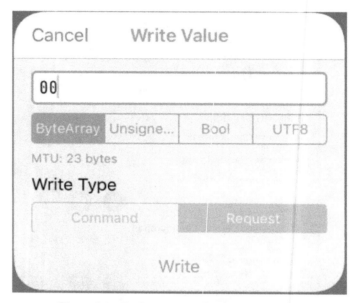

Figure 8.8 – Dialog to write the descriptor value

6. We enter the `00` value in the textbox and send it with the **Write** button. It disables the notification and we see **Value Sent** as follows:

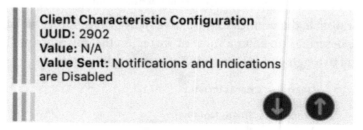

Figure 8.9 – Notifications are disabled

7. If we send the `01` value to be written, then it enables the notification, and we start to see the temperature values automatically updated in the characteristic again.

> **Important note**
> The mobile applications on different platforms show some differences. The screenshots in this example are from the iOS version of nRF Connect. The Android version, unfortunately, doesn't support direct write operations to the Client Characteristic Configuration but you can still enable or disable it by using the notification toggle button (three down arrows on the characteristic) as in *Step 4*.

Great! We have a temperature sensor that we can use with any BLE-compatible device. In the next example, we are going to set up a BLE Mesh network.

Setting up a BLE Mesh network

The Bluetooth Classic and BLE protocols define point-to-point device communications. However, the BLE Mesh protocol defines a complete wireless networking, having a many-to-many topology. The following depicts a BLE Mesh network:

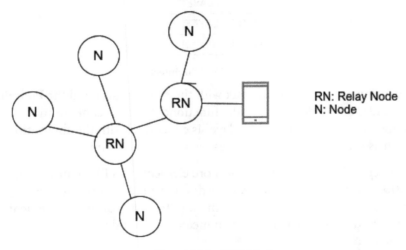

Figure 8.10 – BLE Mesh

In this figure, there are two types of network nodes:

- Node: An ordinary node in the network
- Relay node: A node that is capable of relaying messages to other nodes in the network

BLE Mesh also defines:

- Low-power nodes: Battery-operated nodes that operate with a low-duty cycle

- Friend nodes: 100% duty nodes that keep messages for the low-power nodes they support

- Proxy nodes: These provide a means of communication for mobile devices with no BLE Mesh stack running.

The BLE Mesh network runs on top of the BLE protocol. The architecture of the stack is as follows:

MODELS
FOUNDATION MODELS
ACCESS LAYER
TRANSPORT LAYER
NETWORK LAYER
BEARER LAYER
BLE PROTOCOL

Figure 8.11 – BLE Mesh architecture

As application developers, we mostly interact with the **Models** layer and the **Foundation Models** layer. Foundation Models provide the functionality of the configuration and management of a network. The Models layer is concerned with the application functionality such as the device behavior, states, messages, and so on.

Each node in the network can contain one or more elements. An **Element** corresponds to a separate entity in a node. For instance, if we develop a multisensor device, each type of sensor can be implemented as a separate element in the application. An element has a **Unicast Address** in the mesh network, which means other nodes in the network can directly interact with an element.

BLE Mesh supports group addressing as well. Elements in a group exchange data between them by a publish/subscribe mechanism. The Bluetooth SIG defines four **Fixed Group Addresses**, which are All-proxies, All-friends, All-relays, and All-nodes. We can also define custom group addresses in applications.

One last crucial concept is **provisioning**. A device must be provisioned by a provisioner to join a BLE Mesh network. During the provisioning process, the provisioner shares the **network key** (**NetKey**) with the device, then the device becomes a network node. A node also needs to have an **application key** (**AppKey**) to participate in a specific application. Therefore, a single mesh network can contain distinct applications, for example, a light application and a security application can run in the same mesh network.

There is a perfect paper for developers about BLE Mesh networking. It is on the Bluetooth website and can be downloaded here: `https://www.bluetooth.com/bluetooth-resources/bluetooth-mesh-networking-an-introduction-for-developers/`.

Let's see an example of BLE Mesh in action.

The goal of this example is to develop an LED node that can operate in a BLE Mesh network. The LED element will report its on/off status in the network. The hardware connections are in the following Fritzing diagram:

Figure 8.12 – The Fritzing diagram of the hardware

We have an LED connected to GPIO2 and a button at GPIO5. The button will toggle the LED status.

Let's create a PlatformIO project and edit `platformio.ini` as follows:

```
[env:az-delivery-devkit-v4]
platform = espressif32
board = az-delivery-devkit-v4
framework = espidf

monitor_speed = 115200
```

The ESP-IDF configuration, sdkconfig, should have the following settings in it:

```
CONFIG_BLE_MESH_CFG_CLI=y
CONFIG_BLE_MESH_FRIEND=y
CONFIG_BLE_MESH_GATT_PROXY_SERVER=y
CONFIG_BLE_MESH_GATT_PROXY=y
CONFIG_BLE_MESH_HCI_5_0=y
CONFIG_BLE_MESH_HEALTH_CLI=y
CONFIG_BLE_MESH_IV_UPDATE_TEST=y
CONFIG_BLE_MESH_MEM_ALLOC_MODE_INTERNAL=y
CONFIG_BLE_MESH_NET_BUF_POOL_USAGE=y
CONFIG_BLE_MESH_NET_BUF_TRACE_LEVEL_WARNING=y
CONFIG_BLE_MESH_NODE=y
CONFIG_BLE_MESH_PB_ADV=y
CONFIG_BLE_MESH_PB_GATT=y
CONFIG_BLE_MESH_PROV=y
CONFIG_BLE_MESH_PROXY=y
CONFIG_BLE_MESH_RELAY=y
CONFIG_BLE_MESH_RX_SEG_MSG_COUNT=10
CONFIG_BLE_MESH_SCAN_DUPLICATE_EN=y
CONFIG_BLE_MESH_SELF_TEST=y
CONFIG_BLE_MESH_SETTINGS=y
CONFIG_BLE_MESH_TEST_AUTO_ENTER_NETWORK=y
CONFIG_BLE_MESH_TRACE_LEVEL_WARNING=y
CONFIG_BLE_MESH_TX_SEG_MSG_COUNT=10
CONFIG_BLE_MESH_USE_DUPLICATE_SCAN=y
CONFIG_BLE_MESH=y
CONFIG_BT_BTU_TASK_STACK_SIZE=4512
CONFIG_BTDM_BLE_MESH_SCAN_DUPL_EN=y
CONFIG_BTDM_CTRL_MODE_BLE_ONLY=y
CONFIG_BTDM_CTRL_MODE_BR_EDR_ONLY=n
CONFIG_BTDM_CTRL_MODE_BTDM=n
CONFIG_BTDM_MODEM_SLEEP=n
CONFIG_BTDM_SCAN_DUPL_TYPE_DATA_DEVICE=y
CONFIG_BT_ENABLED=y
CONFIG_BT_GATTS_SEND_SERVICE_CHANGE_MANUAL=y
```

It would be easier just to copy `sdkconfig` from the project repository here: `https://github.com/PacktPublishing/Internet-of-Things-with-ESP32/blob/main/ch8/ble_mesh_ex/sdkconfig`.

There are some libraries and supporting source files to be copied from the project repository as well. They are the following:

- `lib/appbt_init/appbt_init.{c,h}`: They implement the Bluetooth initialization.

- `src/board.{c,h}`: They manage the LED and button.

- `src/appmesh_setup.{c,h}`: They implement the BLE Mesh setup by defining the provisioning configuration and the BLE Mesh element.

When we put everything in place, we should have the following directory structure:

```
$ ls -R
.:
CMakeLists.txt  include  lib  platformio.ini  sdkconfig  src
test

./include:
README

./lib:
appbt_init  README

./lib/appbt_init:
appbt_init.c  appbt_init.h

./src:
appmesh_setup.c  appmesh_setup.h  board.c  board.h  CMakeLists.
txt  main.c
```

Let's develop the application in `main.c`:

```
#include "esp_log.h"
#include "nvs_flash.h"

#include "esp_ble_mesh_defs.h"
#include "esp_ble_mesh_common_api.h"
```

```
#include "esp_ble_mesh_networking_api.h"
#include "esp_ble_mesh_provisioning_api.h"
#include "esp_ble_mesh_config_model_api.h"
#include "esp_ble_mesh_generic_model_api.h"
#include "esp_ble_mesh_local_data_operation_api.h"

#include "board.h"
#include "appmesh_setup.h"
#include "appbt_init.h"

#define TAG "app"
```

In ESP-IDF, the BLE Mesh APIs start with esp_ble_mesh*. We include them in addition to the helper headers, board.h, appmesh_setup.h, and appbt_init.h.

Let's jump to app_main in order to understand the overall application structure:

```
void app_main(void)
{
    esp_err_t err;

    board_init(update_element_cb);
    err = nvs_flash_init();
    if (err == ESP_ERR_NVS_NO_FREE_PAGES)
    {
        ESP_ERROR_CHECK(nvs_flash_erase());
        ESP_ERROR_CHECK(nvs_flash_init());
    }
    ESP_ERROR_CHECK(appbt_init());

    esp_ble_mesh_register_prov_callback(provisioning_cb);
    esp_ble_mesh_register_config_server_callback(config_server_
cb);
    esp_ble_mesh_register_generic_server_callback(generic_
server_cb);
    ESP_ERROR_CHECK(appmesh_init());
}
```

We start with the `board_init` function to initialize the LED and button. We pass a callback function, `update_element_cb`, to be called by the button ISR to update the mesh element with the current state of the LED. After initializing the `nvs` partition and the Bluetooth stack by calling `appbt_init`, we set the BLE Mesh callbacks. The BLE Mesh stack heavily depends on callbacks to interface applications. In our application, we use a provisioning callback to know about provisioning events, a configuration callback, which handles configuration events, and a server callback to handle LED change-state requests from clients. Finally, we call `appmesh_init` to initialize the BLE Mesh stack and create the BLE Mesh element of the application. Let's see what happens in `provisioning_cb` next:

```
static void provisioning_cb(esp_ble_mesh_prov_cb_event_t event,
esp_ble_mesh_prov_cb_param_t *param)
{
    switch (event)
    {
    case ESP_BLE_MESH_NODE_PROV_COMPLETE_EVT:
        ESP_LOGI(TAG, "provisioned. addr: 0x%04x", param->node_
prov_complete.addr);
        break;
    case ESP_BLE_MESH_NODE_PROV_RESET_EVT:
        ESP_LOGI(TAG, "node reset");
        esp_ble_mesh_node_local_reset();
        break;
    default:
        break;
    }
}
```

In `provisioning_cb`, we handle only two events. The first one is when the device joins a network by a provisioner and the other one is when it is removed. When the node is removed, we clear the network information by calling `esp_ble_mesh_node_local_reset` to make it available for another provisioning.

Another callback function that we implement is `config_server_cb`, which handles node configuration events:

```
static void config_server_cb(esp_ble_mesh_cfg_server_cb_event_t
event, esp_ble_mesh_cfg_server_cb_param_t *param)
{
    if (event == ESP_BLE_MESH_CFG_SERVER_STATE_CHANGE_EVT)
    {
        switch (param->ctx.recv_op)
        {
        case ESP_BLE_MESH_MODEL_OP_APP_KEY_ADD:
            ESP_LOGI(TAG, "config: app key added");
            break;
        default:
            break;
        }
    }
}
```

Actually, there is only one event for a configuration server, which is ESP_BLE_MESH_CFG_SERVER_STATE_CHANGE_EVT. We can check the underlying reason with the help of the `param->ctx.recv_op` parameter value, which shows the received opcode, for example, add network key, add application key, set node role, and so on.

The next callback is for handling generic server events:

```
static void generic_server_cb(esp_ble_mesh_generic_server_cb_
event_t event, esp_ble_mesh_generic_server_cb_param_t *param)
{
    switch (event)
    {
    case ESP_BLE_MESH_GENERIC_SERVER_STATE_CHANGE_EVT:
        ESP_LOGI(TAG, "event name: state-changed");
        if (param->ctx.recv_op == ESP_BLE_MESH_MODEL_OP_GEN_
ONOFF_SET ||
            param->ctx.recv_op == ESP_BLE_MESH_MODEL_OP_GEN_
ONOFF_SET_UNACK)
        {
            board_set_led(param->value.state_change.onoff_set.
```

```
onoff);
        }
        break;
    default:
        ESP_LOGW(TAG, "unexpected event");
        break;
    }
}
```

In this callback, we handle `ESP_BLE_MESH_GENERIC_SERVER_STATE_CHANGE_EVT` and if the received opcode is a generic on/off model set command, we update the LED state with the received value. The Bluetooth SIG defines many models in the BLE Mesh protocol. We use the generic on/off model for our device, which perfectly makes sense since an LED has only two states: on or off. The BLE Mesh protocol also allows vendor-defined models where needed. We can find all Bluetooth SIG-defined models here: `https://www.bluetooth.com/bluetooth-resources/bluetooth-mesh-models/`.

We need one more callback to link the actual state of the LED and the element:

```
static void update_element_cb(uint8_t led_s)
{
    esp_ble_mesh_model_t *model = appmesh_get_onoff_model();
    esp_ble_mesh_gen_onoff_srv_t *srv = appmesh_get_onoff_server();
    srv->state.onoff = led_s;

    esp_ble_mesh_model_publish(model, ESP_BLE_MESH_MODEL_OP_GEN_ONOFF_STATUS, sizeof(srv->state.onoff), &srv->state.onoff, ROLE_NODE);
}
```

To clarify the abstraction hierarchy, each node has one or more elements and each element contains one or more models. The functionality is provided by servers and/or clients enclosed in models. `update_element_cb` is called in the button ISR as a FreeRTOS task. In this callback, we update the server's on/off state and call `esp_ble_mesh_model_publish` to inform any bound clients about the state change.

We have completed the application code and are ready to test it. After flashing the firmware on a devkit, we start the nRF Mesh mobile application:

1. nRF Mesh comes with a pre-configured provisioner. When we tap on the + (*add*) button to add a new device in the network, this provisioner is employed:

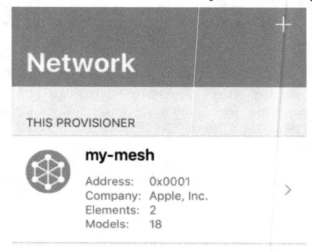

Figure 8.13 – nRF Mesh provisioner

2. Our devkit is listed as ESP-BLE-MESH. We select it to proceed:

Figure 8.14 – BLE-Mesh-enabled devices ready to provision

3. The application shows the device's capabilities after selecting it. We rename the device to dev1 and tap on the top-right button, **Provision**:

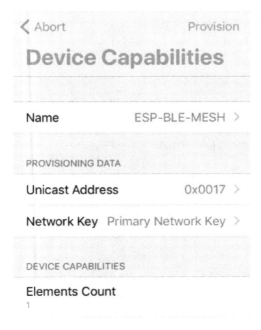

Figure 8.15 – Device Capabilities

4. A success dialog pops up after provisioning. Our device has become a network node at that point. We continue by tapping **OK**:

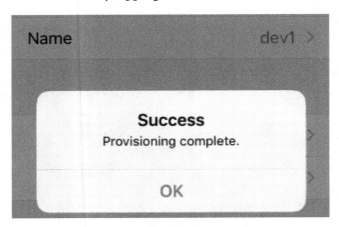

Figure 8.16 – Provisioning complete

5. The node has a network key, but it doesn't have an application key yet. We provide one by selecting **Application Keys** on the UI:

Name	dev1 >
Unicast Address	0x0017
Default TTL	7 >
Device Key 51C8A61BFADE10D83CA79...	
Network Keys	1 >
Application Keys	0 >

Figure 8.17 – Provisioned node

6. Tap on the top-right + to add the application key. We may need to create a new one if there is no defined application key yet:

Figure 8.18 – Add the application key

7. Now, it is time to configure our only element by selecting it in the properties view:

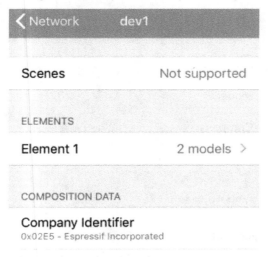

Figure 8.19 – dev1 properties

8. We rename it to `dev1-led` first, then proceed to configure `Generic OnOff Server`:

Figure 8.20 – Element (renamed to dev1-led)

9. We bind the application key to `Generic OnOff Server` as well:

Figure 8.21 – Configuring Generic OnOff Server

10. Next, we define a publication to `All Nodes`. `All Nodes` is a fixed group address by Bluetooth SIG. With this configuration, any status change will be delivered in the network:

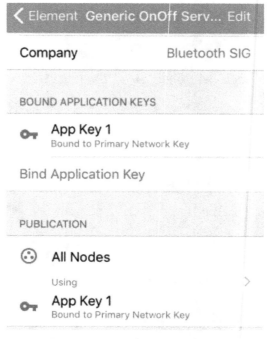

Figure 8.22 – Define a publication

Having the configuration done, we can move on to the tests now:

1. There are several tests that we can apply to see if our application works properly. First, we should be able to read the element status. We tap on **Read** in the bottom-right corner:

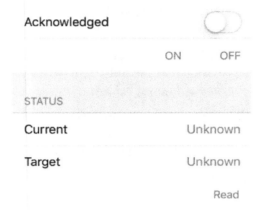

Figure 8.23 – Element controls

2. nRF Mesh shows the status as **OFF** after querying the node:

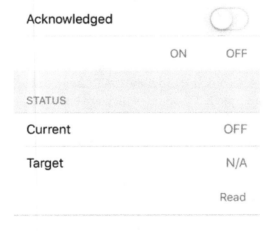

Figure 8.24 – OFF status

Here are some other experiments that we could do:

- When we toggle the LED state by pressing the physical button of the device, the status on the mobile application should update automatically since we have configured the element publication.

- There are two controls on the mobile application: **ON** and **OFF**. When we tap on them, the physical LED status should change accordingly.

We have a mesh node that we can control and monitor via the mobile application. You can flash another devkit and provision it in the BLE Mesh network to do further tests, for example, without a publication, and see how it behaves.

This example finalizes the BLE chapter. Although we have covered many aspects of the ESP32 BLE capabilities, there is more to learn. For example, we can develop a provisioner device, or use other predefined models in our applications. You can check the ESP-IDF repository for more examples here: `https://github.com/espressif/esp-idf/tree/master/examples/bluetooth/esp_ble_mesh`.

Summary

This chapter explained an important feature of ESP32, BLE. BLE has many advantages over other wireless protocols. Probably the key advantage is the compatibility with mobile devices. Every mobile device manufacturer supports BLE in their designs, which eliminates the need for a separate gateway device to communicate with the sensor network. Therefore, it is super easy to develop impressive IoT products with powerful GUI applications for end users. Although BLE is a massive subject, we had a good start in this chapter by covering beacons, a standalone GATT server device, and setting up a BLE Mesh network for multiple IoT devices, which are extremely useful when local connectivity is needed.

In the next chapter, we will develop a full-fledged smart home by employing ESP32's networking capabilities.

Questions

Here are some questions to review what we have learned in this chapter:

1. Which layer is not on the host side of the BLE stack?

    a) **Generic Access Profile (GAP)**

    b) **Generic Attribute Profile (GATT)**

    c) Link layer

    d) **Security Manager Protocol (SMP)**

2. Which layer of the BLE stack provides the API for advertisement configuration and management?

    a) **Generic Access Profile (GAP)**

    b) **Generic Attribute Profile (GATT)**

    c) Link layer

    d) **Security Manager Protocol (SMP)**

3. Which layer of the BLE stack provides the API for defining characteristics?

    a) **Generic Access Profile (GAP)**

    b) **Generic Attribute Profile (GATT)**

    c) Link layer

    d) **Security Manager Protocol (SMP)**

4. Which one is wrong for the BLE Mesh?

    a) It is a networking protocol.

    b) It is a point-to-point protocol.

    c) It has a many-to-many topology.

    d) It defines different node types.

5. Which one defines the sensor functionality of a BLE Mesh node?

    a) Node type

    b) Model

    c) Application key

    d) Network address

Further reading

Please refer to the following for more information about what was covered in the chapter:

- *Building Bluetooth Low Energy Systems, Muhammad Usama bin Aftab, Packt Publishing* (https://www.packtpub.com/product/building-bluetooth-low-energy-systems/9781786461087): In *Chapter 1, BLE and the Internet of Things*, the key concepts are explained, such as ATT, GATT, security features, and so on. *Chapter 4, Bluetooth Low Energy Beacons*, discusses BLE beacons, and the mesh technology is covered in *Chapter 6, Bluetooth Mesh Technology*.

9
Practice – Making Your Home Smart

The second project in this book is a smart home application. Here, we are going to put the wireless communication knowledge we attained in the previous chapters into practice. A basic smart home product usually contains three groups of devices. There are sensor devices such as temperature, light, and motion sensors, actuator devices such as alarms, switches, and dimmers, and usually a gateway that provides access to the home device. This grouping doesn't necessarily apply to all smart home solutions, though. Many smart home products combine sensors and actuators into a single device with a direct IP connection to the local network, which lets its users connect directly to the device itself via a web browser or mobile application. We can find smart thermostats (such as Google Nest Thermostat) or smart doorbells (such as Ring Video Doorbell) on the market as examples of this approach.

However, when the sensors and actuators need to be physically located in different locations of a house and communicate with each other, **wireless personal area networks (WPANs)** come in handy. The IEEE 802.15 series standards define such networks. You can find a good explanation of WPAN standards on Wikipedia here: `https://en.wikipedia.org/wiki/IEEE_802.15`. In this project, we will develop a light sensor, a switch, and a gateway for our smart home product and set up a BLE mesh network with them.

In this chapter, we will cover the following topics:

- Feature list
- Solution architecture
- Implementation

Technical requirements

You can find the code for this chapter in this book's GitHub repository, here: `https://github.com/PacktPublishing/Internet-of-Things-with-ESP32/tree/main/ch9`.

The external libraries can be found here: `https://github.com/PacktPublishing/Internet-of-Things-with-ESP32/tree/main/common`.

In terms of hardware, you will need the following:

- Three devkits: One for each node in the BLE mesh network
- Three LEDs: One for each node
- A relay: For the switch node
- A TLS2561 light sensor: For the light sensor node

To set up the BLE network and test the project, we will use a mobile application from Nordic Semiconductor ASA called **nRF Mesh**. It is available on both iOS and Android platforms.

Check out the following video to see the code in action: `https://bit.ly/3yxFBae`

Feature list

Our smart home product will have the following features:

- Support BLE mesh networking.
- During provisioning, a node blinks an LED indicator to distinguish itself visually.
- A light sensor will be provided. This broadcasts a message to the network when the light level drops below a certain threshold.
- A switch will be provided. When the switch receives an ON/OFF message or a level change notification from the light sensor, it will turn the connected lamp on/off accordingly.

- A gateway will be provided. This provides a web user interface for controlling the switch's state.

Now that we've covered the feature list, we can propose our solution.

Solution architecture

In this section, we will discuss each node type and show how all the components work together to accomplish the project's goals. Although the feature list described some of the common functionality of the nodes, it would be much clearer to discuss each node separately. Let's start with the light sensor.

Light sensor

The light sensor device will have the following features and functionality:

- It integrates a TLS2561 sensor to measure the ambient light level.
- It reads from TLS2561 every second and compares the reading against a predetermined threshold level.
- When the level goes below or above the threshold, it broadcasts a message to the BLE network, indicating a high/low status of the light reading.
- The user can provision the device in a BLE network by using a mobile app. During provisioning, it blinks an integrated LED indicator.

For this set of features, we can design and implement the following software modules in the light sensor firmware:

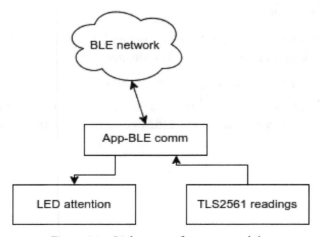

Figure 9.1 – Light sensor firmware modules

The LED attention module abstracts the LED state management. The BLE communication module calls the ON/OFF functions of the LED attention API during provisioning. The TLS2561 module pushes light level changes to the BLE communication module so that they can be broadcasted in the BLE network. The BLE communication module does all the hard work here. It should implement the following BLE mesh models to achieve the intended functionality:

- **Configuration server model**: This model is mandatory for interoperability. A configuration client, typically a mobile application, sends configuration data, including keys, to the device over this model.

- **Health server model**: The main purpose of the health server model is fault reporting and diagnostics. In addition to this, it also helps provision for user attention. We use the LED indicator for this purpose by implementing a callback for the health server events.

- **Generic OnOff server model**: This is the model that delivers a high/low light value in the mesh network.

Any **Generic OnOff client** can receive the light level changes from the light sensor node when the changes are broadcasted in the mesh network via the **Generic OnOff server** model.

The next device we will look at is the switch node, which controls the connected lamp.

Switch

The switch provides the actuator role for the solution. Whenever the light level changes or it is instructed to change by the user, the switch will turn the lamp on/off. The following are its features and functionality:

- The user can provision the device in a BLE network by using a mobile app. During provisioning, it blinks an integrated LED indicator.

- It integrates a relay to control the power of the attached lamp.

- When an ON/OFF message comes from the BLE network, it changes the relay state accordingly. The message source can be the light sensor or a user command.

The switch's firmware will contain the following software modules:

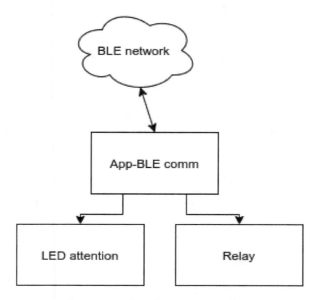

Figure 9.2 – Switch software modules

The BLE communication module has a central role in the firmware. It stands between the BLE network and all the other modules. When a state message comes from the BLE network, it calls the Relay module functions to control the physical relay. The same LED attention module is used in the switch firmware for provisioning.

Let's see which BLE mesh models are included in the implementation of the BLE communication module:

- Configuration server model.

- Health server model.

- **Generic OnOff server model**: This model provides a communication mechanism for changing the state of the integrated relay via other network nodes that implement the Generic OnOff client model.

- **Generic OnOff client model**: This model can connect or listen to the Generic OnOff server models in the network. In our case, the light sensor is the OnOff data source. When a state change notification is published by the light sensor in the network, the Generic OnOff client model will capture it and trigger any related actions.

We will implement both the Generic OnOff server and the client in the switch firmware since the switch serves as the relay controller and consumes the light state changes.

The last node we'll look at is the gateway.

Gateway

One important feature of ESP32 is that it allows us to enable Wi-Fi and Bluetooth simultaneously, which makes it possible to implement a gateway node in our project. This gateway provides a web interface for end users to change the switch state manually via a web browser. The features and functionality of this gateway are as follows:

- It connects to the local Wi-Fi network.

- It runs a web server that publishes a simple HTML form where the user can turn the switch on or off.

- The user can provision the device in a BLE network by using a mobile app. During provisioning, it blinks an integrated LED indicator.

The following diagram shows the modules in the gateway firmware:

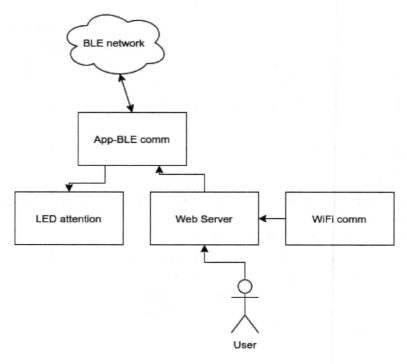

Figure 9.3 – Gateway software modules

In the gateway firmware, we have two additional modules for Wi-Fi communication and the web server. After connecting to the local Wi-Fi, the web server module handles all requests coming from the user and passes switch ON/OFF commands to the BLE communication module.

The following BLE mesh models will be implemented in the firmware:

- Configuration server model.

- Health server model.

- **Generic OnOff client model**: It sends **OnOff** messages to the switch. The **OnOff** parameter comes from the web server.

Before the implementation, let's take a look at the solution:

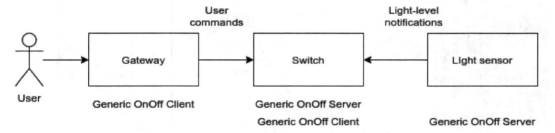

Figure 9.4 – Gateway firmware modules

For the switch, both the gateway and light sensor provide input to change the relay's state. However, the relationship between the gateway and the switch is different from the relationship between the light sensor and the switch. The light sensor, as a server, provides input to the switch in the form of notifications, whereas the gateway sends **OnOff** requests as a client.

In the next section, we will develop the project.

Implementation

Having discussed the solution architecture, next, we will look at the firmware for each device. Let's retain the order we used while discussing the solution and start with the light sensor.

Light sensor

Here, we will integrate a TLS2561 light sensor module into the light sensor device and use an LED as the indicator during provisioning. The following Fritzing diagram shows the connections:

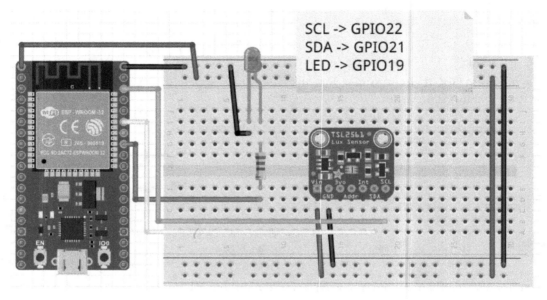

SCL -> GPIO22
SDA -> GPIO21
LED -> GPIO19

Figure 9.5 – Light sensor diagram

Let's prepare the development environment before coding. Here are the steps:

1. Create a PlatformIO project with the following `platformio.ini` file:

```
[env:az-delivery-devkit-v4]
platform = espressif32
board = az-delivery-devkit-v4
framework = espidf

monitor_speed = 115200
lib_extra_dirs =
    ../../common/esp-idf-lib/components
    ../common
build_flags =
    -DCONFIG_I2CDEV_TIMEOUT=100000
```

`lib_extra_dirs` shows the directories of the external libraries that we will be using`../../common/esp-idf-lib/components` is where the TLS2561 driver resides. The `../common` directory contains the common libraries for all three devices. We will discuss these common libraries later while developing the application.

2. In `sdkconfig`, enable some Bluetooth-related parameters. However, the list is quite long, so we can just copy it from the repository.

3. Activate the virtual environment by using the `pio` command-line tool:

```
$ source ~/.platformio/penv/bin/activate
(penv)$ pio --version
PlatformIO Core, version 5.1.0
```

Now that our development environment is ready, we can start coding. As a spoiler, I want to share the list of source code files so that it will be easier to map them to the solution architecture that we discussed previously:

```
(penv)$ ls src/
app_ble.c  app_ble.h  app_sensor.c  app_sensor.h  CMakeLists.
txt  component.mk  main.c
(penv)$ ls -R ../common/
../common/:
ble  led
../common/ble:
app_blecommon.c  app_blecommon.h
../common/led:
app_ledattn.c  app_ledattn.h
```

The `src/app_ble.{c,h}` files implement the BLE communication module, along with `../common/ble/app_blecommon.{c,h}`. `src/app_sensor.{c,h}` are for the TLS2561 module. Lastly, the LED attention module is implemented in `../common/led/app_ledattn.{c,h}`.

The C source files for the module implementations are a bit lengthy to include here, so we will only talk about the API functions and structures, as declared in the headers. Let's start with `../common/led/app_ledattn.h`:

```
#ifndef appled_attn_h_
#define appled_attn_h_
```

```
#include <stdbool.h>

#define ATTN_LED_PIN 19

void appled_init(void);
void appled_set(bool);

#endif
```

The LED attention API contains only two functions. `appled_init` initializes the GPIO pin of the LED indicator, while `appled_set` updates its state to on or off. The LED attention module is common to all devices.

The next one is `../common/ble/app_blecommon.h`. It declares several BLE functions, all of which are common to all device implementations:

```
#ifndef app_blecommon_h_
#define app_blecommon_h_

#include <stdint.h>
#include "esp_ble_mesh_defs.h"
#include "esp_ble_mesh_config_model_api.h"
#include "esp_ble_mesh_health_model_api.h"

void appble_get_dev_uuid(uint8_t *dev_uuid);
```

First, we must include the `esp_ble_mesh*` header files for the BLE-related structure definitions that we will use in the library functions. `appble_get_dev_uuid` reads the device unique identifier into memory, pointed to by the parameter. The device UUID is needed during provisioning. We have several more functions in this header file, as follows:

```
esp_err_t appble_bt_init(void);

void appble_provisioning_handler(esp_ble_mesh_prov_cb_event_t
event, esp_ble_mesh_prov_cb_param_t *param);

void appble_config_handler(esp_ble_mesh_cfg_server_cb_event_t
event, esp_ble_mesh_cfg_server_cb_param_t *param);
```

```
void appble_health_evt_handler(esp_ble_mesh_health_server_cb_
event_t event, esp_ble_mesh_health_server_cb_param_t *param);
```

appble_bt_init initializes the Bluetooth hardware. The others are BLE event handlers, which are common to all device implementations. They handle provisioning, configuration, and health operation events. We also need the attention callback functions, as follows:

```
typedef void (*appble_attn_on_f)(void);
typedef void (*appble_attn_off_f)(void);
typedef struct
{
    appble_attn_on_f attn_on;
    appble_attn_off_f attn_off;
} appble_attn_cbs_t;

void appble_set_attn_cbs(appble_attn_cbs_t);

#endif
```

appble_set_attn_cbs sets the attention callbacks, which are called in the health event handler. We can use any type of attention indicator here, such as a buzzer or LED. The health event handler doesn't need to know what it is; just on and off functions are enough for the handler.

Let's move on to the light sensor-specific APIs. The src/app_ble.h header file defines the API for the BLE communication module:

```
#ifndef app_ble_h_
#define app_ble_h_

#include <stdlib.h>
#include <stdbool.h>
#include "app_blecommon.h"

void init_ble(appble_attn_cbs_t);
void appble_update_state(bool onoff);

#endif
```

The BLE communication module has a very simple API. It is initialized with `init_ble`, which takes attention callback functions as the parameter. To update the internal state of the Generic OnOff server, `appble_update_state` is called. It also publishes the state change in the BLE network in the form of a notification to be processed by clients. We won't talk about the whole implementation, but it is worth mentioning the models defined in `src/app_ble.c`:

```
static esp_ble_mesh_model_t root_models[] = {
    ESP_BLE_MESH_MODEL_CFG_SRV(&config_server),
    ESP_BLE_MESH_MODEL_GEN_ONOFF_SRV(&onoff_pub_0, &onoff_
server_0),
    ESP_BLE_MESH_MODEL_HEALTH_SRV(&health_server, &health_
pub_0),
};
```

`root_models` is a global array that holds the server models of the light sensor. It contains a configuration server, a health server, and a Generic OnOff server. ESP-IDF provides macros to declare models easily.

Another important point in the source file is that we must register some callback functions as BLE event handlers in `init_ble`:

```
    esp_ble_mesh_register_prov_callback(appble_provisioning_
handler);
    esp_ble_mesh_register_config_server_callback(appble_config_
handler);
    esp_ble_mesh_register_generic_server_callback(generic_
server_cb);
    esp_ble_mesh_register_health_server_callback(appble_health_
evt_handler);
```

The registered callbacks for the BLE events are as follows:

- **Provisioning handler**: This is declared in `app_blecommon.h`.

- **Configuration server handler**: This is declared in `app_blecommon.h`.

- **Generic server handler**: This is implemented in `app_ble.c`.

- **Health server handler**: This is declared in `app_blecommon.h`.

These handlers manage the whole data flow according to the events coming from the ESP-IDF BLE layer.

`src/app_sensor.h` defines the TLS2561 sensor API. Let's see what is inside:

```
#ifndef app_sensor_h_
#define app_sensor_h_

#include "tsl2561.h"

#define LIGHT_THRESHOLD 30
#define LIGHT_SDA 21
#define LIGHT_SCL 22
#define LIGHT_ADDR TSL2561_I2C_ADDR_FLOAT


typedef void (*light_changed_f)(bool);
void init_hw(light_changed_f);
bool is_light_low(void);

#endif
```

The threshold value to report a change is 30 lux. When the light level goes below this value, the library reports it as low-level light, and vice versa. The `init_hw` function initializes the TLS2561 sensor with I²C pins. It also takes a callback function as its parameter, which is to be called when the light level changes.

Now that we've discussed all the libraries, we are ready to develop the application in `main.c`:

```
#include <stdio.h>
#include <string.h>
#include "esp_log.h"

#include "app_sensor.h"
#include "app_ble.h"
#include "app_ledattn.h"
```

First, we must include the header files of the modules. They are as follows:

- `app_ble.h` for the BLE communication module
- `app_sensor.h` for the TLS2561 sensor module
- `app_ledattn.h` for the LED attention module

Then, we define the attention callbacks:

```
#define TAG "sensor"


static void attn_on(void)
{
    appled_set(true);
}
static void attn_off(void)
{
    appled_set(false);
}
```

We call the `appled_set` function with `true` and `false` to change the attention state to on and off respectively. Finally, we define the `app_main` function:

```
void app_main(void)
{
    init_hw(appble_update_state);
    appled_init();
     appble_attn_cbs_t cbs = {attn_on, attn_off};
    init_ble(cbs);
}
```

In `app_main`, we call `init_hw` to initialize TLS2561. The callback function for the light level change is `appble_update_state`, which broadcasts this change in the BLE network. The other initialization function, `init_ble`, is called with the attention callbacks. We connected all the modules at this level by passing the callbacks to each other.

At this point, our program is ready to be compiled and flashed into the devkit. Make sure you have all the source code in place, as I showed at the beginning of this section:

```
(penv)$ pio run -t upload && pio device monitor
```

If everything goes well, we should be able to see the light level printed on the serial terminal every second. The light sensor is ready, so we will develop the switch next.

Switch

For the switch, we will use a relay and an LED. The ultimate purpose is, of course, to control a lamp, but we are good without it in this example.

> **Tip**
>
> If you decide to control a lamp with the relay, you can follow the instructions at `https://ncd.io/relay-logic`. It also explains more interesting connections with relays; for instance, how to connect a three-way light switch so that either relay toggles the lamp. Please make sure you take all the necessary precautions while working with the high voltage.

The hardware connections are as follows:

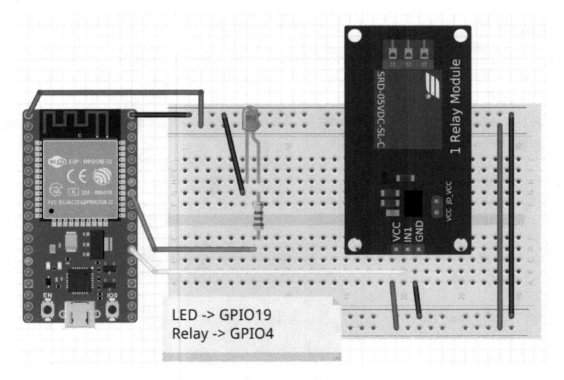

LED -> GPIO19
Relay -> GPIO4

Figure 9.6 – Fritzing diagram for the switch

The steps to prepare the development environment are the same as the ones for the light sensor, so we only need to see platformio.ini:

```
[env:az-delivery-devkit-v4]
platform = espressif32
board = az-delivery-devkit-v4
framework = espidf

monitor_speed = 115200
lib_extra_dirs = ../common
```

We have only set the baud rate for the serial monitor and specified the common library folder.

For the source code, we have the following files:

```
(penv)$ ls src/
app_ble.c  app_ble.h  app_sw.c  app_sw.h  CMakeLists.txt
main.c
```

app_ble.{c,h} implement the BLE communication module, while app_sw.{c,h} implement the relay driving module. Let's see what we have in app_ble.h for the BLE communication API:

```
#ifndef app_ble_h_
#define app_ble_h_

#include <stdlib.h>
#include <stdbool.h>
#include "app_blecommon.h"

typedef void (*switch_set_f)(bool);
typedef bool (*switch_get_f)(void);

typedef struct {
    switch_set_f sw_set;
    switch_get_f sw_get;
    appble_attn_on_f attn_on;
    appble_attn_off_f attn_off;
```

```
} app_ble_cb_t;
```

```
void init_ble(app_ble_cb_t callbacks);
```

```
#endif
```

init_ble takes a parameter that contains a list of callback functions. These are as follows:

- sw_set and sw_get: Switch state get/set functions

- attn_on and attn_off: Attention indicator ON/OFF functions

The init_ble function also registers some functions as the BLE event handlers in its implementation in app_ble.c, as shown here:

```
esp_ble_mesh_register_prov_callback(appble_provisioning_
handler);
    esp_ble_mesh_register_config_server_callback(appble_config_
handler);
    esp_ble_mesh_register_health_server_callback(appble_health_
evt_handler);
    esp_ble_mesh_register_generic_server_callback(generic_
server_cb);
    esp_ble_mesh_register_generic_client_callback(generic_
client_cb);
```

generic_server_cb is used to handle requests coming from any Generic OnOff client in the network. In our case, it is the gateway, which directs the user commands to the switch as BLE messages. generic_client_cb catches the notifications from the light switch. These functions use sw_set to change the switch state.

The models of the switch also reside in app_ble.c as a global variable, as shown in the following code snippet:

```
static esp_ble_mesh_model_t root_models[] = {
    ESP_BLE_MESH_MODEL_CFG_SRV(&config_server),
    ESP_BLE_MESH_MODEL_GEN_ONOFF_SRV(&onoff_pub_0, &onoff_
server_0),
    ESP_BLE_MESH_MODEL_GEN_ONOFF_CLI(&onoff_cli_pub, &onoff_
client),
```

```
    ESP_BLE_MESH_MODEL_HEALTH_SRV(&health_server, &health_
pub_0),
};
```

Again, we are using the same macros to define the models. This time, we have a new addition to the club: the Generic OnOff client.

Let's see what the Relay API provides in app_sw.h:

```
#ifndef app_sw_h_
#define app_sw_h_

#include <stdbool.h>
 #define RELAY_PIN 4

void init_hw(void);
void switch_set(bool);
bool switch_get(void);

#endif
```

This is a very clear API with three functions. init_hw initializes the GPIO pin that the relay is connected to. We can set the relay state by using switch_set and we can call switch_get when we need to know its state.

Now that we've looked at all the APIs, we will discuss the main application, which is implemented in main.c:

```
#include <stdio.h>
#include <string.h>

#include "esp_log.h"

#include "app_ble.h"
#include "app_sw.h"
#include "app_ledattn.h"
```

We must include the necessary module headers here, which are as follows:

- `app_ble.h` for the BLE communication module
- `app_sw.h` for the Relay module
- `app_ledattn.h` for the LED attention module

Next, we define the attention callback functions:

```
#define TAG "switch"

static void attn_on(void)
{
    appled_set(true);
}
static void attn_off(void)
{
    appled_set(false);
}
```

Now that the attention callbacks are ready, we can continue with `app_main`:

```
void app_main(void)
{
    init_hw();
    appled_init();

    app_ble_cb_t cbs = {
        .sw_set = switch_set,
        .sw_get = switch_get,
        .attn_on = attn_on,
        .attn_off = attn_off,
    };
    init_ble(cbs);
}
```

After initializing the relay and the LED in app_main, we must call the init_ble function with the callbacks. The most important callback is sw_set, which is connected to switch_set of the Relay API. It will run any time the BLE communication module receives a notification or a command from the BLE network to change the state of the relay.

Now that the application is complete, we can upload the firmware, as shown here:

```
(penv)$ pio run -t upload
```

That's it. Next, we can develop the last device in the project: the gateway.

Gateway

In terms of setting up the hardware, we don't need anything except the LED connection to the devkit. After attaching an LED to GPIO19, we can start to develop the application. Let's prepare the development environment:

1. Create a PlatformIO project with the following platformio.ini:

    ```
    [env:az-delivery-devkit-v4]
    platform = espressif32
    board = az-delivery-devkit-v4
    framework = espidf

    monitor_speed = 115200
    lib_extra_dirs = ../common
    board_build.partitions = partitions.csv
    build_flags =
        -DWIFI_SSID=${sysenv.WIFI_SSID}
        -DWIFI_PASS=${sysenv.WIFI_PASS}
    ```

    In platformio.ini, we need to provide a custom partitions file because the firmware size will exceed 1 MB, which is the maximum size in the default partitions table. Therefore, we need to increase the size of the app partition to 2 MB in partitions.csv.

2. Add the partition file, called `partitions.csv`:

nvs,	data,	nvs,	0x9000,	16k
otadata,	data,	ota,	0xd000,	8k
phy_init,	data,	phy,	0xf000,	4k
factory,	**app**,	factory,	0x10000,	**2M**

We have set the size of the `app` partition to 2 MB here.

3. Copy `sdkconfig` to the root of the project from this project's GitHub repository. It includes all the necessary settings for the custom partitions file, Bluetooth, and BLE.

4. Activate the virtual environment to be able to use the `pio` tool and set the environment variables for the Wi-Fi SSID and password:

```
$ source ~/.platformio/penv/bin/activate
(penv)$ export WIFI_SSID='\"<your_ssid>\"'
(penv)$ export WIFI_PASS='\"<your_passwd>\"'
```

5. Run `menuconfig` and increase the HTTP header length to `4096` for requests. It is located at **(Top) | Component config | HTTP server | Max HTTP Request Header Length**:

```
(penv)$ pio run -t menuconfig
```

Before discussing the code, let's see which source files we have in the project:

```
$ ls src/
app_ble.c  app_ble.h  app_ip.c  app_ip.h  app_web.c  app_web.h
CMakeLists.txt  main.c
```

`app_ble.{c,h}` implement the BLE communication module, while `app_ip.{c,h}` implement the Wi-Fi connection module, as described in the solution architecture. The web server module is implemented in `app_web.{c,h}` and the `app_main` function resides in `main.c` as usual.

Let's start by implementing BLE communication. `app_ble.h` contains the function declarations:

```
#ifndef app_ble_h_
#define app_ble_h_


#include <stdlib.h>
#include <stdbool.h>
```

```
#include "app_blecommon.h"

void init_ble(appble_attn_cbs_t);
void appble_set_switch(bool);

#endif
```

`init_ble` initializes the BLE mesh communication and registers the event handlers. `appble_set_switch` sends Generic OnOff messages to the BLE network. The purpose is to pass the user requests from the IP network to the BLE network. In `app_ble.c`, we also declare the models to achieve the necessary BLE mesh features, as follows:

```
static esp_ble_mesh_model_t root_models[] = {
    ESP_BLE_MESH_MODEL_CFG_SRV(&config_server),
    ESP_BLE_MESH_MODEL_GEN_ONOFF_CLI(&onoff_cli_pub, &onoff_
client),
    ESP_BLE_MESH_MODEL_HEALTH_SRV(&health_server, &health_
pub_0),
};
```

Here, we have the following:

- Configuration server model
- Health server model
- Generic OnOff client model

`app_ip.h` contains the functions and types for connecting to the local Wi-Fi network, as shown here:

```
#ifndef app_ip_h_
#define app_ip_h_

typedef void (*on_connected_f)(void);
typedef void (*on_failed_f)(void);

typedef struct {
    on_connected_f on_connected;
    on_failed_f on_failed;
} connect_wifi_params_t;
```

```
void appip_connect_wifi(connect_wifi_params_t);

#endif
```

appip_connect_wifi is the only function that's declared in this header file. It takes a parameter that specifies the callbacks to be called when the Wi-Fi is connected or failed to connect. This lets any client code know about its status.

app_web.h is used to manage the web server running on the gateway:

```
#ifndef app_web_h_
#define app_web_h_

#include <stdbool.h>

typedef void (*set_switch_f)(bool);

void appweb_init(set_switch_f);
void appweb_start_server(void);

#endif
```

This provides a simple API for the web server. appweb_init takes a parameter of the type set_switch_f, which is the function to be called when the user sends an ON/OFF request via the web interface. appweb_start_server starts the web server, hence its name.

In app_web.c, both HTTP GET and HTTP PUT handlers are implemented for user requests. The web server publishes the following web page:

```
static const char *HTML_FORM = "<html><form action=\"/\"
method=\"post\">"
"<label for=\"switch_state\">Set switch:</label>"
"<select id=\"switch_state\" name=\"switch_state\">"
"<option value=\"ON\">ON</option>"
"<option value=\"OFF\">OFF</option>"
"</select>"
"<input type=\"submit\" value=\"Submit\">"
"</form></html>";
```

This is a simple form that shows an **ON/OFF** option group, along with a **Submit** button.

Finally, we will discuss the main application in `main.c`:

```c
#include <stdio.h>
#include <string.h>

#include "esp_log.h"
#include "app_ble.h"
#include "app_ip.h"
#include "app_web.h"
#include "app_ledattn.h"
```

First, we must include the `app_*.h` files to use the module implementations and continue with implementing the callbacks, as follows:

```c
#define TAG "gateway"

void wifi_connected(void)
{
    ESP_LOGI(TAG, "wifi connected");
    appweb_start_server();
}

void wifi_failed(void)
{
    ESP_LOGE(TAG, "wifi failed");
}
```

When the local Wi-Fi network is connected, we start the web server. We also need the attention callbacks, which we'll implement here:

```c
static void attn_on(void)
{
    appled_set(true);
}
static void attn_off(void)
{
```

```
        appled_set(false);
}
```

Now that all the callbacks are ready, we can glue all the components in `app_main` together, as follows:

```
void app_main(void)
{
    appled_init();
    appweb_init(appble_set_switch);

    connect_wifi_params_t p = {
        .on_connected = wifi_connected,
        .on_failed = wifi_failed,
    };
    appip_connect_wifi(p);

    appble_attn_cbs_t cbs = {attn_on, attn_off};
    init_ble(cbs);
}
```

In `app_main`, we initialize all of the modules. We pass the user requests to the BLE network by calling `appweb_init` with `appble_set_switch` as the callback. The HTTP PUT handler inside the web server will call `appble_set_switch` with ON/OFF commands from the user.

Now, the application is ready to be compiled and flashed into the devkit:

```
(penv)$ pio run -t upload && pio device monitor
```

In the serial output, we can see the ON/OFF requests when we connect to the web server via a browser and press the **Submit** button.

With that, we have set up the applications for all our devices. In the next section, we will set up a BLE network with the devices and test them to see how they behave in different scenarios.

Testing

Testing has two stages: setting up the BLE network and testing the scenarios. We will use our mobile phone during these tests. Follow these steps to set up the BLE network and configure the nodes:

1. Power up the devices and run the nRF Mesh application on your mobile phone. When we go to the **Network** tab of the app and tap on the + (*add*) button, we will see all of our devices waiting to be provisioned:

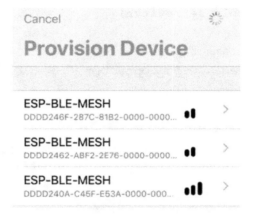

Figure 9.7 – BLE mesh devices ready to be provisioned

2. We can select any of them. When the application connects, the LED indicator will turn on so that we can see which one is connected. In my case, this is the gateway. Rename it gateway and tap **Provision** in the top right:

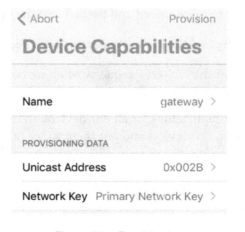

Figure 9.8 – Provisioning

3. After provisioning it successfully, specify an application key to be used by the Generic OnOff server and client models of all devices. It is the shared key of our application:

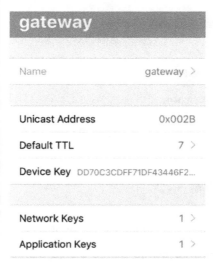

Figure 9.9 – Specifying the application key

4. Select **Element 1** on the page to see the models that have been implemented in the gateway:

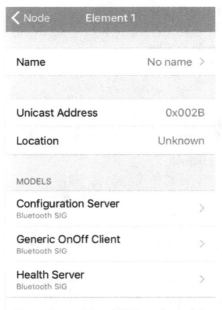

Figure 9.10 – List of BLE mesh models

5. Bind the application key to **Generic OnOff Client**:

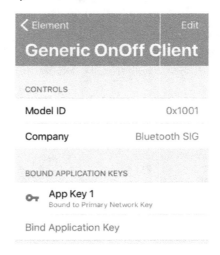

Figure 9.11 – Binding the application key

6. Mark the gateway as **Configured**:

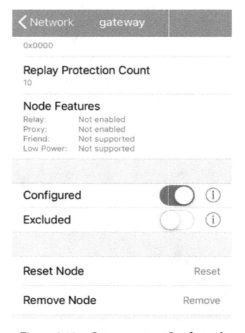

Figure 9.12 – Gateway set to Configured

7. Return to the **Network** view to see the gateway in the **Configured Nodes** list:

Figure 9.13 – Network view

8. Configure the switch and the light sensor in the same way. Note that there is a slight difference in binding the application key to the models. For the switch, we need to bind the application key to both the Generic OnOff client and the server. For the light sensor, we need to set the publication to **All Nodes** after binding the key to the Generic OnOff server:

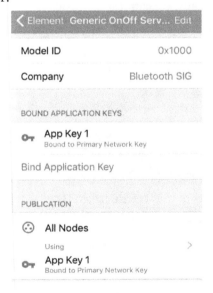

Figure 9.14 – Light sensor publication to All Nodes

Once we have configured all the devices, we can see them as nodes in the BLE network:

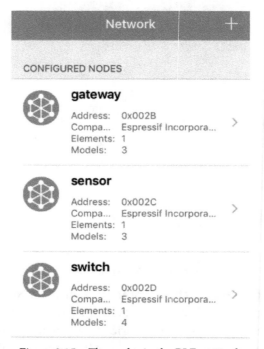

Figure 9.15 – The nodes in the BLE network

Now that the BLE network is ready, we can test the product. There are four basic scenarios that we can test:

1. Sending ON messages from the web interface by connecting to the local IP of the gateway. The switch should set the relay **ON**:

Figure 9.16 – Sending an ON message via the web interface

2. Sending OFF messages from the web interface. The switch should set the relay **OFF**.

3. The light sensor in the dark. The switch should set the relay **ON**.

4. The light sensor in the light. The switch should set the relay **OFF**.

Although we only have three types of nodes in our smart home project, it is open to new types being added to extend the capabilities of the solution. Bluetooth SIG defines more BLE mesh models and if they are not enough, the BLE mesh standard supports vendor-defined models as well.

This project finalizes this section. We are going to learn how to use ESP32 in cloud platforms to harness the real power of IoT in the next chapter.

Summary

With this project, we have completed the part where we explore the wireless connectivity capabilities of ESP32. For IP networks, ESP32 can connect to Wi-Fi. When we need to set up a WPAN to exchange data between devices, it supports BLE mesh networking. As we discussed earlier, IoT cannot be defined without connectivity and communication considerations. In this chapter, we gained important hands-on experience with the networking capabilities of ESP32, which we can leverage in any real-life IoT project.

The next chapter is devoted to cloud platforms and services, and how we utilize ESP32 as an IoT device in cloud solutions to interact with the physical environment remotely. Integration with cloud platforms and services closes the loop for any IoT solution, where all devices can be accessed from anywhere in the world and data coming from those IoT devices is stored for further processing.

Section 3: Cloud Communication

Most IoT applications require cloud connectivity to transfer and store data coming from IoT devices for further processing or analytics, or maybe simply to configure, monitor, or control them remotely. In this section, you will learn how to connect ESP32 to cloud services and transfer data between ESP32 and those services.

This part of the book comprises the following chapters:

- *Chapter 10, No Cloud, No IoT – Cloud Platforms and Services*
- *Chapter 11, Connectivity Is Never Enough – Third-Party Integrations*
- *Chapter 12, Practice – A Voice-Controlled Smart Fan*

10
No Cloud, No IoT – Cloud Platforms and Services

One of the biggest enablers of **Internet of Things** (**IoT**) is cloud computing. We can do all kinds of magic with ESP32 in a local network. We collect data, share them between nodes, interact with users via the physical switches and displays of the devices, and add more interesting features based on collective sensor data of the local device network. However, the missing part here is the connectivity. We should be able to access our devices remotely from anywhere in the world and analyze device data to gain insights into our product in a more fruitful manner. As a matter of fact, the analysis of IoT data and any insight resulting from this analysis can provide more benefits than the direct use of the devices themselves in some cases. Cloud technologies make all these benefits available in IoT products.

This chapter explains some common and well-supported IoT communication protocols. All cloud platforms provide endpoints for these protocols and we are going to learn how to use them in our ESP32 projects.

We will also briefly discuss some popular cloud platforms from different technology companies to understand what a cloud platform means and what we can expect from them. As a final example in the chapter, we are going to develop an application that connects to the AWS cloud.

In this chapter, we will cover the following:

- IoT protocols with ESP32
- Understanding cloud IoT platforms
- Developing on AWS IoT

Technical requirements

As hardware, we only need an ESP32 devkit and a DHT11 sensor.

You can find the code for the chapter examples at this link: `https://github.com/PacktPublishing/Internet-of-Things-with-ESP32/tree/main/ch10`.

The common libraries are located here: `https://github.com/PacktPublishing/Internet-of-Things-with-ESP32/tree/main/common`.

We need a new external library while developing the AWS example, which can be cloned from this repository: `https://github.com/espressif/esp-aws-iot.git`.

An AWS account and an **Identity and Access Management** (**IAM**) user are required. This documentation explains how to do that if you don't have an AWS account: `https://docs.aws.amazon.com/polly/latest/dg/setting-up.html`.

Eclipse Mosquitto is the MQTT message broker that we will use in this chapter. It also provides the client applications to connect to any message broker. This page helps with the installation: `https://mosquitto.org/download/`.

In the CoAP server example, we need a CoAP client to test the application. We can use any CoAP client, but one is here: `https://libcoap.net/install.html`.

Check out the following video to see the code in action: `https://bit.ly/3jVbOUM`

IoT protocols with ESP32

There are a number of application layer protocols for IoT devices to communicate with remote servers. Their design principles and architectures are quite different, so it is really a matter of requirements and constraints which one to choose in an IoT project. Let's discuss some popular protocols and their features with examples.

MQTT

Message Queue Telemetry Transport (MQTT) is a many-to-many communication protocol with a message broker as the mediator. There are publishers that send messages to the topics on the broker, and there are subscribers that receive messages from the topics that they have subscribed to. A node can be a publisher and subscriber at the same time:

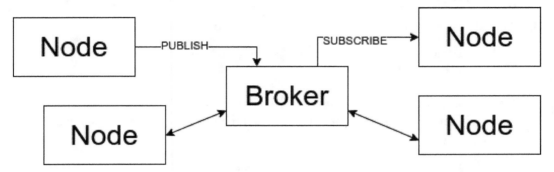

Figure 10.1 – MQTT communication model

For MQTT, TCP is the underlying transport protocol and TLS can be configured for communication security.

Let's see how MQTT works with a simple example. We will develop a sensor device with DHT11. It will publish temperature and humidity values to separate topics on an MQTT broker.

The hardware setup is easy. We only connect a DHT11 to the GPIO17 pin of our devkit. Then, we are ready to configure the development environment as follows:

1. Create a project with the following `platformio.ini`:

```
[env:az-delivery-devkit-v4]
platform = espressif32
board = az-delivery-devkit-v4
framework = espidf

monitor_speed = 115200
lib_extra_dirs =
    ../../common/esp-idf-lib/components
    ../common
build_flags =
    -DWIFI_SSID=${sysenv.WIFI_SSID}
```

```
-DWIFI_PASS=${sysenv.WIFI_PASS}
-DMQTT_BROKER_URL=${sysenv.MQTT_BROKER_URL}
```

2. Copy the common libraries of this chapter to `../common`. The GitHub link is here: `https://github.com/PacktPublishing/Internet-of-Things-with-ESP32/tree/main/ch10/common`.

3. Activate the virtual environment to use the `pio` tool:

```
$ source ~/.platformio/penv/bin/activate
(penv)$
```

4. Define the environment variables for Wi-Fi and the MQTT broker. We will install a broker later on our development PCs but it can be any MQTT broker that we have access to:

```
(penv)$ export WIFI_SSID='\"<your_ssid>\"'
(penv)$ export WIFI_PASS='\"<your_pass>\"'
(penv)$ export MQTT_BROKER_URL='\"mqtt://<your_PC_ip>\"'
```

Notice that the broker URL starts with the `mqtt://` prefix.

Having the development environment ready, we can continue with the application code. Let's see what we have in the common libraries briefly. It is enough to check the header files to understand their APIs. The first one is `../common/sensor/app_temp.h`:

```
#ifndef app_temp_h_
#define app_temp_h_

#define DHT11_PIN 17

typedef void (*temp_ready_f)(int, int);
void apptemp_init(temp_ready_f cb);

#endif
```

The sensor library initializes DTH11 with a callback that is called for each reading. Both temperature and humidity values are provided as the parameters to the callback.

The next library is `../common/wifi/app_wifi.h`:

```c
#ifndef app_wifi_h_
#define app_wifi_h_

typedef void (*on_connected_f)(void);
typedef void (*on_failed_f)(void);

typedef struct {
    on_connected_f on_connected;
    on_failed_f on_failed;
} connect_wifi_params_t;

void appwifi_connect(connect_wifi_params_t);

#endif
```

It declares a function, `appwifi_connect`, to connect to the local Wi-Fi with a parameter of callbacks to be called when ESP32 is connected or failed.

Having these libraries ready, we can move on to the application in `src/main.c` as follows:

```c
#include <string.h>
#include <stdbool.h>
#include <stdlib.h>
#include "freertos/FreeRTOS.h"
#include "freertos/task.h"
#include "esp_log.h"

#include "mqtt_client.h"

#include "app_temp.h"
#include "app_wifi.h"
```

We start with including the necessary header files. The header file for the MQTT library that comes with ESP-IDF is `mqtt_client.h`.

We then define the macros and the global variables as follows:

```
#define TAG "app"


#ifndef MQTT_BROKER_URL
#define MQTT_BROKER_URL "mqtt://<your_broker_url>"
#endif


#define SENSOR_NO "1"
#define ENABLE_TOPIC "home/" SENSOR_NO "/enable"
#define TEMP_TOPIC "home/temperature/" SENSOR_NO
#define HUM_TOPIC "home/humidity/" SENSOR_NO


static esp_mqtt_client_handle_t client = NULL;
static bool enabled = false;
```

We reserve an MQTT topic to enable or disable the sensor device. Our sensor will subscribe to the topic, ENABLE_TOPIC, to set/reset the enabled global variable. When enabled, the sensor device will publish to TEMP_TOPIC and HUM_TOPIC and any other client in the network can subscribe to these topics to receive the readings.

At this point, let's talk a little bit about MQTT topics. Topics are how we organize information in MQTT. Here are some rules and best practices about them:

- / (**slash**) is the level separator. We don't start with / to name a topic since it introduces an unnecessary level.

- + (**plus**) is the single-level wildcard. It corresponds to all topic names where it is used. For example, when we subscribe to home/+/light, we receive from all topics matching this pattern, such as home/kitchen/light or home/bedroom/light.

- # (**sharp**) is the multi-level wildcard and can be used only at the end. It matches all topics at that level and below it.

- No space or non-printable characters in topic names.

- Naming and levels depend on the context.

Let's continue with `app_main` to see the execution flow:

```
void app_main()
{
    esp_event_loop_create_default();

    connect_wifi_params_t cbs = {
        .on_connected = handle_wifi_connect,
        .on_failed = handle_wifi_failed};
    appwifi_connect(cbs);
}
```

In `app_main`, we first create the default event loop. It is necessary to receive MQTT events in the application. Next, we call `appwifi_connect` to connect to the local Wi-Fi. `handle_wifi_connect` is the function to be called when the Wi-Fi connection is established. The implementation of that function is as follows:

```
static void handle_wifi_connect(void)
{
    esp_mqtt_client_config_t mqtt_cfg = {
        .uri = MQTT_BROKER_URL,
    };
    client = esp_mqtt_client_init(&mqtt_cfg);
    esp_mqtt_client_register_event(client, ESP_EVENT_ANY_ID,
handle_mqtt_events, NULL);
    esp_mqtt_client_start(client);
    apptemp_init(publish_reading);
}


static void handle_wifi_failed(void)
{
    ESP_LOGE(TAG, "wifi failed");
}
```

We initialize the MQTT client when the local Wi-Fi is connected and register the MQTT event handler function, `handle_mqtt_events`, for the events coming from `client`. We can start the MQTT client to connect to the broker by calling `esp_mqtt_client_start`. Lastly, we initialize the DHT11 readings with `publish_reading` as the callback function. Let's see how the MQTT event handler works first, then we will discuss `publish_reading`, where we send readings to the topics on the broker:

```
static void handle_mqtt_events(void *handler_args,
                               esp_event_base_t base,
                               int32_t event_id,
                               void *event_data)
{
    esp_mqtt_event_handle_t event = event_data;
    switch ((esp_mqtt_event_id_t)event_id)
    {
    case MQTT_EVENT_CONNECTED:
        ESP_LOGI(TAG, "mqtt broker connected");
        esp_mqtt_client_subscribe(client, ENABLE_TOPIC, 0);
        break;
```

The first event in the list is `MQTT_EVENT_CONNECTED`, where we subscribe to `ENABLE_TOPIC` in order to listen to messages for enable/disable sensor commands. Then, we continue with the `MQTT_EVENT_DATA` case next:

```
    case MQTT_EVENT_DATA:
        if (!strncmp(event->topic, ENABLE_TOPIC, event->topic_len))
        {
            enabled = event->data[0] - '0';
        }
        break;
```

When `MQTT_EVENT_DATA` happens, it means we have received a message from a topic that we have subscribed to. In this case, there is only one topic, but we check anyway whether it is really `ENABLE_TOPIC`. We expect message data in string format. We can also handle the error case as follows:

```
    case MQTT_EVENT_ERROR:
        ESP_LOGE(TAG, "errtype: %d", event->error_handle->error_type);
```

```
            break;
        default:
            ESP_LOGI(TAG, "event: %d", event_id);
            break;
    }
}
```

The last event that we handle explicitly is `MQTT_EVENT_ERROR`. We only print the error type on the serial console if this event happens.

Next comes publishing readings to the topics:

```
static void publish_reading(int temp, int hum)
{
    char buffer[5];

    if (client != NULL && enabled)
    {
        esp_mqtt_client_publish(client, TEMP_TOPIC, itoa(temp,
buffer, 10), 0, 1, 0);
        esp_mqtt_client_publish(client, HUM_TOPIC, itoa(hum,
buffer, 10), 0, 1, 0);
    }
}
```

To publish a message to a topic, we call `esp_mqtt_client_publish`. It takes several parameters, including the MQTT client, topic name, and data to be published. One parameter specifies the **quality of service**, or **QoS**. There are three valid options for QoS:

- **QoS level-0**: This means no delivery guarantee to subscribers. The subscribers don't have to acknowledge receipt of the message.

- **QoS level-1**: Guarantees the delivery but subscribers may receive several copies of the message.

- **QoS level-2**: Subscribers receive exactly one copy of the message.

We select QoS according to the requirements of the application. For instance, if skipping a reading is not so important, we can select QoS-0. QoS-1 and QoS-2 are achieved by additional **acknowledge** (**ACK**) messages, which introduce some overhead on the communication. Therefore, it can be a good idea to discuss this decision with the product owner in some cases if nothing is specified or there is no hint about it in the requirements.

We have completed the application and it is ready to test. Let's do this in the following steps:

1. We will use Mosquitto as the broker, publisher, and subscriber clients. Here are the installers for different platforms if you don't have Mosquitto on your PC: `https://mosquitto.org/download/`.

2. Start the broker and make sure it works properly by checking the services on the PC. Additionally, the default port for MQTT is `1883`. We can also check the open ports to understand whether the service is up and running:

```
$ systemctl | grep -i mosquitto
mosquitto.service loaded active        running    Mosquitto
MQTT v3.1/v3.1.1 Broker
$ sudo netstat -tulpn | grep -i mosquitto
tcp       0       0 0.0.0.0:1883               0.0.0.0:*
LISTEN       2245/mosquitto
```

3. Test the subscriber and publisher applications of Mosquitto. We open a command line and start `mosquitto_sub` listening on the `home/test` topic. The documentation about the tools is at `https://mosquitto.org/documentation/`:

```
$ mosquitto_sub -h localhost -t home/test
```

4. In another command line, publish a message on the same topic by using `mosquitto_pub`:

```
$ mosquitto_pub -h localhost -t home/test -m "test message"
```

If we see the message on the subscriber, it means we can continue testing ESP32 with the same broker.

5. Start a subscriber to listen to the application topics:

```
$ mosquitto_sub -h localhost -t "home/+/1" -d
```

6. Go back to the VSCode command line where we have activated the PlatformIO virtual environment. There, we flash the devkit and start a serial monitor:

```
(penv)$ pio run -t upload && pio device monitor
```

7. As the final step, enable the sensor by publishing an enable message to the `home/1/enable` topic:

```
$ mosquitto_pub -h localhost -t home/1/enable -m "1"
```

That is all! The sensor should start to publish readings on both MQTT topics, and we can see them in the subscriber window.

> **Tip**
>
> If you run Mosquitto 2.0, you will need a configuration file to allow clients to connect to the broker remotely, which is explained in detail here: `https://mosquitto.org/documentation/migrating-to-2-0/`.

We will discuss another popular IoT communication protocol, CoAP, in the next topic.

CoAP

Constrained Application Protocol (CoAP) is a client-server protocol in which servers expose resources in the network and clients send HTTP requests to get or set the state of the resources on the servers. CoAP is specifically designed for resource-limited low-power IoT devices as a **Representational State Transfer (REST)** communication protocol with low overheads:

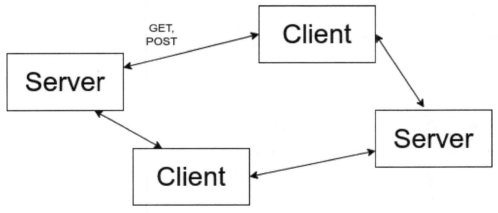

Figure 10.2 – CoAP communication model

CoAP is originally depicted to run on top of UDP but it can work with any transport protocols. For example, when CoAP is ported into a proprietary wireless network, it is quite easy for nodes to communicate with an external IP network when a proper gateway is included. The gateway translates messages at the transport level and the applications on both sides can exchange messages as if they are in the same network.

In terms of communication security, we can use DTLS as a secure transport layer for CoAP.

Let's have an example. The hardware setup and development environment configuration are the same as the MQTT example, so I won't repeat them here. We can just start with the application code in src/main.c:

```c
#include <string.h>
#include <stdint.h>
#include <sys/socket.h>

#include "freertos/FreeRTOS.h"
#include "freertos/task.h"
#include "freertos/event_groups.h"

#include "esp_log.h"
#include "esp_event.h"

#include "app_temp.h"
#include "app_wifi.h"

#include "coap.h"

const static char *TAG = "app";

static int temperature, humidity;
```

We include the header files first. coap.h defines the CoAP library API. We have two global variables to hold temperature and humidity values.

We jump into app_main to see how the story starts:

```c
void app_main()
{
    connect_wifi_params_t cbs = {
        .on_connected = handle_wifi_connect,
        .on_failed = handle_wifi_failed};
    appwifi_connect(cbs);
}
```

We connect to the local Wi-Fi by calling `appwifi_connect`. Its callbacks come next:

```
static void update_reading(int temp, int hum)
{
    temperature = temp;
    humidity = hum;
}

static void handle_wifi_connect(void)
{
    xTaskCreate(sensor_server, "coap", 8 * 1024, NULL, 5,
NULL);
    apptemp_init(update_reading);
}

static void handle_wifi_failed(void)
{
    ESP_LOGE(TAG, "wifi failed");
}
```

`handle_wifi_connect` is the callback function that is called when the devkit connects to the local Wi-Fi. In the function, we start a FreeRTOS task for the CoAP server and initialize the DHT11 sensor library by passing the `update_reading` function as the callback, in which we update the global variables with readings from DHT11. We implement `sensor_server` as follows:

```
static void sensor_server(void *p)
{
    coap_context_t *ctx = NULL;
    coap_address_t serv_addr;
    coap_resource_t *temp_resource = NULL;
    coap_resource_t *hum_resource = NULL;
```

We start with defining the local variables. `ctx` holds the CoAP context. It is the central data source for all CoAP library functions. We declare a server address variable and pointers for two CoAP resources to be exposed on the CoAP server. Next, we start the server:

```
coap_set_log_level(LOG_DEBUG);

while (1)
{
    coap_address_init(&serv_addr);
    serv_addr.addr.sin.sin_family = AF_INET;
    serv_addr.addr.sin.sin_addr.s_addr = INADDR_ANY;
    serv_addr.addr.sin.sin_port = htons(COAP_DEFAULT_PORT);

    ctx = coap_new_context(NULL);
    coap_new_endpoint(ctx, &serv_addr, COAP_PROTO_UDP);
```

The `while` loop is a fail-safe loop that restarts the server in case of any failure. We initialize the server address structure and create a new context. By passing them as parameters to `coap_new_endpoint`, we create an endpoint for clients to connect. The endpoint runs on top of UDP at the default port, which is `5683` for CoAP. Then we create the resources as follows:

```
    temp_resource = coap_resource_init(coap_make_str_
const("temperature"), 0);
    coap_register_handler(temp_resource, COAP_REQUEST_GET,
handle_sensor_get);
    coap_add_resource(ctx, temp_resource);

    hum_resource = coap_resource_init(coap_make_str_
const("humidity"), 0);
    coap_register_handler(hum_resource, COAP_REQUEST_GET,
handle_sensor_get);
    coap_add_resource(ctx, hum_resource);
```

The first resource is the temperature resource. After initializing it, we register a handler for the COAP_REQUEST_GET requests. We complete the resource configuration by adding the temperature resource to the CoAP context with the help of coap_add_resource. We repeat the same process for the humidity resource. Next comes the message processing:

```
        while (1)
        {
            int result = coap_run_once(ctx, 2000);
            if (result < 0)
            {
                break;
            }
        }
        coap_free_context(ctx);
        coap_cleanup();
    }

    vTaskDelete(NULL);
}
```

The second while loop is for the message processing. coap_run_once waits for a new request to the server. If any error occurs, the inner loop breaks, the CoAP context and resources are cleared, and a new instance is started by the outer loop.

We have completed the server task. Let's see how the GET handler works:

```
static void
handle_sensor_get(coap_context_t *ctx,
                  coap_resource_t *resource,
                  coap_session_t *session,
                  coap_pdu_t *request,
                  coap_binary_t *token,
                  coap_string_t *query,
                  coap_pdu_t *response)
{
    char buff[100];
    memset(buff, 0, sizeof(buff));
    if (!strcmp("temperature", (const char *) (resource->uri_
```

```
path->s)))
    {
        sprintf(buff, "{\"temperature\": %d}", temperature);
    }
    else
    {
        sprintf(buff, "{\"humidity\": %d}", humidity);
    }
    coap_add_data_blocked_response(resource, session,
request, response, token, COAP_MEDIATYPE_APPLICATION_JSON, 0,
strlen(buff), (const uint8_t *)buff);
}
```

In `handle_sensor_get`, we check which resource is queried and arrange JSON data accordingly. We update the response with this JSON data by calling `coap_add_data_blocked_response`.

The application is ready. Let's test it using the following steps:

1. Flash the firmware to the devkit:

    ```
    (penv)$ pio run -t upload && pio device monitor
    ```

    When the application starts, ESP32 connects to the local Wi-Fi and starts the CoAP server with the temperature and humidity resources. The IP of the device is printed on the serial monitor.

2. We need a CoAP client. I will use `coap-client` from the `libcoap` project here: `https://libcoap.net/`. You can also download and compile it on your development PC or install any other CoAP client application for your system. There are some mobile applications that you can try as well.

3. We open another command line and send a GET request to the temperature resource on the server:

    ```
    $ coap-client -m get coap://192.168.1.85/temperature
    {"temperature": 22}
    ```

4. We can query the humidity as well using the following:

    ```
    $ coap-client -m get coap://192.168.1.85/humidity
    {"humidity": 52}
    ```

Great! We have a working example of a CoAP server with two resources. We can also develop client applications to run on ESP32. When it comes to wireless sensor networks, CoAP presents a good option to exchange data between nodes as well as the outside world.

The next protocol that we will discuss is WebSocket.

WebSocket

WebSocket brings full-duplex messaging power to the internet. As we know, HTTP communication is a simple client-server model where a client connects to a web server and requests data and the server replies. The client always has to poll for any updates on the server side. This is an issue when the server needs to update the client in real time. WebSocket solves this problem. After an HTTP handshake, parties can switch to WebSocket communication, which is a binary data exchange method running on top of TCP. The underlying TCP connection is preserved during the communication and both ends can pass data in real time. All modern web servers and web browsers support WebSocket.

When it comes to IoT devices, using WebSocket can have significant advantages in some use cases. For example, when we need to have a web-based dashboard that needs to receive real-time data from IoT gateways behind a firewall or other security network elements, a WebSocket connection is likely to be the easiest and most effective solution to deal with traffic filters since HTTP is usually allowed through firewalls and all other ports are mostly blocked.

WebSocket provides a raw full-duplex connection between parties. Although it is quite possible to use WebSocket as a direct communication channel, we can also run other application layer protocols on top of it, such as MQTT or CoAP. In this way, we can leverage the advantages of both WebSocket and the application layer protocol, whatever we choose for our project.

Let's try the pure WebSocket method in an example. The goal of the next application is to start a web server on ESP32 with a WebSocket endpoint. ESP32 will have a DHT11 attached to it. When a client connects, it can enable/disable readings and see the readings on the page without refreshing it.

The hardware setup is not different from the previous example. A DHT11 sensor is connected to the devkit at GPIO17. The development environment configuration is a bit tricky, so we will follow the given steps:

1. Create a new PlatformIO project with the following `platformio.ini`:

```
[env:az-delivery-devkit-v4]
platform = espressif32
board = az-delivery-devkit-v4
framework = espidf

monitor_speed = 115200
lib_extra_dirs =
    ../../common/esp-idf-lib/components
    ../common
build_flags =
    -DWIFI_SSID=${sysenv.WIFI_SSID}
    -DWIFI_PASS=${sysenv.WIFI_PASS}

board_build.partitions = partitions.csv
```

We will use a custom partitions table to save the `index.html` file on the flash.

2. Create `partitions.csv` with the following content:

```
nvs,       data, nvs,      ,         0x6000,
phy_init,  data, phy,      ,         0x1000,
factory,   app,  factory,  ,         1M,
spiffs,    data, spiffs,   0x210000,         1M,
```

We will upload `index.html` on the `spiffs` partition.

3. Create a `data` folder to save `index.html`. Here is the link to download `index.html`: https://github.com/PacktPublishing/Internet-of-Things-with-ESP32/blob/main/ch10/websocket_ex/data/index.html:

```
$ mkdir data && chdir data && wget https://github.com/
PacktPublishing/Internet-of-Things-with-ESP32/blob/main/
ch10/websocket_ex/data/index.html
```

4. Edit `CMakeLists.txt` to specify the `data` folder as the `spiffs` source:

```
cmake_minimum_required(VERSION 3.16.0)
include($ENV{IDF_PATH}/tools/cmake/project.cmake)
project(websocket_ex)
spiffs_create_partition_image(spiffs data)
```

5. Enable the virtual environment for `pio` and set the Wi-Fi SSID and password:

```
$ source ~/.platformio/penv/bin/activate
(penv)$ export WIFI_SSID='\"<your_ssid>\"'
(penv)$ export WIFI_PASS='\"<your_passwd>\"'
```

6. When all files are in place, we should have the following directory structure:

```
(penv)$ ls -R
.:
CMakeLists.txt   data   include   lib   partitions.csv
platformio.ini   sdkconfig   sdkconfig.old   src   test
./data:
index.html
./src:
CMakeLists.txt   main.c
```

7. Run `menuconfig` to set the partitions file and enable WebSocket:

```
(penv)$ pio run -t menuconfig
```

8. Specify the custom partitions file first:

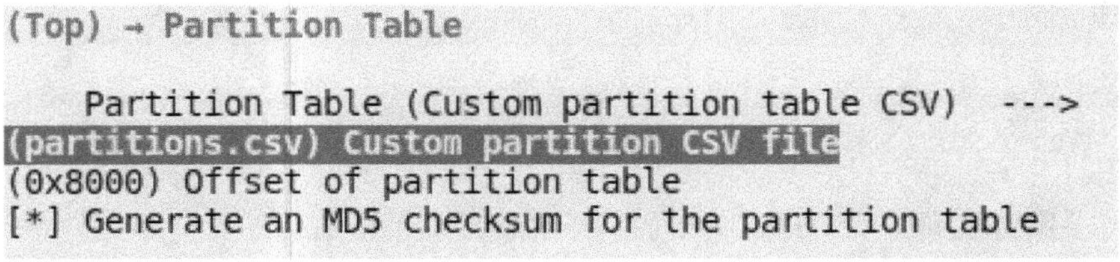

```
(Top) → Partition Table

    Partition Table (Custom partition table CSV)  --->
(partitions.csv) Custom partition CSV file
(0x8000) Offset of partition table
[*] Generate an MD5 checksum for the partition table
```

Figure 10.3 – Custom partitions file

9. Enable WebSocket by navigating to **Component config | HTTP Server**:

```
(Top) → Component config → HTTP Server

(512) Max HTTP Request Header Length
(512) Max HTTP URI Length
[*] Use TCP_NODELAY socket option when sending HTTP error responses
(32) Length of temporary buffer for purging data
[ ] Log purged content data at Debug level
[*] WebSocket server support
```

Figure 10.4 – WebSocket server support

10. Update Max HTTP Request Header Length to 4096 on the same menu.

The configuration of the development environment is done. We can start to code the application in src/main.c now:

```c
#include <string.h>
#include <stdint.h>
#include <sys/stat.h>


#include "esp_log.h"


#include "app_temp.h"
#include "app_wifi.h"


#include "esp_spiffs.h"
#include "esp_http_server.h"


const static char *TAG = "app";
```

We include the necessary header files. esp_http_server.h has the API to start a web server with WebSocket support. Let's define the globals next:

```c
#define INDEX_HTML_PATH "/spiffs/index.html"
static char index_html[4096];


static int temperature, humidity;
static bool enabled = true;
```

```
static httpd_handle_t server = NULL;
static int ws_fd = -1;
```

We define `server` and `ws_fd` as globals to be able to send asynchronous WebSocket messages. `ws_fd` denotes the WebSocket descriptor, which is a simple integer value. Let's see `app_main` to understand the execution flow:

```
void app_main()
{
    init_html();

    connect_wifi_params_t cbs = {
        .on_connected = handle_wifi_connect,
        .on_failed = handle_wifi_failed};
    appwifi_connect(cbs);
}
```

`init_html` opens the `spiffs` partition and reads the `index.html` file. `appwifi_connect` is the function that we use to connect to the local Wi-Fi. It calls `handle_wifi_connect` when the Wi-Fi is connected. Let's continue with the implementation of `init_html`:

```
static void init_html(void)
{
    esp_vfs_spiffs_conf_t conf = {
        .base_path = "/spiffs",
        .partition_label = NULL,
        .max_files = 5,
        .format_if_mount_failed = true};

    ESP_ERROR_CHECK(esp_vfs_spiffs_register(&conf));
```

We call `esp_vfs_spiffs_register` to initialize the `spiffs` partition. Then we check whether `index.html` exists on this partition, as follows:

```
    memset((void *)index_html, 0, sizeof(index_html));
    struct stat st;
    if (stat(INDEX_HTML_PATH, &st))
    {
```

```
        ESP_LOGE(TAG, "index.html not found");
        return;
    }
```

The `stat` function stores the file information in the `st` variable and returns an error code if the file doesn't exist. If the file exists, we open the file next:

```
    FILE *fp = fopen(INDEX_HTML_PATH, "r");
    if (fread(index_html, st.st_size, 1, fp) != st.st_size)
    {
        ESP_LOGE(TAG, "fread failed");
    }
    fclose(fp);
}
```

We read the `index.html` file from the flash into the `index_html` global variable to send it when a GET request comes to the web server.

Let's implement the Wi-Fi callbacks:

```
static void handle_wifi_connect(void)
{
    start_server();
    apptemp_init(update_reading);
}


static void handle_wifi_failed(void)
{
    ESP_LOGE(TAG, "wifi failed");
}
```

In `handle_wifi_connect`, we start the web server and readings from DHT11. If any client is connected, the `update_reading` function will send the readings over WebSocket.

Next, we discuss how `start_server` works:

```
static void start_server(void)
{
    httpd_config_t config = HTTPD_DEFAULT_CONFIG();
```

```
    config.open_fn = handle_socket_opened;
    config.close_fn = handle_socket_closed;
```

We first define an HTTP configuration variable. We will use it to start the web server.
`handle_socket_opened` and `handle_socket_closed` are two callback functions
to track the latest active WebSocket and they are specified in `config`. Then, we try to
start the web server:

```
    if (httpd_start(&server, &config) == ESP_OK)
    {
        httpd_uri_t uri_get = {
            .uri = "/",
            .method = HTTP_GET,
            .handler = handle_http_get,
            .user_ctx = NULL};
        httpd_register_uri_handler(server, &uri_get);
```

If `httpd_start` succeeds in starting a web server, we register a handler to reply GET
requests sent to the root URL. We also register another handler for WebSocket requests
that are sent to the /ws, endpoint as follows:

```
        httpd_uri_t ws = {
            .uri = "/ws",
            .method = HTTP_GET,
            .handler = handle_ws_req,
            .user_ctx = NULL,
            .is_websocket = true};
        httpd_register_uri_handler(server, &ws);
    }
}
```

We have to specify that this endpoint is a WebSocket by setting the is_websocket
field to `true`. When `start_server` finishes running, we will have a web server with
WebSocket support. Let's implement the socket opened/closed handlers next:

```
static esp_err_t handle_socket_opened(httpd_handle_t hd, int
sockfd)
{
    ws_fd = sockfd;
    return ESP_OK;
```

```
}

static void handle_socket_closed(httpd_handle_t hd, int sockfd)
{
    if (sockfd == ws_fd)
    {
        ws_fd = -1;
    }
}
```

When a WebSocket connection is established, we store the socket descriptor in the `ws_fd` global variable. If the same socket is closed later, we set `ws_fd` to -1, which shows there is no active socket to use. Before moving on to the WebSocket request handler, let's take a look at the following HTML code snippet from `index.html`:

```
<p class="state">State: <span id="state">%STATE%</span></p>
<p class="state">Temp: <span id="temp">%TEMP%</span></p>
<p class="state">Hum: <span id="hum">%HUM%</span></p>
<p><button id="button" class="button">Toggle</button></p>
```

We have four UI elements on the web page. We show the state of the device as on or off, temperature and humidity values, and a button to send a WebSocket message in order to toggle the state of the sensor. The WebSocket communication is achieved with the help of several JavaScript functions implemented on this web page, but we won't list them here since they are out of the scope of the book.

Having this information, we can continue with the `handle_ws_req` function where we handle WebSocket messages from the client:

```
static esp_err_t handle_ws_req(httpd_req_t *req)
{
    enabled = !enabled;

    httpd_ws_frame_t ws_pkt;
    uint8_t buff[16];
    memset(&ws_pkt, 0, sizeof(httpd_ws_frame_t));
    ws_pkt.payload = buff;
    ws_pkt.type = HTTPD_WS_TYPE_BINARY;
```

```
    httpd_ws_recv_frame(req, &ws_pkt, sizeof(buff));


    if (!enabled)
    {
        httpd_queue_work(server, send_async, NULL);
    }
    return ESP_OK;
}
```

When a WebSocket request is received from the client, it is for toggling the state, so we toggle the `enabled` global variable. We need to consume the transmitted data to free the internal buffer of the web server. To do that, we define a variable of the `httpd_ws_frame_t` type and call `httpd_ws_recv_frame` to store the data in that variable. We can check the payload if needed. If we disable the device as a result of toggling, we update the client with this information by calling `httpd_queue_work`. The web server has asynchronous operation capability, so we pass a callback function, `send_async`, to be scheduled by the web server. Next, we implement `send_async`, in which we send a WebSocket message asynchronously to the client:

```
static void send_async(void *arg)
{
    if (ws_fd < 0)
    {
        return;
    }

    char buff[128];
    memset(buff, 0, sizeof(buff));
    sprintf(buff, "{\"state\": \"%s\", \"temp\": %d, \"hum\":
%d}", enabled ? "ON" : "OFF", temperature, humidity);

    httpd_ws_frame_t ws_pkt;
    memset(&ws_pkt, 0, sizeof(httpd_ws_frame_t));
    ws_pkt.payload = (uint8_t *)buff;
    ws_pkt.len = strlen(buff);
    ws_pkt.type = HTTPD_WS_TYPE_TEXT;
```

```
        httpd_ws_send_frame_async(server, ws_fd, &ws_pkt);
}
```

If we have an active socket, we prepare JSON-formatted data to be sent to the client in send_async. httpd_ws_send_frame_async sends this data over the socket.

Let's see the callback where we share DHT11 readings with the client. It also uses send_async to share readings:

```
static void update_reading(int temp, int hum)
{
    temperature = temp;
    humidity = hum;

    if (server != NULL && enabled)
    {
        httpd_queue_work(server, send_async, NULL);
    }
}
```

update_reading is called by the DHT11 library that we have for this chapter. The library takes a reading every 2 seconds and calls this function. In the function, we set the global variables with the temperature and humidity values, and if the device is in the enabled state, we call httpd_queue_work to schedule a send_async call.

The last function that we haven't discussed yet is handle_http_get. Here it comes:

```
static esp_err_t handle_http_get(httpd_req_t *req)
{
    if (index_html[0] == 0)
    {
        httpd_resp_set_status(req, HTTPD_500);
        return httpd_resp_send(req, "no index.html", HTTPD_
RESP_USE_STRLEN);
    }
    return httpd_resp_send(req, index_html, HTTPD_RESP_USE_
STRLEN);
}
```

If `index_html` contains nothing, it means ESP32 has failed to read the `index.html` file from its flash memory. Therefore, we set the status code of the reply to `HTTP-500`, `Internal Server Error`. If `index_html` contains the web page, we simply send it to the client.

It is done! Now, we can test the application as follows:

1. Compile the project first and make sure there is no error:

    ```
    (penv)$ pio run
    ```

2. Build and upload the filesystem that contains the `index.html` file:

    ```
    (penv)$ pio run -t buildfs && pio run -t uploadfs
    ```

3. Upload the firmware to the devkit and start the serial monitor:

    ```
    (penv)$ pio run -t upload && pio device monitor
    ```

4. We can see the IP of the devkit on the serial monitor when it connects to the local Wi-Fi. After the web server starts, connect it from any web browser with the IP of the devkit:

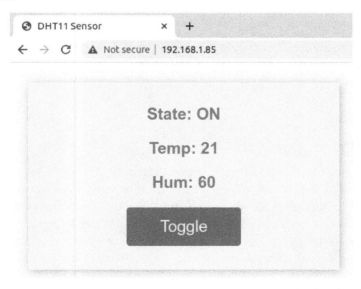

Figure 10.5 – The web interface of the WebSocket application

5. Observe that the temperature and humidity values are updated automatically when the state is ON. We can change the state by clicking on the **Toggle** button.

We have learned about some popular IoT communication protocols with examples. MQTT has a special place among them since it is the de facto standard to communicate with cloud platforms. All platforms provide MQTT endpoints for IoT devices to connect. In the next topic, we are going to talk about the cloud platforms that we can integrate with in our ESP32 projects.

Understanding cloud IoT platforms

We can use ESP32 with a wide range of cloud platforms. The most popular ones are the following:

- AWS IoT
- Azure IoT
- Google IoT Core
- Alibaba Cloud IoT Platform

The best way to understand what an IoT platform means is to look at its offerings and services. Let's see briefly what they provide for us to develop IoT projects.

AWS IoT

AWS IoT provides many services to help developers in their IoT endeavors. The services in the AWS cloud can be grouped into three categories:

- Control services
- Device software
- Data services

The control services cover the device management capabilities of AWS IoT. The most basic one, **AWS IoT Core**, is the central service for IoT solutions. IoT devices connect to the whole AWS infrastructure through AWS IoT Core. **AWS IoT Device Management** lets IoT vendors track and manage their IoT devices in bulk. **AWS IoT Device Defender** is responsible for the security of IoT devices by ensuring security best practices. **AWS IoT Things Graph** helps developers to design interactions and data flow between IoT devices and web services. It provides a visual drag-and-drop flow design interface that reduces the development time and increases efficiency.

The device software group provides open source software components or SDKs that run on IoT devices. The main purpose is to accelerate IoT device development and integration with the AWS IoT services. **AWS IoT Greengrass** brings a limited set of AWS data processing capabilities to edge devices, which reduces the volume of data transferred between devices and the cloud services. **FreeRTOS** is supported officially by AWS IoT as the RTOS for microcontrollers. **AWS IoT Device SDK** is the group of open source libraries and SDKs to connect devices to AWS IoT. Finally, **AWS IoT Device Tester** enables developers to test their devices to see whether they will interoperate with AWS IoT services.

The data services group is composed of data collection and analysis services. **AWS IoT SiteWise** provides a gateway software to collect on-premises data and sends it to the AWS cloud for further processing. **AWS IoT Analytics** is the service to preprocess unstructured IoT data in high volumes before storing. **AWS IoT Events** monitors a fleet of devices for failures or changes in operation and triggers actions based on defined rules.

These are the IoT-specific services. After we integrate our ESP32 devices into AWS IoT, all other AWS cloud services are available for any type of application.

For the documentation of the AWS IoT services, you can refer to the following link: `https://docs.aws.amazon.com/iot/latest/developerguide/aws-iot-how-it-works.html`.

Azure IoT

Azure IoT provides similar services to develop IoT applications and manage IoT devices in the cloud.

IoT Hub is the front service of Azure IoT. It provides endpoints for IoT devices to integrate with other Azure cloud services. **Device Provisioning Service** is responsible for provisioning IoT devices by validating their unique identities with a zero-touch strategy, which means there is no need for any human intervention. **IoT Plug and Play** removes the need for manual configuration by introducing device models that describe device capabilities. **Device Update** is the service for OTA updates of IoT devices. **IoT Central** enables developers to develop their own custom IoT solutions on the Azure cloud. **Azure IoT Edge** aims to move the preprocessing of data and data analytics to edge devices to handle data management on the edge. **Azure Digital Twins** is an analytics tool to model and analyze the whole IoT solution to have an overall view and gain insights. **Azure Time Series Insights Gen2** is another analytics service that works with time series data to reveal any anomaly or trend.

You can see the Azure IoT documentation here: `https://docs.microsoft.com/en-gb/azure/iot-fundamentals`.

Google IoT Core

Google IoT Core provides a single API to manage millions of devices. When we enable the API, it provides two main components:

- The **device manager** to register and configure devices
- **Protocol bridges** to which our devices connect in order to communicate with Google IoT Core

After we register a device and configure it to connect to Google IoT Core, we can enable other Google services for further processing.

More information is on the documentation pages here: `https://cloud.google.com/iot/docs/concepts`.

Alibaba Cloud IoT Platform (Aliyun IoT)

IoT Platform of Alibaba Cloud has the following features to develop IoT applications:

- Device connection
- Message communication
- Device management
- Monitoring and maintenance
- Data analysis

The platform provides SDKs and other software components, letting developers easily connect IoT devices to the cloud. The services of Alibaba Cloud IoT Platform are all comprehensive in terms of device development and management. After connecting the device, we can use other Alibaba Cloud services, or we can redirect messages to our own on-premises servers.

To learn more about Aliyun IoT, you can read the documentation here: `https://www.alibabacloud.com/help/product/30520.htm`.

It is possible to use ESP32 with other cloud providers as well. They all provide SDKs and tools to connect IoT devices to their infrastructures and therefore let developers use IoT data in their applications. No matter which IoT platform we choose for a project, the communication with the platform is always encrypted and secured as a common feature of all platforms.

Let's see an example of an AWS cloud connection with ESP32.

Developing on AWS IoT

In this example, we will adapt our previous MQTT application to the AWS cloud.

Before starting the example, we need to have an AWS account and install the `aws` command-line tool. If you haven't done so yet, the AWS documentation provides excellent guidance:

- Getting started with AWS IoT Core: `https://docs.aws.amazon.com/iot/latest/developerguide/iot-gs.html`

- Installing, updating, and uninstalling the AWS CLI version 2: `https://docs.aws.amazon.com/cli/latest/userguide/install-cliv2.html`

- Configuring the AWS CLI: `https://docs.aws.amazon.com/cli/latest/userguide/cli-configure-quickstart.html`

After installing `aws`, we will create a **thing** in AWS IoT Core. A thing is the representation of a physical IoT device in the cloud. We create and configure it as follows:

1. First check that the `aws` command-line tool works:

   ```
   $ aws --version
   aws-cli/2.1.31 Python/3.8.8 Linux/5.4.0-65-generic exe/
   x86_64.ubuntu.20 prompt/off
   ```

2. Create a thing using the following command:

   ```
   $ aws iot create-thing --thing-name my_sensor1
   ```

   The name of the thing is `my_sensor1`.

3. Create a policy description file. The content is as follows:

   ```
   {
       "Version": "2012-10-17",
       "Statement": [
           {
               "Effect": "Allow",
               "Action": [
                   "iot:Connect",
                   "iot:Publish",
                   "iot:Subscribe",
                   "iot:Receive"
   ```

```
        ],
        "Resource": "arn:aws:iot:*:*:*"
    }
    ]
}
```

The policy file says that any thing associated with this policy has the permissions of connecting, publishing, subscribing, and receiving on any AWS IoT Core resource. This policy is too permissive for an application in production but fine for our testing purposes.

4. Create a policy with the policy file that we had in the previous step:

```
$ aws iot create-policy \
    --policy-name my_sensor1_policy \
    --policy-document file://policy.json
```

The name of the policy is my_sensor1_policy.

5. Create private and public keys and a certificate:

```
$ aws iot create-keys-and-certificate \
    --certificate-pem-outfile "my_sensor1.cert.pem" \
    --public-key-outfile "my_sensor1.public.key" \
    --private-key-outfile "my_sensor1.private.key" \
    --set-as-active
```

The command generates three files in the directory. One is for the certificate, one is the public key, and the last one contains the private key. The command also prints the **Amazon Resource Name (ARN)** of the certificate on the screen. We take note of this ARN since we will need it to glue parts to each other. It is something like this:

```
"certificateArn": "arn:aws:iot:<your_
region>:******:cert/*****"
```

6. Attach the policy to the certificate so that any thing that uses this certificate and cryptographic keys can have the permissions in the associated policy:

```
$ aws iot attach-policy \
    --policy-name my_sensor1_policy \
    --target <cert_arn>
```

7. The last step is to attach the same certificate to `my_sensor1`:

```
$ aws iot attach-thing-principal \
    --thing-name my_sensor1 \
    --principal <cert_arn>
```

> **Tip**
> AWS also has a nice web GUI for all these steps and to manage our devices.
> We can choose any of the methods to accomplish the AWS-related steps in
> this example. You can log in to the AWS Management Console at this URL:
> `https://aws.amazon.com/console/`.

We have created a thing, a policy, and a certificate. They work together as a whole, allowing us to connect our device to AWS IoT Core. Let's test them to see whether we did everything right:

1. Download the Amazon root certificate:

```
$ wget https://www.amazontrust.com/repository/
AmazonRootCA1.pem
```

2. Find the AWS IoT endpoint address to connect:

```
$ aws iot describe-endpoint --endpoint-type iot:Data-ATS
{
    "endpointAddress": "XXXXX.iot.<region>.amazonaws.com"
}
```

3. Run a subscriber. It listens to the topic of `test/topic1`:

```
$ mosquitto_sub --cafile AmazonRootCA1.pem --cert my_
sensor1.cert.pem --key my_sensor1.private.key -d -h
<endpointAddress> -p 8883 -t test/topic1
```

4. Publish a message to `test/topic1`. We should see this message on the subscriber side as follows:

```
$ mosquitto_pub --cafile AmazonRootCA1.pem --cert my_
sensor1.cert.pem --key my_sensor1.private.key -d -h
<endpointAddress> -p 8883 -t test/topic1 -m hi
```

We will use the Amazon root certificate in *step 1* and the endpoint address in *step 2* in our application as well.

The cloud setup is completed, and we can move on to the application. After connecting DHT11 to GPIO17, we follow the given steps to prepare the development environment:

1. Create a PlatformIO project with the following `platformio.ini`:

```
[env:az-delivery-devkit-v4]
platform = espressif32
board = az-delivery-devkit-v4
framework = espidf

monitor_speed = 115200
lib_extra_dirs =
    ../../common/esp-idf-lib/components
    ../common
build_flags =
    -DWIFI_SSID=${sysenv.WIFI_SSID}
    -DWIFI_PASS=${sysenv.WIFI_PASS}
    -DAWS_ENDPOINT=${sysenv.AWS_ENDPOINT}

board_build.embed_txtfiles =
    ./tmp/my_sensor1.private.key
    ./tmp/my_sensor1.cert.pem
    ./tmp/AmazonRootCA1.pem
```

In addition to Wi-Fi credentials, we define a new environment variable for the AWS IoT endpoint. We will set them next. We also specify the paths for the cryptographic files that we will copy later.

2. Activate the `pio` tool and set the environment variables:

```
$ source ~/.platformio/penv/bin/activate
(penv)$ export WIFI_SSID='\"<your_ssid>\"'
(penv)$ export WIFI_PASS='\"<your_passwd>\"'
(penv)$ export AWS_ENDPOINT='\"<your_endpoint>\"'
```

The endpoint comes from the `aws iot describe-endpoint` command that we used while testing `my_device1`.

3. Copy the cryptographic files into the temporary directory:

```
(penv)$ mkdir tmp && cp <crpyto_dir>/* tmp/
(penv)$ ls -1 tmp
AmazonRootCA1.pem
my_sensor1.cert.pem
my_sensor1.private.key
my_sensor1.public.key
```

The tmp directory is in the .gitignore list so that the files will not be committed. It is important not to share them in the code repository; otherwise, it would be a potential security vulnerability.

4. Update src/CMakeLists.txt with the paths. After the update, the file contains the following:

```
FILE(GLOB_RECURSE app_sources ${CMAKE_SOURCE_DIR}/
src/*.*)
set(COMPONENT_ADD_INCLUDEDIRS ".")

idf_component_register(SRCS ${app_sources})

target_add_binary_data(${COMPONENT_TARGET} "../tmp/
AmazonRootCA1.pem" TEXT)
target_add_binary_data(${COMPONENT_TARGET} "../tmp/my_
sensor1.cert.pem" TEXT)
target_add_binary_data(${COMPONENT_TARGET} "../tmp/my_
sensor1.private.key" TEXT)
```

We specify the paths for the cryptographic files in src/CMakeLists.txt as well.

5. The GitHub repository contains the AWS device SDK in ../../common/
components/esp-aws-iot. Edit the CMakeLists.txt file under the project root with the following content:

```
cmake_minimum_required(VERSION 3.16.0)
list(APPEND EXTRA_COMPONENT_DIRS "../../common/
components/esp-aws-iot")
include($ENV{IDF_PATH}/tools/cmake/project.cmake)
project(aws_ex)
```

The `list` directive appends the AWS device SDK path to the extra components list so that ESP-IDF can find the SDK.

6. When we have all files in place, we should have the following directory structure:

```
(penv)$ ls -R
.:
CMakeLists.txt  components  include  lib  platformio.ini
sdkconfig  sdkconfig.defaults  src  test  tmp
./components:
esp-aws/* # all files from the SDK
./src:
CMakeLists.txt  main.c
./tmp:
AmazonRootCA1.pem  my_sensor1.cert.pem  my_sensor1.
private.key  my_sensor1.public.key
```

Now, we are ready to develop the application. Let's edit `src/main.c`:

```
#include <string.h>
#include <stdbool.h>
#include <stdlib.h>
#include "freertos/FreeRTOS.h"
#include "freertos/task.h"
#include "esp_log.h"

#include "app_temp.h"
#include "app_wifi.h"

#include "aws_iot_config.h"
#include "aws_iot_log.h"
#include "aws_iot_version.h"
#include "aws_iot_mqtt_client_interface.h"
```

We start with including the necessary header files. `aws_iot_*` comes from the AWS device SDK. Next, we define the MQTT topics that we will use in our application:

```
#define TAG "app"
#define SENSOR_NO "1"
#define ENABLE_TOPIC "home/" SENSOR_NO "/enable"
```

```
#define TEMP_TOPIC "home/temperature/" SENSOR_NO
#define HUM_TOPIC "home/humidity/" SENSOR_NO
```

After the topic definitions, we continue with the globals:

```
extern const uint8_t aws_root_ca_pem_start[] asm("_binary_
AmazonRootCA1_pem_start");
extern const uint8_t aws_root_ca_pem_end[] asm("_binary_
AmazonRootCA1_pem_end");
extern const uint8_t certificate_pem_crt_start[] asm("_binary_
my_sensor1_cert_pem_start");
extern const uint8_t certificate_pem_crt_end[] asm("_binary_my_
sensor1_cert_pem_end");
extern const uint8_t private_pem_key_start[] asm("_binary_my_
sensor1_private_key_start");
extern const uint8_t private_pem_key_end[] asm("_binary_my_
sensor1_private_key_end");

static char endpoint_address[] = AWS_ENDPOINT;
static char client_id[] = "my_sensor1";

static AWS_IoT_Client aws_client;
static bool enabled = false;
```

All cryptographic files are embedded in the firmware and we define their start addresses
as externals. The value of endpoint_address comes from the environment variable
that we have defined during the environment setup. aws_client is the variable that
holds all AWS IoT connection information. We will initialize it before connecting to AWS
IoT Core. Let's see app_main and the Wi-Fi connection handlers next:

```
static void handle_wifi_connect(void)
{
    xTaskCreate(connect_aws_mqtt, "connect_aws_mqtt", 15 *
configMINIMAL_STACK_SIZE, NULL, 5, NULL);
    apptemp_init(publish_reading);
}
static void handle_wifi_failed(void)
{
    ESP_LOGE(TAG, "wifi failed");
```

```
}

void app_main()
{
    connect_wifi_params_t cbs = {
        .on_connected = handle_wifi_connect,
        .on_failed = handle_wifi_failed};
    appwifi_connect(cbs);
}
```

In app_main, we try to connect to the local Wi-Fi network. When the Wi-Fi connection becomes successful, we start a FreeRTOS task to connect to the AWS MQTT broker in handle_wifi_connect. We also initialize DHT11 with the publish_reading callback to send readings to the AWS MQTT broker. connect_aws_mqtt is implemented as follows:

```
void connect_aws_mqtt(void *param)
{
    memset((void *)&aws_client, 0, sizeof(aws_client));

    IoT_Client_Init_Params mqttInitParams =
iotClientInitParamsDefault;
    mqttInitParams.pHostURL = endpoint_address;
    mqttInitParams.port = AWS_IOT_MQTT_PORT;
    mqttInitParams.pRootCALocation = (const char *)aws_root_ca_
pem_start;
    mqttInitParams.pDeviceCertLocation = (const char *)
certificate_pem_crt_start;
    mqttInitParams.pDevicePrivateKeyLocation = (const char *)
private_pem_key_start;
    mqttInitParams.disconnectHandler = disconnected_handler;
    aws_iot_mqtt_init(&aws_client, &mqttInitParams);
```

We first initialize the global AWS client, aws_client. In the initialization, we specify the following:

- AWS endpoint address
- MQTT port

- Cryptographic data
- A handler to be called when the client disconnects

Next, we will try to connect to the endpoint:

```
    IoT_Client_Connect_Params connectParams =
iotClientConnectParamsDefault;
    connectParams.keepAliveIntervalInSec = 10;
    connectParams.pClientID = client_id;
    connectParams.clientIDLen = (uint16_t)strlen(client_id);
    while (aws_iot_mqtt_connect(&aws_client, &connectParams) !=
SUCCESS)
    {
        vTaskDelay(1000 / portTICK_RATE_MS);
    }
    ESP_LOGI(TAG, "connected");
```

We call `aws_iot_mqtt_connect` with the connection parameters in a loop until it succeeds. Then, we continue with the topic subscription as follows:

```
    aws_iot_mqtt_subscribe(&aws_client, ENABLE_TOPIC,
strlen(ENABLE_TOPIC), QOS0, subscribe_handler, NULL);

    while (1)
    {
        aws_iot_mqtt_yield(&aws_client, 100);
        vTaskDelay(1000 / portTICK_PERIOD_MS);
    }
}
```

After the client connects, we subscribe to `ENABLE_TOPIC` by calling `aws_iot_mqtt_subscribe`. It also takes a callback parameter, `subscribe_handler`, to be called when a message comes from the topic. It will enable/disable sending messages to the MQTT broker. `aws_iot_mqtt_yield` is the function that processes incoming messages in a loop. It will call the subscription message handler when a new message comes from a topic. Let's see how we define this handler:

```
void subscribe_handler(AWS_IoT_Client *pClient,
                    char *topicName, uint16_t topicNameLen,
                    IoT_Publish_Message_Params *params,
```

```
                    void *pData)
{
    enabled = ((char *)params->payload)[0] - '0';
}
```

In `subscribe_handler`, we simply check the message payload to see whether it is `'0'` or not to disable/enable the device. We don't need to check `topicName` here since there is only one topic that we have subscribed to. The other event handler function is `disconnected_handler`, which can be implemented as follows:

```
void disconnected_handler(AWS_IoT_Client *pClient, void *data)
{
    ESP_LOGW(TAG, "reconnecting...");
}
```

In the disconnect event handler, we do nothing but print a warning message. Actually, the default initialization parameter of the AWS client contains an auto-connect field, which is set to `true` by default. Therefore, we don't need to do anything special about the disconnect event in this case. The last function that we implement is `publish_reading`, which is the callback for DHT11 readings. Here is the implementation:

```
static void publish_reading(int temp, int hum)
{
    IoT_Error_t res = aws_iot_mqtt_yield(&aws_client, 100);
    if (res != SUCCESS && res != NETWORK_RECONNECTED)
    {
        return;
    }
    if (!enabled)
    {
        return;
    }
}
```

We again call `aws_iot_mqtt_yield` to process any incoming messages. It returns the connection status. If the client doesn't have a connection to the AWS MQTT broker, `publish_reading` exits. It also exits when the device is disabled. Now, we are ready to publish a message as follows:

```
    char buffer[5];
    IoT_Publish_Message_Params message;
```

```
    memset((void *)&message, 0, sizeof(message));

    itoa(temp, buffer, 10);
    message.qos = QOS0;
    message.payload = (void *)buffer;
    message.payloadLen = strlen(buffer);
    aws_iot_mqtt_publish(&aws_client, TEMP_TOPIC, strlen(TEMP_
TOPIC), &message);

    itoa(hum, buffer, 10);
    message.payloadLen = strlen(buffer);
    aws_iot_mqtt_publish(&aws_client, HUM_TOPIC, strlen(HUM_
TOPIC), &message);
}
```

We first define a variable, message, which shows the QoS level and the data buffer. We use aws_iot_mqtt_publish with this variable to publish a message on a topic. We call it twice here to publish both temperature and humidity readings to their respective topics.

The application is ready to flash the devkit and test. Let's do it step by step:

1. Upload the firmware and start the serial monitor to see the logs as follows:

    ```
    (penv)$ pio run -t upload && pio device monitor
    ```

2. Start a mosquitto_sub client on the command line to wait for messages at home/temperature/1:

    ```
    $ mosquitto_sub --cafile AmazonRootCA1.pem --cert my_
    sensor1.cert.pem --key my_sensor1.private.key -d -h
    <endpointAddress> -p 8883 -t home/temperature/1
    ```

3. Enable the device by publishing a '1' message on home/1/enable on another command line:

    ```
    $ mosquitto_pub --cafile AmazonRootCA1.pem --cert my_
    sensor1.cert.pem --key my_sensor1.private.key -d -h
    <endpointAddress> -p 8883 -t home/1/enable -m '1'
    ```

4. Observe that when we enable the device, the subscriber starts to receive temperature readings. Similarly, when we disable it, the readings stop:

```
$ mosquitto_pub --cafile AmazonRootCA1.pem --cert my_
sensor1.cert.pem --key my_sensor1.private.key -d -h
<endpointAddress> -p 8883 -t home/1/enable -m '0'
```

Nice! We have completed the chapter with this important example. In the next chapter, we will carry on with more cloud services in which we can integrate ESP32.

Summary

There are many ways to connect to cloud platforms. No cloud platform can provide endpoints for all available IoT protocols but some of those protocols are quite common and well-supported by cloud vendors. They are MQTT, CoAP, and WebSocket, which we have discussed with examples in this chapter. We can choose any of them according to the technical requirements of a given project. We also had a brief overview of some major cloud providers. We examined their features and offerings to understand what to expect from an IoT platform. To exemplify cloud integration, we developed a simple application that connects and communicates with the AWS IoT platform over the MQTT protocol. Although this chapter barely scratches the surface of what we can do with an IoT platform, it explains the fundamentals of cloud communication techniques that we can apply in any IoT project with any IoT platform vendor.

In the next chapter, we will talk about other cloud services that we can integrate ESP32 with. We can add voice capabilities to our ESP32 products by using voice assistants or we can interface with thousands of other products by integrating with an online rule engine service. The examples of the next chapter will allow us to practice these subjects.

Questions

Let's review the chapter by answering the following questions:

1. Which protocol makes use of topics to publish and subscribe?

    a) HTTP

    b) WebSocket

    c) CoAP

    d) MQTT

2. Which one is not correct for CoAP?

    a) It is a server-client protocol.

    b) It provides RESTful communication for IoT devices.

    c) Only runs on top of UDP.

    d) A client sends HTTP requests.

3. Which problem is solved by WebSocket?

    a) Polling server for status updates

    b) The need for a server

    c) Lowers the energy consumption of constrained devices

    d) Replaces TCP for IoT devices

4. Which one is not a common feature of IoT platforms?

    a) They provide secure endpoints.

    b) Security is an optional feature.

    c) We can use more services after authenticating an IoT device.

    d) Data analytics in the cloud.

5. What is not correct about an MQTT connection to AWS IoT?

    a) A policy file is needed to define permissions.

    b) A device must be authenticated to communicate.

    c) A policy file is automatically generated when a thing is created.

    d) The AWS device SDK can be used to publish an MQTT message.

11
Connectivity Is Never Enough – Third-Party Integrations

Developing an IoT product doesn't mean that we make every piece of the product by ourselves. On the contrary, it is impossible and not the right way of developing a valuable product. After analyzing the required features, we decide which parts we'll make and which parts we'll integrate with others to add a feature. In that manner, we have endless options and support from third-party service providers when it comes to connectivity. With the right selection of third-party services, we can create outstanding IoT products for our users.

During the last decade, voice assistants have assumed an important place in our lives as a new type of machine interface. We have them on our PCs, on our mobile phones, and many other smart devices. Therefore, it would be a wise approach to think about whether we need integration with a voice service when we develop a new IoT product. Integrating with a voice service doesn't only mean that our product has a voice feature that we can put as a label on the box. Such integration is a gateway to many other possibilities where our product can be used in combination with many other products from other developers, which provides more value for end users than a single product does. This applies to any type of third-party integration and creates an ecosystem where all people benefit from taking part in that ecosystem by supporting each other.

We will use Amazon Alexa as the voice service in this chapter. If you want to learn more about how to develop with Amazon Alexa, you can find resources in the *Further reading* section.

In this chapter, we're going to cover the following main topics:

- Using voice assistants
- Integrating with Amazon Alexa
- Defining rules with IFTTT

Technical requirements

The chapter projects are located here: https://github.com/PacktPublishing/Internet-of-Things-with-ESP32/tree/main/ch11

We need developer accounts on AWS. The prerequisites section provides the links to the pages that explain how to create Alexa and AWS developer accounts, here: https://developer.amazon.com/en-US/docs/alexa/smarthome/steps-to-build-a-smart-home-skill.html#prerequisites.

We also need an IFTTT and a Google account for the last example of the chapter where we integrate ESP32 with the IFTTT service.

As hardware, we will use an ESP32 devkit and a DHT11 sensor. It would also be helpful to have an Alexa built-in device, such as Amazon Echo, but it is not mandatory to complete the example.

Check out the following video to see the code in action: https://bit.ly/2ST8ePW

Using voice assistants

Voice assistants provide another dimension in human-machine interaction. The classical means of interaction is to use a **graphical user interface (GUI)**. In addition to this, a voice assistant introduces a **voice user interface (VUI)**, where a user gives commands via voice and receives spoken responses. Although there are many enabler technologies, the modern voice assistant systems basically make use of **speech recognition**, **natural language processing (NLP)**, and **speech synthesis**. Today, we can find many voice assistant products on the market from tech giants, such as Google Assistant, Amazon Alexa, Apple Siri, and IBM Watson, which are all examples of voice assistant solutions.

How it works

The following diagram shows the main components of a voice solution:

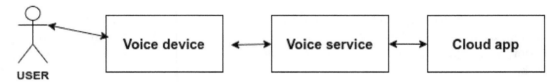

Figure 11.1 – Voice solution components

When a user says the wake word or phrase, for instance, **OK, Google**, it activates the voice device and then the voice device starts to capture the voice command. The device could be any hardware with a microphone and a speaker, such as a computer, a mobile phone, or a smart speaker. Then the device sends the audio data to the voice service where speech-to-text conversion happens. The NLP engine in the voice service tries to extract a command from the utterance. If it successfully matches the utterance to any available application in the user account, the command is forwarded to the cloud application to act on the command.

On the response side, the cloud application returns the result to the voice service in the form of text. The voice service converts the text to audio data by using speech synthesis techniques and sends the output audio back to the device to be played to the user.

In this chapter, we will see an example with Amazon Alexa. Before starting to develop, let's see what **Alexa Voice Service (AVS)** provides for developers.

Amazon Alexa concepts

In the Alexa nomenclature, a voice application is called a **skill**. As developers, we develop skills for our users and publish them on the Alexa Skills Store to be available publicly.

There are several skill types that we can choose from when we create a skill, for example, a custom skill or a smart home skill. Fundamentally, a skill has **intents**, which are user requests that our skill can respond to. We provide **sample utterances** of an intent as a guideline to AVS. An intent can have **slots**. We can think of a slot as a parameter of an intent that the user can fill up freely. When there are many slots in an intent, AVS can collect them by asking questions, thanks to **Alexa Conversations**. Alexa Conversations is an AI tool that uses deep learning to find out dialog paths. When AVS matches an intent successfully, the backend function is triggered for that intent. We implement what to do when an intent is matched. AVS provides the **Alexa Skills Kit (ASK)** SDK for this purpose. We use the ASK SDK to handle requests. Currently, the ASK SDK comes with three programming language options: Java, Node.js, and Python.

Let's discuss a sample utterance and its components. Let's say the user says the following:

Alexa, ask History Teacher what happened on January 10.

AVS looks for the **History Teacher** skill and whether there is any matching intent for this utterance in the skill. If it finds one, then the request handler is called for that intent with the slot value of **January 10**. In this example, History Teacher is the **invocation name** of the skill.

For more information about how to develop a custom skill, you can refer to the online documentation here: `https://developer.amazon.com/en-US/docs/alexa/custom-skills/understanding-custom-skills.html`.

A smart home skill is a specialized form of Alexa skill. The voice interaction model is ready to use in AVS, which means we don't need to think about intents or sample utterances, but simply integrate our device with AWS and develop a handler to be called by AVS when a request comes from the user. An example architecture for such a solution could be the following:

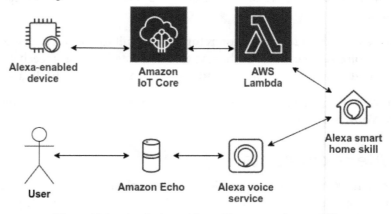

Figure 11.2 – A solution with an Alexa smart home skill

In this diagram, we use an Amazon Echo as the voice device to get commands from the user. If AVS matches the utterance to the Alexa smart home skill, it invokes the skill, which in turn calls the AWS Lambda function to get the state of the requested Alexa-enabled device, such as an ESP32 sensor. Amazon IoT Core sits between the Alexa-enabled device, for example, a temperature sensor, and the Lambda function, which retrieves the state of the temperature sensor from Amazon IoT Core. For example, let's say the user says the following:

Alexa, what is the temperature inside?

AVS will look for any enabled skill in the user account that can return this information. In this utterance, there is no invocation name of a skill. AVS still can discern that it is a valid utterance because there is a skill that can reply to temperature queries in the user account.

In the next section, we will get our hands dirty and implement an example integration together.

Integrating with Amazon Alexa

As we have discussed, AVS allows us to add voice features to our connected devices. When we integrate with AVS, ESP32 can report to voice commands and take action if it is commanded to do so. In this section, we will see how to develop an Alexa-enabled temperature sensor by using ESP32. Although developing the sensor firmware is a relatively easy task, creating an Alexa skill requires attention. The following is what we need to do:

1. Create a smart home skill in the Alexa development environment.

2. Create a Lambda function as the backend service of the smart home skill.

3. Link the Amazon account to the skill.

4. Enable the skill.

5. Create a thing in AWS IoT Core.

6. Develop the Lambda function.

7. Test the skill.

8. Develop the sensor firmware.

9. Test the project with voice commands.

There are many concepts to learn regarding Alexa development, which we are going to cover while we do all these steps one by one. Let's start with the smart home skill.

Creating the smart home skill

Unfortunately, the **Alexa Skills Kit Command Line Interface** (**ask-cli**) doesn't support smart home skills as of writing this book. Therefore, we are going to use a web-based development environment for this purpose. Let's do so in the following steps:

1. Navigate to the Alexa developer console and log in: `https://developer.amazon.com/alexa/console/ask`.

2. In the **Skills** tab, click on the **Create skill** button. It will open a page where we can enter the skill name and select the model of the new skill:

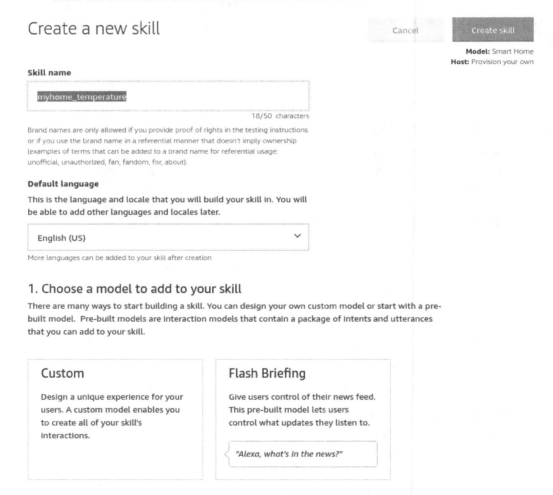

Figure 11.3 – The Create a new skill page

Enter the skill name as `myhome_temperature`, select **Smart Home** as the model, and click on the **Create skill** button on this page.

3. At this point, we have our smart home skill created and the configuration page opens:

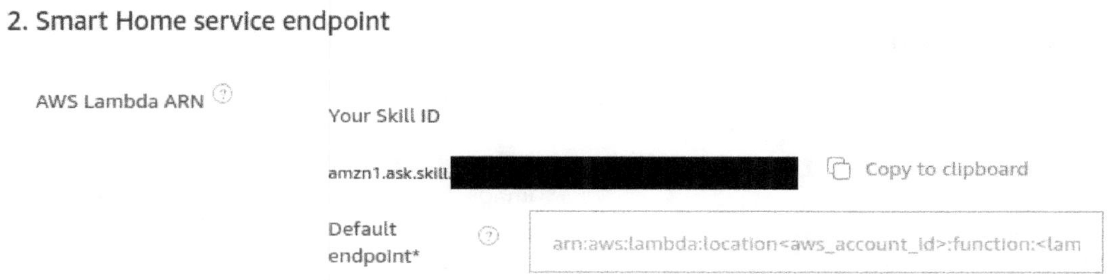

2. Smart Home service endpoint

AWS Lambda ARN ⓘ

Your Skill ID

amzn1.ask.skill▆▆▆▆▆▆▆▆▆▆▆▆▆▆▆▆▆▆▆▆▆▆▆▆▆▆   ⎘ Copy to clipboard

Default
endpoint*   ⓘ   arn:aws:lambda:location<aws_account_id>:function:<lam

Figure 11.4 – Endpoint configuration

The page contains the skill ID that we need during the Lambda function configuration and an input box to enter the Lambda function ARN to forward requests to. We'll keep this page open since we will return here when we have the Lambda function.

Let's create the Lambda function next.

Creating the Lambda function

We use a Lambda function to handle requests from the smart home skill. Here is how we create it:

1. Navigate to the AWS Management Console and log in: `https://aws.amazon.com/console/`.

2. Go to the Lambda functions service from **AWS Management Console** and click on the **Create function** button.

> **Important note**
> The region of the Lambda function matters. Please select the correct region for your Lambda function, as explained in the AWS documentation, here: `https://developer.amazon.com/en-US/docs/alexa/smarthome/develop-smart-home-skills-in-multiple-languages.html#deploy`. In my case, I have selected **eu-west-1** to host my Lambda function, but you may want to choose **us-east-1** or **us-west-2**.

On the next page, select **Author from scratch**, set **Function name** as myhome_
temperature_lambda, and set **Runtime** as **Python 3.8**. When we click on the
Create button at the end of the page, it will open the Lambda configuration:

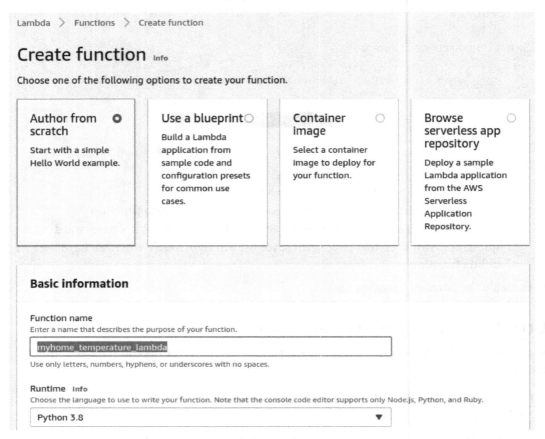

Figure 11.5 – The Create function page

3. Add a trigger by clicking on the + **Add trigger** button in the **Function overview**
    section of the Lambda configuration page after creating it. We select **Alexa Smart
    Home** in the search box and configure the trigger with the smart home skill ID:

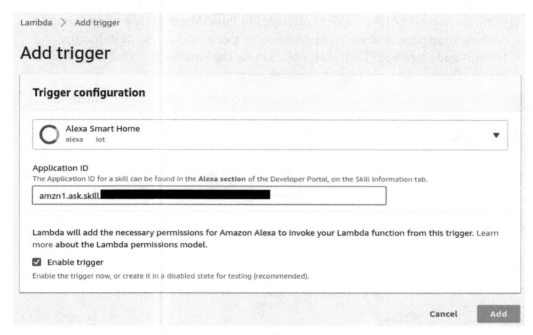

Figure 11.6 – Adding a trigger

Application ID is the smart home skill ID. You can copy it from the Alexa developer console, which we kept open. We click on the **Add** button to complete the trigger configuration.

4. We also need to specify the Lambda ARN on the smart home skill:

Figure 11.7 – The skill page with Default endpoint

Copy the Lambda ARN, which is displayed in **Function overview** of the Lambda configuration page, and go to the Alexa developer console to paste it into the **Default endpoint** box. Then save it by clicking the **Save** button. Our skill now knows where to forward requests by looking at the Lambda ARN.

5. Go back to the AWS Management Console to configure the Lambda function permissions. Navigate to **Configuration | Permissions | Execution role** and edit it by clicking on the **Role name** link:

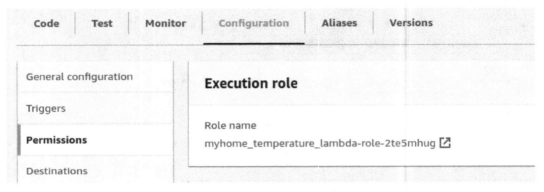

Figure 11.8 – Execution role

When we click on the **Role name** link, it navigates to IAM where we can set the policy for the Lambda function.

6. On the role page, we can see the policy of our Lambda function. Click on the name of the policy and then the **Edit policy** button to update the policy when the policy is displayed:

Figure 11.9 – The policy

7. On the next page, go to the **JSON** tab where we can edit this policy:

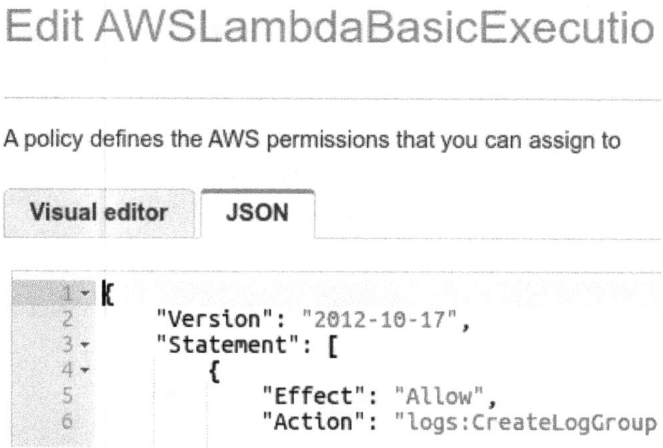

Edit AWSLambdaBasicExecutio

A policy defines the AWS permissions that you can assign to

Visual editor | **JSON**

```
1    {
2        "Version": "2012-10-17",
3        "Statement": [
4            {
5                "Effect": "Allow",
6                "Action": "logs:CreateLogGroup
```

Figure 11.10 – Edit policy in JSON format

8. Paste the following policy into the editor:

```json
{
    "Version": "2012-10-17",
    "Statement": [
        {
            "Effect": "Allow",
            "Action": [
                "logs:CreateLogStream",
                "logs:CreateLogGroup",
                "logs:PutLogEvents"
            ],
            "Resource": "*"
        },
        {
            "Effect": "Allow",
            "Action": [
                "iot:Connect",
                "iot:Receive",
                "iot:UpdateThingShadow",
                "iot:GetThingShadow"
            ],
```

```
                    "Resource": "arn:aws:iot:*:*:*"
            }
        ]
    }
```

This policy allows the Lambda function to write logs and to perform some IoT operations, including `UpdateThingShadow` and `GetThingShadow`. We will discuss what a shadow is later when creating a thing.

Click on the **Review** and **Save changes** buttons to finish the policy update.

We are done with the Lambda function for now. Account linking comes next.

Linking an Amazon account to the skill

We have the link between the Lambda function and the skill, but the skill still needs an authorized account for the purpose of testing. The process of providing an authorized account is called **Account Linking**. Here are the steps to do that:

1. Navigate to `https://developer.amazon.com/dashboard`.

2. Click on **Login with Amazon** on the page:

Figure 11.11 – Login with Amazon

3. Click on the **Create a New Security Profile** button:

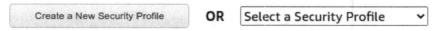

Figure 11.12 – Create a New Security Profile

4. Set the name as `myhome_sec_profile` and click on **Save**:

Name your new Security Profile

Choose a name for this security profile. You can create multiple security profiles. You
of data (for example, a "My App - Free" and a "My App - HD" could share data). For
More

* Indicates a required field

Security Profile Name *	myhome_sec_profile
Security Profile Description *	myhome_sec_profile
Consent Privacy Notice URL *	https://mevoo.co.uk
Consent Logo Image	UPLOAD IMAGE

Figure 11.13 – New security profile

5. We have a client ID and client secret for our skill now. We will enter these
credentials in the smart home skill:

Login with Amazon Configurations

Security Profile Name	OAuth2 Credentials
myhome_sec_profile	**Client ID:** amzn1.application-oa2-client.db
	Client Secret: ██████████████████

Figure 11.14 – OAuth2 Credentials

6. Go back to the Alexa developer console and navigate to the **Account Linking** page:

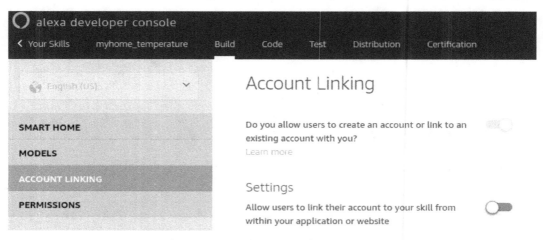

Figure 11.15 – The Account Linking page of the Alexa developer console

7. Fill in the form on this page with the credentials from the security profile. The values to be entered on this page are as follows:

a) **Your Web Authorization URI**: `https://www.amazon.com/ap/oa`

b) **Access Token URI**: `https://api.amazon.com/auth/o2/token`

c) **Your Client ID**: The client ID from the security profile

d) **Your Secret**: The client secret from the security profile

e) **Your Authentication Scheme**: `HTTP basic`

f) **Scope**: `profile:user_id`

Click on the **Save** button to send the form.

8. At the end of the **Account Linking** page, there are three **Alexa Redirect URLs**. As the name implies, the user is redirected to these links after the authorization process. We will share this information with the security profile:

Figure 11.16 – Alexa Redirect URLs

9. Return to the security profile page to enter these URLs. There is a **Manage** button on this page. Select **Web Settings** from the list:

Figure 11.17 – Web Settings selection

10. The web settings of the security profile are displayed on the screen. Click the **Edit** button and enter the redirect URLs there in the **Allowed Return URLs** box. After entering the URLs, click on **Save**:

Figure 11.18 – Allowed Return URLs for the security profile

This concludes account linking. Next, we will enable the skill in our Alexa user account.

Enabling the skill

Before any tests, we have to enable the skill in our Alexa user account. The steps are as follows:

1. Navigate to `https://alexa.amazon.com/` and log in.

2. Select **Skills | Your Skills** on the page and then go to the **DEV SKILLS** tab.

3. Our skill should be listed in **DEV SKILLS**:

Figure 11.19 – myhome_temperature skill

4. After selecting the skill, click the **ENABLE** button on the next page:

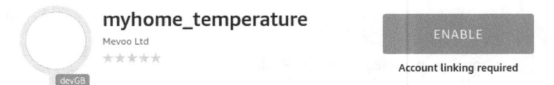

Figure 11.20 – The ENABLE button of the skill

5. The **ENABLE** button redirects to the Amazon login page. When we log in, it shows a success message:

myhome_temperature has been successfully linked.

What to do next:

→ Close this window to discover smart home devices you can control with Alexa.

Figure 11.21 – Linking is successful

6. Close the message page and return to the Alexa user account. Another message pops up to start the discovery process of the new Alexa device. However, it cannot succeed since we haven't implemented the Lambda function yet. So, we just cancel it:

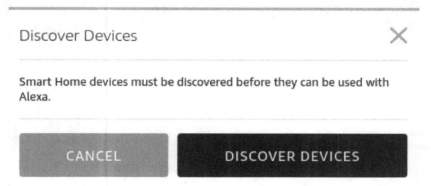

Figure 11.22 – The Discover Devices dialog

Now we have our skill enabled, it is time to add a thing in AWS IoT Core.

Creating a thing

We can create a new thing in AWS IoT Core either by using the AWS CLI tool or the web interface. This time, we are going to use the web interface. Let's do it step by step:

1. In the AWS Management Console, navigate to **AWS IoT | Manage | Things** and then click on the **Create** button. It opens a new page where we can create a single thing or create them in bulk. Click on **Create a single thing**:

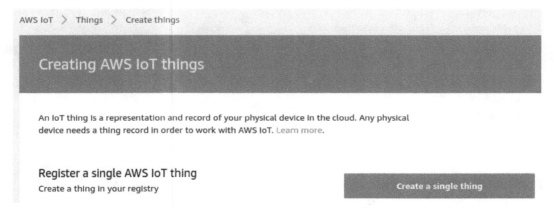

Figure 11.23 – Create a single thing

2. Name the device myhome_sensor1.

3. Create a certificate for it:

A certificate is used to authenticate your device's connection to AWS IoT.

One-click certificate creation (recommended)

This will generate a certificate, public key, and private key using AWS IoT's certificate authority.

Create certificate

Figure 11.24 – One-click certificate creation

4. Download all cryptographic keys and activate the certificate. We also need the root certificate for AWS IoT. The link is provided on the same page. After downloading all the keys, complete the process by clicking **Done**:

Certificate created!

Download these files and save them in a safe place. Certificates can be retrieved at any time, but the private and public keys cannot be retrieved after you close this page.

In order to connect a device, you need to download the following:

A certificate for this thing	0ea009c503.cert.pem	Download
A public key	0ea009c503.public.key	Download
A private key	0ea009c503.private.key	Download

You also need to download a root CA for AWS IoT:
A root CA for AWS IoT Download

Activate

Cancel   Done   Attach a policy

Figure 11.25 – Certificate created

Please keep the certificates in a secure place. We are going to use them when we develop the ESP32 sensor.

5. Create a new policy for the thing. The policy will specify the permissions for the thing. To do this, navigate to **Secure | Policies** and then click on the **Create** button:

Figure 11.26 – Policies

6. A form opens where we can enter policy statements. The values on the form are as follows:

a) **Name**: myhome_thing_policy

b) **Action**: iot:*

c) **Resource ARN**: arn:aws:iot:*:*:*

d) **Effect**: Allow

Then, continue by clicking on **Create**:

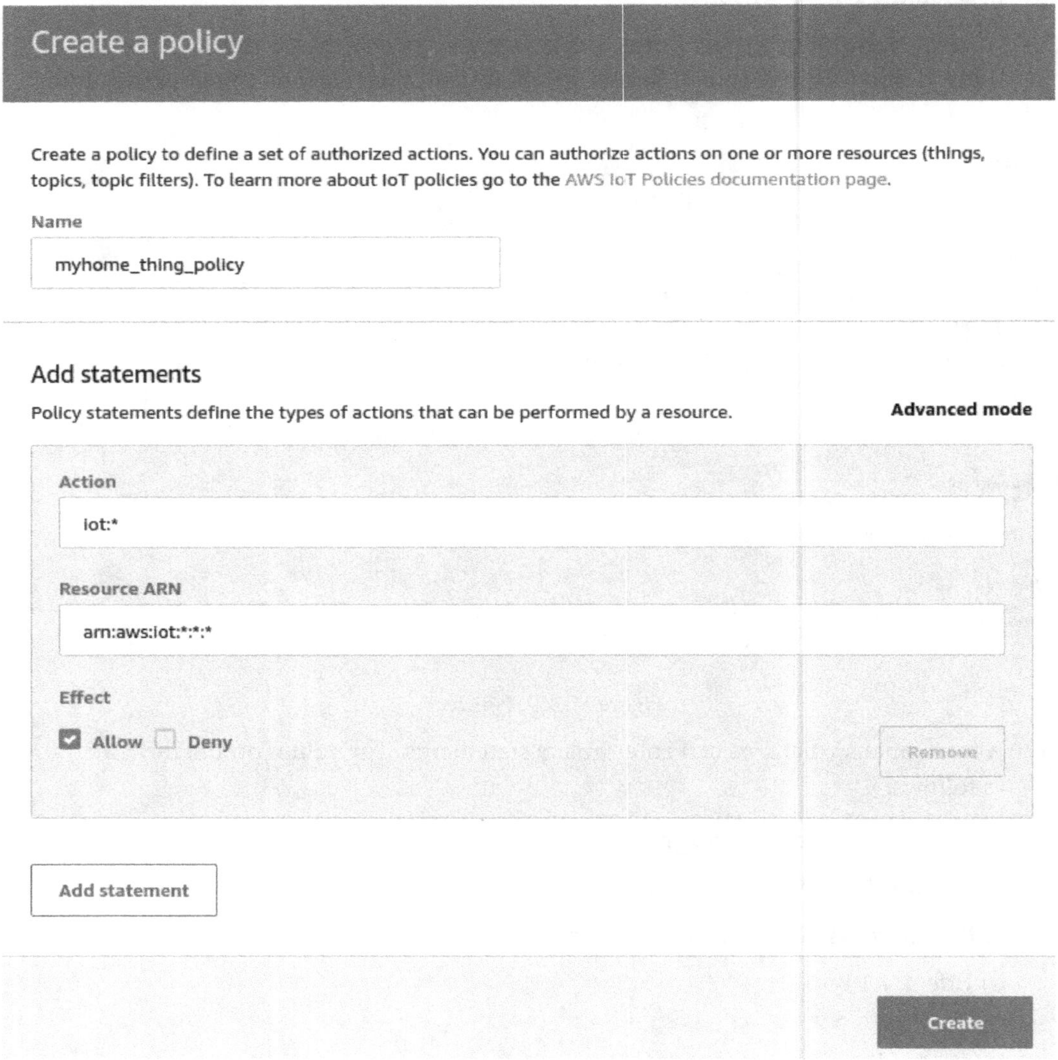

Create a policy

Create a policy to define a set of authorized actions. You can authorize actions on one or more resources (things, topics, topic filters). To learn more about IoT policies go to the AWS IoT Policies documentation page.

Name

myhome_thing_policy

Add statements

Policy statements define the types of actions that can be performed by a resource.   **Advanced mode**

Action

iot:*

Resource ARN

arn:aws:iot:*:*:*

Effect

☑ Allow ☐ Deny   Remove

Add statement

Create

Figure 11.27 – Create a policy

7. We need to associate the policy with the thing certificate. To do that, navigate to **Secure | Certificates** and select the certificate that we have created in *step 5*. Then, select **Actions | Attach policy** on the certificate details page:

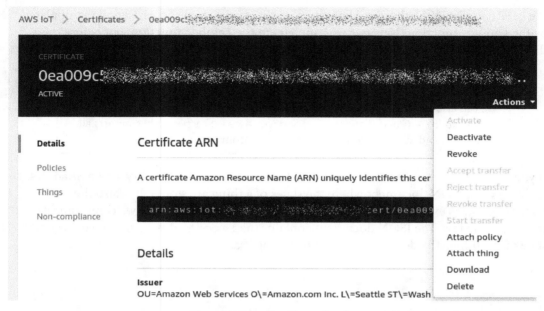

Figure 11.28 – Certificate details

8. In the pop-up window, select myhome_thing_policy and click on the **Attach** button:

Figure 11.29 – Attaching the policy

We have completed the thing configuration and it is ready to be accessed and manipulated by the Lambda function. Next, we will implement the Lambda function, but before this, there is an AWS IoT concept that we need to discuss.

> **Tip**
> We can also use the AWS CLI to create a new thing as we did in *Chapter 10, No Cloud, No IoT – Cloud Platforms and Services*. `aws-cli` perfectly supports all these steps and allows us to manage our things from the command line.

If you remember, we allowed the Lambda function to access and modify **Thing Shadows**. A shadow is a JSON document where the states of a thing are stored. It is also the document that is exchanged during any interaction with a thing when we communicate through a shadow. The JSON document contains the `reported` state and the `desired` state of the thing. The default shadow of our thing is as follows:

```
{
  "desired": {
    "welcome": "aws-iot"
  },
  "reported": {
    "welcome": "aws-iot"
  }
}
```

The idea is that we set the states of a shadow by using the `desired` group, and we get the states from the `reported` group.

Let's edit the shadow and add a new state in it for temperature:

1. Navigate to the thing by selecting **Manage | Things** from the left menu of AWS IoT and click on the thing name, `myhome_sensor1`.

2. Select **Shadows** from the left menu and **Classic Shadow** from the list:

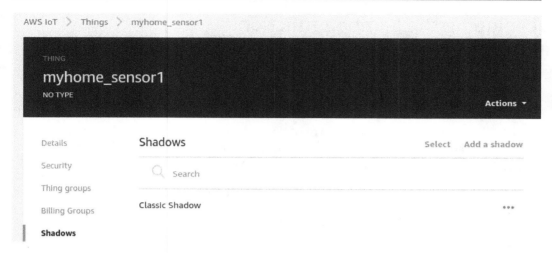

AWS IoT > Things > myhome_sensor1

THING

myhome_sensor1

NO TYPE

Actions ▾

Details	Shadows		Select	Add a shadow
Security				
Thing groups	Search			
Billing Groups	Classic Shadow			•••
Shadows				

Figure 11.30 – The Shadows list

3. Edit the shadow document by clicking on **Edit**. Add a new state in the document
    with a random temperature value. After the modification, we should have the
    following shadow:

Shadow Document

Delete   Edit

Last update: April 09, 2021, 21:15:59 (UTC+0100)

Shadow state:

```
{
  "desired": {
    "welcome": "aws-iot"
  },
  "reported": {
    "welcome": "aws-iot",
    "temperature": 20
  }
}
```

Figure 11.31 – Updated shadow document

Finally, we have a thing to use in our application. We are ready to develop the Lambda
function, which is the bridge between the thing and the Alexa smart home skill.

Developing the Lambda function

The Lambda function that we will develop in this section has two main purposes:

- Handling the discovery request from AVS
- Handling the GET requests for the temperature from the smart home skill

As usual, all these requests are in the form of JSON documents. The Lambda function will reply to a request by generating a JSON document that contains the information in a specific format as listed in the AWS documentation.

Let's see what these requests and responses are. The first one is the discovery request by AVS, as follows:

```
{
    "directive": {
        "header": {
            "namespace": "Alexa.Discovery",
            "name": "Discover",
            "payloadVersion": "3",
            "messageId": "1bd5d003-31b9-476f-ad03-71d471922820"
        },
        "payload": {
            "scope": {
                "type": "BearerToken",
                "token": "access-token-from-skill"
            }
        }
    }
}
```

The request has two parts: a header and a payload. We will check the name of the request in the header. If the name of the request is Discover, then we reply with a JSON document that contains the identification of our device.

> **Important note**
> Please take note of this JSON request. We are going to need it while testing the Lambda function.

Here is the response template for a discovery request:

```
{
    "event": {
        "header": {
            "namespace": "Alexa.Discovery",
            "name": "Discover.Response",
            "payloadVersion": "3",
            "messageId": "<message id>"
        },
```

In the header section of the response, we say it is a `Discover.Response` event. Then we add a payload to the response:

```
        "payload": {
            "endpoints": [{
                "endpointId": "myhome_sensor1",
                "manufacturerName": "iot-with-esp32",
                "description": "Smart temperature sensor",
                "friendlyName": "Temperature sensor",
                "displayCategories": ["TEMPERATURE_SENSOR"],
                "cookie": {},
```

A discovery response can have multiple endpoints. In our case, we have a single thing and therefore a single endpoint, which is myhome_sensor1. We also need to share the capabilities of the thing, as follows:

```
                "capabilities": [{
                    "type": "AlexaInterface",
                    "interface": "Alexa.TemperatureSensor",
                    "version": "3",
                    "properties": {
                        "supported": [{
                            "name": "temperature"
                        }],
                        "proactivelyReported": true,
                        "retrievable": true
                    }
                },
```

We list all capabilities of our thing. The first interface implemented by the thing is `Alexa.TemperatureSensor` and the thing has a property named `temperature` for this purpose. We had added this property to the thing's shadow. The next capability in the list is `Alexa.EndpointHealth`. This interface has to be implemented by all Alexa-enabled devices. Here is how we specify this interface:

```
                    {
                        "type": "AlexaInterface",
                        "interface": "Alexa.EndpointHealth",
                        "version": "3",
                        "properties": {
                            "supported": [{
                                "name": "connectivity"
                            }],
                            "proactivelyReported": true,
                            "retrievable": true
                        }
                    },
```

The last interface is `Alexa`, which is again a mandatory capability for all devices, as follows:

```
                    {
                        "type": "AlexaInterface",
                        "interface": "Alexa",
                        "version": "3"
                    }
                ]
            }]
        }
    }
}
```

After the discovery, AVS adds the skill to its database and whenever the user asks what the temperature is, AVS will forward this request to the smart home skill, which triggers the Lambda function in turn as we have configured it. Let's see what a temperature request looks like:

```json
{
  "directive": {
    "endpoint": {
      "cookie": {},
      "endpointId": "myhome_sensor1",
      "scope": {
        "token": "some_random_token_here",
        "type": "BearerToken"
      }
    },
    "header": {
      "correlationToken": "a_correlation_token_here",
      "messageId": "ad6578b0-0608-4963-9e28-7708942934be",
      "name": "ReportState",
      "namespace": "Alexa",
      "payloadVersion": "3"
    },
    "payload": {}
  }
}
```

In the endpoint section of the request, we specify the thing name as myhome_sensor1. The header contains the name of the request, which is a ReportState request.

> **Important note**
> This JSON request will also be used in the Lambda function tests. We will send it to the Lambda function and check whether it replies successfully.

When the Lambda function receives this message, it replies with a state report similar to the following:

```json
{
    "event": {
        "header": {
            "namespace": "Alexa",
            "name": "StateReport",
            "messageId": "<message id>",
            "correlationToken": "comes_from_request",
            "payloadVersion": "3"
        },
        "endpoint": {
            "endpointId": "myhome_sensor1"
        },
        "payload": {}
    },
```

In the response, we say it comes from `myhome_sensor1` and that it is a `StateReport` event. `correlationToken` connects this response to the request by setting the same value in the request. In the context section of the response, we return the temperature value from the thing:

```json
    "context": {
        "properties": [{
            "namespace": "Alexa.TemperatureSensor",
            "name": "temperature",
            "value": {
                "value": 20,
                "scale": "CELSIUS"
            },
            "timeOfSample": "2017-02-03T16:20:50.52Z",
            "uncertaintyInMilliseconds": 1000
        },
```

In the Lambda function, we will update value with whatever the thing has at that moment. The response also contains the health status as reported OK, as follows:

```
        {
            "namespace": "Alexa.EndpointHealth",
            "name": "connectivity",
            "value": {
                "value": "OK"
            },
            "timeOfSample": "2017-02-03T16:20:50.52Z",
            "uncertaintyInMilliseconds": 0
        }
      ]
    }
}
```

All these requests and responses may sound a bit confusing, but AWS has great documentation for all of them, here: https://developer.amazon.com/en-US/docs/alexa/device-apis/smart-home-general-apis.html.

We already set the Lambda function runtime to Python 3.8 while creating it, so we will develop in Python. You can use any editor for this purpose as well as VSCode.

With this background knowledge, we can implement the Lambda function as follows:

```
import logging
import time
import json
import uuid
import boto3

endpoint_id = "myhome_sensor1"
discovery_response = {
...
state_report = {
...
accept_grant_response = {
...
```

We start by importing some Python modules. The notable one is `boto3`. It is the Python SDK for AWS. We access all AWS services by using `boto3`. After the modules, we define the global variables. `endpoint_id` shows the thing name. The other three globals are the templates of the responses from the Lambda function. We have already discussed `discovery_response` and `state_report`. `accept_grant_response` is new. It is used when we need to send asynchronous messages or change reports. Although we are not going to implement change reports in this Lambda function, it is possible to notify AVS of any changes in temperature. We have more global variables, as follows:

```
logger = logging.getLogger()
logger.setLevel(logging.INFO)
client = boto3.client('iot-data')
```

`logger` and `client` are another two global variables. We will use `client` to retrieve the temperature value from the thing.

> **Tip**
> It is a best practice to define any client objects globally in serverless development. The execution environment reuses them for Lambda invocations, which increases the performance and reduces the cost. You can find other best practices here: https://docs.aws.amazon.com/lambda/latest/dg/best-practices.html

`lambda_handler` is the Python function that handles the requests from AVS. We define `lambda_handler` next:

```
def lambda_handler(request, context):
    try:
        logger.info("Directive:")
        logger.info(json.dumps(request, indent=4, sort_
keys=True))

        version = get_directive_version(request)
        response = ""
        if version != "3":
            logger.error("not a version 3 request")
            return response
```

We first check whether the request directive version is 3. The version number indicates the JSON schema of the messages. The latest one is 3 as of writing this book. The handler function filters out older versions. Then, we select the request namespace and request name to arrange an appropriate response accordingly, as in the following code snippet:

```
        request_namespace = request["directive"]["header"]
["namespace"]
        request_name = request["directive"]["header"]["name"]
```

Now, we can generate a response for the request:

```
        if request_namespace == "Alexa.Discovery" and request_
name == "Discover":
            response = gen_discovery_response()
        elif request_namespace == "Alexa" and request_name ==
"ReportState":
            response = gen_report_state(request["directive"]
["header"]["correlationToken"])
        elif request_namespace == "Alexa.Authorization" and
request_name == "AcceptGrant":
            response = gen_acceptgrant_response()
        else:
            logger.error("unexpected request")
        return response
```

We generate and send responses according to the request type. We will develop the helper functions used here after lambda_handler. Before returning, we print the response or any errors in the logs for debugging purposes:

```
        logger.info("Response:")
        logger.info(json.dumps(response, indent=4, sort_
keys=True))

        return response

    except ValueError as error:
        logger.error(error)
        raise
```

CloudWatch is the service where all diagnostic messages are collected. Therefore, we go to CloudWatch when we want to see the logs from the Lambda function execution. This ends the `lambda_handler` function. Let's discuss the important helper functions briefly:

```
def gen_report_state(tkn):
    response = state_report
    response["event"]["header"]["messageId"] = get_uuid()
    response["event"]["header"]["correlationToken"] = tkn
    response["context"]["properties"][0]["timeOfSample"] = get_
utc_timestamp()
    response["context"]["properties"][1]["timeOfSample"] = get_
utc_timestamp()
    response["context"]["properties"][0]["value"]["value"] =
read_temp_thing()
    return response
```

In `gen_report_state`, we prepare a state report when `lambda_handler` receives a state report request. The response contains both the temperature value and the endpoint health as we discussed before. We also set the correlation token that matches the request. Let's see what we have in `read_temp_thing`:

```
def read_temp_thing():
    response = client.get_thing_shadow(thingName=endpoint_id)
    streamingBody = response["payload"].read().decode('utf-8')
    jsonState = json.loads(streamingBody)
    return jsonState["state"]["reported"]["temperature"]
```

This function gets the temperature value from the thing's shadow and returns it. We use the `client` variable, which we have defined globally, to access the shadow.

There are several other helper functions, but they are too boring to include here. You can find the complete source code at this link: https://github.com/PacktPublishing/Internet-of-Things-with-ESP32/blob/main/ch11/alexa_sensor/aws/lambda_function.py.

We are done with developing the Lambda handler. Let's deploy it and then test it step by step:

1. In the AWS Management Console, navigate to the Lambda function that we created before. Click on the `lambda_function.py` file and paste the code that we have just developed. Then, deploy the code by clicking on the **Deploy** button. When the deployment finishes, we see the message **Changes deployed** on the UI:

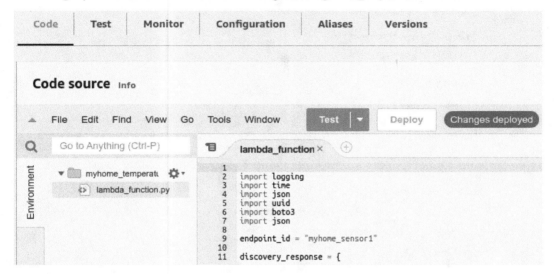

Figure 11.32 – The function is deployed

2. We will create two test events. One is for the discovery, and the other one is for the state report. We will test the Lambda function by sending the test events and see the results. When we click on the **Test** dropdown, it shows a menu. Select **Configure test event**:

Figure 11.33 – Configure test event

3. In the pop-up window, create a new test event with the name `discoverRequest`.
    It is a discovery request that we discussed at the beginning of this section. Paste the
    discovery JSON message into the box and click on the **Create** button:

Figure 11.34 – A new test event

4. After creating the test event, select the test from the **Test** drop-down menu and click
    on the **Test** button:

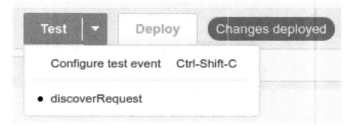

Figure 11.35 – Selection of discoverRequest from the dropdown

5. The **Execution results** tab opens. We can see the response and the logs by scrolling down in the tab:

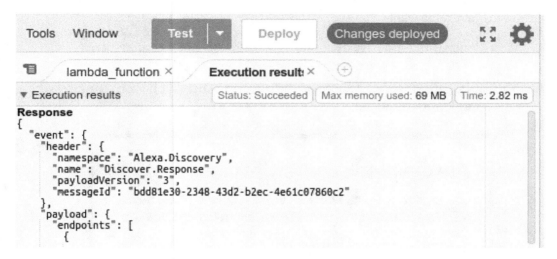

Figure 11.36 – Execution results

6. Repeat *steps 2* to *5* for the state reporting. Create another test event, name it `stateReportRequest`, and paste the JSON message that we discussed at the beginning. The value of `endpointId` should be `myhome_sensor1` in the test event message. When we see the **Succeeded** message on the **Execution results** tab, it means that the Lambda handler has successfully parsed the request and replied with a response.

> **Tip**
> If the execution fails, we can see the error logs in the **Execution results** tab. All the log messages are also collected in the CloudWatch service and we can check CloudWatch any time we want to see them.

We know that the Lambda function works now, so we can test the smart home skill.

Testing the skill

Since we have the Lambda function ready as the backend service of the smart home skill, we are ready to test the whole cloud setup. Let's do it in the following steps:

1. We will start with the device discovery first. Go to our Alexa account here: `https://alexa.amazon.com/`.

2. Navigate to **Smart Home | Devices** and click on the **Discover** button. The discovery pop-up window is displayed:

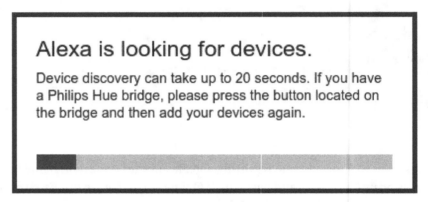

Figure 11.37 – Discovery popup

3. If we completed all the previous steps correctly, we should see the temperature sensor at the end of the discovery process:

Figure 11.38 – The temperature sensor is discovered

4. Go to the Alexa developer console at `https://developer.amazon.com/ alexa/console/ask` and navigate to our skill, `myhome_temperature`. From the top menu, we click on **Test**.

5. We will use the Alexa simulator for testing. We can either write the utterance or use the microphone of our development PC to test the skill. Ask the temperature by writing `what is the temperature inside` in the simulator input box:

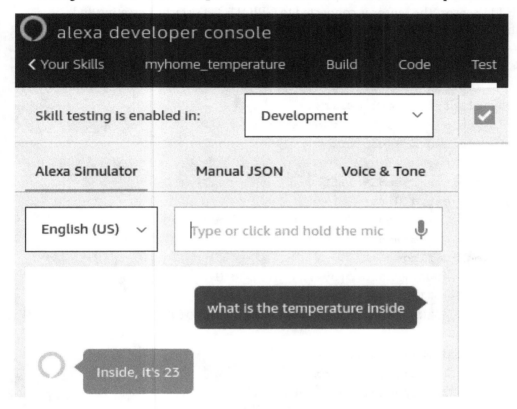

Figure 11.39 – Using the Alexa simulator

> **Tip**
> We can try other utterances such as "the temperature inside" or "tell me the temperature inside." AVS will forward all these queries to our smart home skill. Another test case would be updating the temperature to another value in the thing's shadow and asking Alexa the temperature again to see whether it returns the updated value.

It seems that everything works so far. The next task is to develop the ESP32 firmware.

Developing the firmware

The goal of this development is to measure the ambient temperature and update the thing's shadow with the latest temperature data. We will use our ESP32 devkit with a DHT11 sensor. The sensor is connected to GPIO17. Let's start by creating and configuring a PlatformIO project. Here is how we can do this:

1. Create a project with the following `platformio.ini` file:

```
[env:az-delivery-devkit-v4]
platform = espressif32
board = az-delivery-devkit-v4
framework = espidf

monitor_speed = 115200
lib_extra_dirs =
    ../../common/esp-idf-lib/components
    ../common
build_flags =
    -DWIFI_SSID=${sysenv.WIFI_SSID}
    -DWIFI_PASS=${sysenv.WIFI_PASS}
    -DAWS_ENDPOINT=${sysenv.AWS_ENDPOINT}

board_build.embed_txtfiles =
    ./tmp/private.pem.key
    ./tmp/certificate.pem.crt
    ./tmp/AmazonRootCA1.pem
```

The DHT11 library is in the `../../common/esp-idf-lib/components` folder, and the helper libraries of the chapter are in `../common`.

We define some macros. They are the Wi-Fi credentials and the AWS endpoint to be connected. The values come from the corresponding environment variables.

We will also embed the cryptographic files in the firmware. They will be located under the `tmp` folder. We don't want them exposed in the GitHub repository, so they are in `tmp`, which is itself in the `.gitignore` list.

2. Find the AWS endpoint by using the AWS CLI tool:

```
$ aws iot describe-endpoint --endpoint-type iot:Data-ATS
{
```

```
        "endpointAddress": "XXXXX.iot.<region>.amazonaws.com"
  }
```

3. Activate the virtual environment for the `pio` tool and set the environment variables of the Wi-Fi credentials and the AWS endpoint:

```
$ source ~/.platformio/penv/bin/activate
(penv)$ export WIFI_SSID='\"<your_ssid>\"'
(penv)$ export WIFI_PASS='\"<your_passwd>\"'
(penv)$ export AWS_ENDPOINT='\"<your_endpoint>\"'
```

4. We need the AWS device SDK port of Espressif in our project. It is in the global common directory of components. Add the AWS device SDK to the list of extra components directory in the project by editing `CMakeLists.txt` in the project root:

```
cmake_minimum_required(VERSION 3.16.0)
list(APPEND EXTRA_COMPONENT_DIRS "../../common/
components/esp-aws-iot")
include($ENV{IDF_PATH}/tools/cmake/project.cmake)
project(aws_ex)
```

5. Copy the cryptographic files into the temporary directory and rename them:

```
(penv)$ mkdir tmp && cp <crpyto_dir>/* tmp/
# rename them
(penv)$ ls -1 tmp/
AmazonRootCA1.pem
certificate.pem.crt
private.pem.key
public.pem.key
```

6. Since we will embed the cryptographic files in the firmware, we tell ESP-IDF about this in `src/CMakeList.txt`. Edit the file with the following content:

```
FILE(GLOB_RECURSE app_sources ${CMAKE_SOURCE_DIR}/
src/*.*)
set(COMPONENT_ADD_INCLUDEDIRS ".")

idf_component_register(SRCS ${app_sources})
```

```
target_add_binary_data(${COMPONENT_TARGET} "../tmp/
AmazonRootCA1.pem" TEXT)
```

```
target_add_binary_data(${COMPONENT_TARGET} "../tmp/
certificate.pem.crt" TEXT)
```

```
target_add_binary_data(${COMPONENT_TARGET} "../tmp/
private.pem.key" TEXT)
```

7. We create an `sdkconfig.defaults` file with the following content. Delete any `sdkconfig` file to force PlatformIO to re-create a new one with the defaults that we provide:

```
CONFIG_MBEDTLS_ASYMMETRIC_CONTENT_LEN=y
```

ESP-IDF uses MbedTLS as the default cryptographic library. This option of MbedTLS needs to be set in `sdkconfig`.

8. When we have all the files in place, we should have the following files:

```
(penv)$ ls -R
.:
CMakeLists.txt  include  lib  platformio.ini  sdkconfig.
defaults  src  test  tmp
./src:
CMakeLists.txt  main.c
./tmp:
AmazonRootCA1.pem  certificate.pem.crt  private.pem.key
public.pem.key
```

9. Compile at this point to see whether the entire configuration is correct. The compilation should generate the project's `sdkconfig` file as well:

```
(penv)$ pio run
```

The project configuration is completed. We can now start to work on the source code in `tmp/main.c`:

```
#include <string.h>
#include <stdbool.h>
#include <stdlib.h>
#include "freertos/FreeRTOS.h"
#include "freertos/task.h"
#include "esp_log.h"
```

```
#include "app_temp.h"
#include "app_wifi.h"

#include "aws_iot_config.h"
#include "aws_iot_log.h"
#include "aws_iot_version.h"
#include "aws_iot_mqtt_client_interface.h"
#include "aws_iot_shadow_interface.h"

#define TAG "app"
```

We include the header files first. aws_iot_* files come from the AWS device SDK. To update the thing's shadow, we are going to use the functions in aws_iot_shadow_interface.h. Next, we define the globals:

```
extern const uint8_t aws_root_ca_pem_start[] asm("_binary_
AmazonRootCA1_pem_start");
extern const uint8_t aws_root_ca_pem_end[] asm("_binary_
AmazonRootCA1_pem_end");
extern const uint8_t certificate_pem_crt_start[] asm("_binary_
certificate_pem_crt_start");
extern const uint8_t certificate_pem_crt_end[] asm("_binary_
certificate_pem_crt_end");
extern const uint8_t private_pem_key_start[] asm("_binary_
private_pem_key_start");
extern const uint8_t private_pem_key_end[] asm("_binary_
private_pem_key_end");

static char endpoint_address[] = AWS_ENDPOINT;
static char client_id[] = "myhome_sensor1_cl";
static char thing_name[] = "myhome_sensor1";

static AWS_IoT_Client aws_client;
```

We have access to the cryptographic keys with the help of extern definitions. They point to the key start and end addresses. Then, we define the AWS-related globals. They are the AWS endpoint address, the thing name, the AWS client, and a client ID.

Let's jump into the `app_main` function to see how the story starts:

```
static void handle_wifi_connect(void)
{
    xTaskCreate(connect_shadow, "connect_shadow", 15 *
configMINIMAL_STACK_SIZE, NULL, 5, NULL);
    apptemp_init(publish_reading);
}

static void handle_wifi_failed(void)
{
    ESP_LOGE(TAG, "wifi failed");
}

void app_main()
{
    connect_wifi_params_t cbs = {
        .on_connected = handle_wifi_connect,
        .on_failed = handle_wifi_failed};
    appwifi_connect(cbs);
}
```

When the Wi-Fi is connected, we create a task to connect to AWS IoT Core. The task function is `connect_shadow`, to be scheduled by FreeRTOS. We also provide a callback function, `publish_reading`, to the DHT library so that when it reads from DHT11, it calls `publish_reading` to update the thing's shadow with the latest temperature data. We implement `connect_shadow` as follows:

```
static void connect_shadow(void *param)
{
    memset((void *)&aws_client, 0, sizeof(aws_client));

    ShadowInitParameters_t sp = ShadowInitParametersDefault;
    sp.pHost = endpoint_address;
    sp.port = AWS_IOT_MQTT_PORT;
    sp.pClientCRT = (const char *)certificate_pem_crt_start;
    sp.pClientKey = (const char *)private_pem_key_start;
    sp.pRootCA = (const char *)aws_root_ca_pem_start;
```

```
    sp.disconnectHandler = disconnected_handler;


    aws_iot_shadow_init(&aws_client, &sp);
```

We call `aws_iot_shadow_init` to initialize the AWS client. It also takes a parameter with the initialization information, such as the AWS endpoint address, the MQTT port, and the cryptographic keys. Thing shadows are also communicated via MQTT. AWS IoT Core provides a special group of topics for this purpose. The AWS device SDK abstracts all MQTT access for us with simple function calls, but if you want to learn more about the shadow topics, they are listed here: `https://docs.aws.amazon.com/iot/latest/developerguide/device-shadow-mqtt.html`.

After the client initialization, we connect to the thing's shadow:

```
    ShadowConnectParameters_t scp =
ShadowConnectParametersDefault;
    scp.pMyThingName = thing_name;
    scp.pMqttClientId = client_id;
    scp.mqttClientIdLen = (uint16_t)strlen(client_id);


    while (aws_iot_shadow_connect(&aws_client, &scp) !=
SUCCESS)
    {
        ESP_LOGW(TAG, "trying to connect");
        vTaskDelay(1000 / portTICK_PERIOD_MS);
    }
```

The function for connecting to the shadow is `aws_iot_shadow_connect`. This function needs the name of the thing to connect and the MQTT client ID that we defined at the beginning. Until it succeeds, we call the function in a `while` loop. Finally, `aws_iot_shadow_yield` runs in another loop to collect incoming messages and keep the connection alive, as follows:

```
    while (1)
    {
        aws_iot_shadow_yield(&aws_client, 100);
        vTaskDelay(1000 / portTICK_PERIOD_MS);
    }
}
```

Let's see how we implement the `publish_reading` function next:

```
static void publish_reading(int temp, int hum)
{
    jsonStruct_t temp_json = {
        .cb = NULL,
        .pKey = "temperature",
        .pData = &temp,
        .type = SHADOW_JSON_INT32,
        .dataLength = sizeof(temp) };
```

We first define a JSON structure to describe the temperature data. It shows which property of the thing is to be updated along with the new value. Then, we prepare the JSON document:

```
    char jsondoc_buffer[200];
    aws_iot_shadow_init_json_document(jsondoc_buffer,
sizeof(jsondoc_buffer));
    aws_iot_shadow_add_reported(jsondoc_buffer, sizeof(jsondoc_
buffer), 1, &temp_json);
    aws_iot_finalize_json_document(jsondoc_buffer,
sizeof(jsondoc_buffer));
```

There are some helper functions in the AWS device SDK to convert a JSON description structure into JSON text data. We initialize the designated buffer first, and then call `aws_iot_shadow_add_reported` to append the data in the buffer. Finally, we simply update the shadow by calling the `aws_iot_shadow_update` function, as in the following code snippet:

```
    aws_iot_shadow_update(&aws_client, thing_name, jsondoc_
buffer, NULL, NULL, 4, true);
}
```

The last callback function is `disconnected_handler`:

```
static void disconnected_handler(AWS_IoT_Client *pClient, void
*data)
{
    ESP_LOGW(TAG, "reconnecting...");
}
```

In `disconnected_handler`, we only print a warning message on the serial console. The AWS IoT client will automatically connect if it somehow disconnects from AWS IoT Core by default.

This was the last piece of code after a long development. Now, we have all the pieces in a complete smart home skill. We flash the application into the ESP32 devkit and then test the skill:

```
(penv)$ pio run -t upload && pio device monitor
```

To test the skill, we can either use the Alexa simulator or any Alexa built-in device such as Amazon Echo. Here is the screenshot from testing with the Alexa simulator:

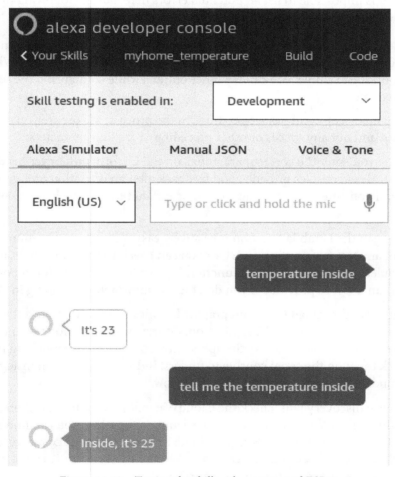

Figure 11.40 – Testing the skill with a connected ESP32

Congratulations! We have just completed a long journey with Alexa. We have covered the whole development cycle; however, when we want to share the skill with our users, we have to certify it through the Alexa certification process. To learn how this is done, the best resource is the Alexa documentation, available here: `https://developer.amazon.com/en-US/docs/alexa/devconsole/test-and-submit-your-skill.html`.

Troubleshooting

Integration with AVS requires many steps to complete the example successfully, and it is quite easy to miss a point that could cause a headache during the integration work. Unfortunately, it is impossible to list all potential errors here, but the following tips can help you to save some time while working on the example:

- If you don't have any previous experience with AWS cloud development, make sure you follow the steps in the exact order, exactly as described in each step. When you have a working example, you can try other options while configuring the services to discover more.

- There are many copy and paste operations in the process. Make sure you copy the exact text, and not any spaces or other preceding or trailing characters.

- Make sure you enter the correct parameters on the UI forms wherever needed. The AWS and Alexa consoles provide good feedback after an operation or configuration; however, if you enter a wrong value, it can be difficult to detect where the problem is.

- The testing of the Lambda function is relatively easy. You can see the immediate output of any test run on the web UI, or you can check **CloudWatch** logs, as well. The complete code of the Lambda function is provided in the GitHub repository, and you can use it as provided if you don't feel comfortable developing in Python.

- Make sure you download the cryptographic key files when you create a thing, and use the same keys in the ESP32 application. Otherwise, ESP32 won't connect to the AWS cloud. You can also modify the application code by adding more log messages and check them on the serial console to understand what is going on inside if ESP32 cannot update the corresponding thing's shadow.

- If the device discovery fails, check the CloudWatch logs. If nothing is there, you can try different AWS regions to host your Lambda function. You can find more information regarding the AWS regions here: `https://developer.amazon.com/en-US/docs/alexa/smarthome/develop-smart-home-skills-in-multiple-languages.html#deploy`.

The next section is about how we integrate ESP32 with another online service, IFTTT.

Defining rules with IFTTT

IFTTT is an online rule engine for any type of application, including IoT projects. We basically define a trigger (if this) and an action (then that). In this example, we will create a webhook on IFTTT, where our ESP32 device publishes temperature readings, and the IFTTT service will record the incoming readings on a Google spreadsheet. As hardware, we simply connect a DHT11 sensor to GPIO17 of the ESP32 devkit. Let's start by defining a rule on IFTTT first.

Preparing the rule

There are several tasks that we need to do at this stage. Here are the steps:

1. Create a Google account if you don't have one and navigate to Google Drive at `https://drive.google.com`.

2. Create a new folder named `ifttt` on Google Drive and a spreadsheet in it, `temperature_log`.

3. Go to `https://ifttt.com` and log in. Then, navigate to `https://ifttt.com/create` to create a new **applet**. An applet is the IFTTT term for a rule. In the free plan, we can create up to three applets:

Figure 11.41 – Creating an IFTTT applet

4. Click on **If This** to add a trigger and search webhook on the next page. Then, set the trigger as **Receive a web request**:

Choose a service

Q   web hook

Webhooks

Figure 11.42 – Choosing Webhooks as the service

5. The configuration page opens. Write down the event name as temperature_ received and click on the **Create trigger** button:

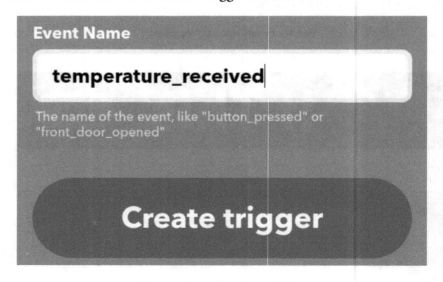

Event Name

temperature_received

The name of the event, like "button_pressed" or "front_door_opened"

Create trigger

Figure 11.43 – Creating a trigger

6. Next, we will add the action. To do that, click on **Then That**. Choose **Google Sheets** as the service this time and **Add row to spreadsheet** as the action:

Choose a service

Q   **google sheets**

Google Sheets

Figure 11.44 – Google Sheets as the service

7. Then the action configuration page opens. Provide the spreadsheet name, row format, and Drive folder as the following and click on **Create action**:

a) **Spreadsheet name**: `temperature_log`

b) **Formatted row**: `{{OccurredAt}} ||| {{Value1}}`

c) **Drive folder path**: `ifttt`:

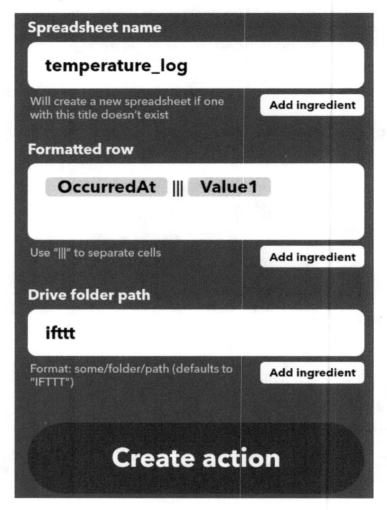

Figure 11.45 – Creating the action

The format describes what we want on the spreadsheet. The first column will have the timestamp and the temperature value will be shown in the second column. After creating the action, we click on the **Continue** button on the next page.

8. Set the applet title to `If temperature_received, then log` and click on the **Finish** button to complete the configuration:

Figure 11.46 – The applet is ready

9. Now, we need the webhook key to construct the URL where we will do POST requests. Go to `https://ifttt.com/maker_webhooks` and click on the **Documentation** button. It opens the page where we can find all the information about the webhook. Make a note of the key since we will need it when developing the firmware:

Figure 11.47 – The webhook key

10. Before moving on to the firmware, we test the applet by using the `curl` tool to make sure everything is properly configured. Let's send a request to the IFTTT endpoint:

```
$ curl -X POST -H "Content-Type: application/json"
-d '{"value1":"0"}' https://maker.ifttt.com/trigger/
temperature_received/with/key/<your_key>
```

```
Congratulations! You've fired the temperature_received
event
```

The request is successful. Let's check whether the Google spreadsheet has the record:

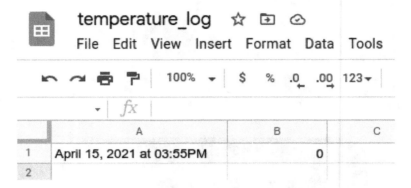

Figure 11.48 – The test log on the spreadsheet

Nice! The IFTTT rule is ready and we can continue with the firmware.

Developing the firmware

In the firmware, we will simply read from DHT11 and do POST requests to the IFTTT endpoint, the same as curl does. Let's start by creating a new PlatformIO project. Here are the steps:

1. Create a new project with the following platformio.ini file:

```
[env:az-delivery-devkit-v4]
platform = espressif32
board = az-delivery-devkit-v4
framework = espidf

monitor_speed = 115200
lib_extra_dirs =
    ../../common/esp-idf-lib/components
    ../common

build_flags =
    -DWIFI_SSID=${sysenv.WIFI_SSID}
    -DWIFI_PASS=${sysenv.WIFI_PASS}
```

```
      -DIFTTT_KEY=${sysenv.IFTTT_KEY}
```

```
board_build.embed_txtfiles =
    src/server_cert.pem
```

We set the macros for the Wi-Fi SSID, password, and the IFTTT key from the environment variables. We will download and keep the IFTTT server certificate in src/server_cert.pem, which will be used during the TLS handshake.

2. Download the IFTTT server certificate and save it in the src/server_cert. pem file:

```
$ openssl s_client -showcerts -connect maker.ifttt.
com:443
```

This command shows all the certificates in the trust chain of maker.ifttt.com. We only need the last one.

3. Edit src/CMakeList.txt to tell ESP-IDF about the server certificate to be embedded in the firmware:

```
FILE(GLOB_RECURSE app_sources ${CMAKE_SOURCE_DIR}/
src/*.*)
idf_component_register(SRCS ${app_sources})
target_add_binary_data(${COMPONENT_TARGET} "./server_
cert.pem" TEXT)
```

4. Activate the virtual environment and define the environment variables:

```
$ source ~/.platformio/penv/bin/activate
(penv)$ export WIFI_SSID='\"<ssid>\"'
(penv)$ export WIFI_PASS='\"<passwd>\"'
(penv)$ export IFTTT_KEY='\"<your_key>\"'
```

Now, we can discuss the application code in src/main.c:

```
#include <string.h>
#include <stdbool.h>
#include <stdlib.h>
#include "freertos/FreeRTOS.h"
#include "freertos/task.h"
#include "freertos/queue.h"
#include "esp_log.h"
```

```
#include "private_include/esp_tls_mbedtls.h"

#include "app_temp.h"
#include "app_wifi.h"
```

We start by including the headers as usual. Then, we define the macros and globals:

```
#define TAG "app"
#define IFTTT_MAKER_URL "https://maker.ifttt.com"

#define QUEUE_SIZE 10
static QueueHandle_t temp_queue;

static const char REQUEST[] = "POST /trigger/temperature_
received/with/key/" IFTTT_KEY " HTTP/1.1\r\n"
"Host: maker.ifttt.com\r\n"
"Content-Type: application/json\r\n"
"Content-Length: %d\r\n"
"\r\n"
"%s";
static const char JSON_DATA[] = "{\"value1\":\"%d\"}";

extern const uint8_t server_root_cert_pem_start[] asm("_binary_
server_cert_pem_start");
extern const uint8_t server_root_cert_pem_end[] asm("_binary_
server_cert_pem_end");
```

We will send the requests to IFTTT_MAKER_URL. REQUEST is the format string that shows the POST request with placeholders. IFTTT_KEY in REQUEST comes from the environment variable. The POST endpoint also includes the event name, temperature_received, which we specified while configuring the IFTTT rule. JSON_DATA is another format string that has a placeholder for temperature. We will apply the producer/consumer pattern to process temperature readings. temp_queue is the global variable for this purpose. Its type is QueueHandle_t, which is declared in freertos/queue.h. We also define the start and end addresses of the server certificate. Let's discuss app_main and the Wi-Fi callbacks next, in order to see the overall execution:

```
static void handle_wifi_connect(void)
{
```

```
    xTaskCreate(do_post, "post_task", 15 * configMINIMAL_STACK_
SIZE, NULL, 5, NULL);
    apptemp_init(publish_reading);
}

static void handle_wifi_failed(void)
{
    ESP_LOGE(TAG, "wifi failed");
}

void app_main()
{
    temp_queue = xQueueCreate(QUEUE_SIZE, sizeof(int16_t));
    connect_wifi_params_t cbs = {
        .on_connected = handle_wifi_connect,
        .on_failed = handle_wifi_failed};
    appwifi_connect(cbs);
}
```

In app_main, we first create the queue by calling xQueueCreate. temp_queue can hold QUEUE_SIZE (10) items of int16_t. When Wi-Fi is connected, we start a FreeRTOS task in which we post the readings and set publish_reading as the callback, which is to be called when a new reading is ready from DHT11. In this design, publish_reading is the producer and it pushes temperature readings to the back of the queue. do_post is the consumer and it removes the readings from the front of the queue. Let's implement publish_reading next:

```
static void publish_reading(int temp, int hum)
{
    if (xQueueSendToBack(temp_queue, (void *)&temp,
(TickType_t)0) != pdPASS)
    {
        ESP_LOGW(TAG, "queue is full");
        xQueueReset(temp_queue);
    }
}
```

xQueueSendToBack is the FreeRTOS function that we use to push a reading to the queue. If the queue is full, we call xQueueReset to discard old readings and make room for new readings. A FreeRTOS queue is thread-safe, so we don't need any guard or mutex mechanism to protect the queue from concurrent access. Now, we can discuss do_post:

```
static void do_post(void *arg)
{
    esp_tls_cfg_t cfg = {
        .cacert_buf = server_root_cert_pem_start,
        .cacert_bytes = server_root_cert_pem_end - server_root_
cert_pem_start,
    };

    int16_t temp;
    char json_data[32];
    char request[256];
    char reply[512];
```

In do_post, we start with a configuration variable for the TLS communication. We provide it with the server certificate information. Then we define other local variables for temperature reading and the buffers. Next, we define a while loop to wait for the readings:

```
    while (1)
    {
        if (xQueueReceive(temp_queue, &(temp), (TickType_t)10)
== pdFALSE)
        {
            ESP_LOGI(TAG, "nothing in the queue");
            vTaskDelay(1000);
            continue;
        }
```

In the loop, we first check whether any reading is waiting in the queue. If not, we add a delay to wait for a new reading to be added to the queue. When we get a new temperature reading, we try to establish a TLS connection as in the following code snippet:

```
        struct esp_tls *tls = esp_tls_conn_http_new(IFTTT_
MAKER_URL, &cfg);
        if (tls == NULL)
```

```
    {
        ESP_LOGE(TAG, "tls connection failed");
        continue;
    }
```

We call the `esp_tls_conn_http_new` function with the IFTTT URL for a new connection. Then, we prepare the request to share the temperature reading:

```
        memset(json_data, 0, sizeof(json_data));
        sprintf(json_data, JSON_DATA, temp);

        memset(request, 0, sizeof(request));
        sprintf(request, REQUEST, strlen(json_data), json_
data);
        int ret = esp_mbedtls_write(tls, request,
strlen(request));
```

First, we prepare the JSON data in the `json_data` buffer and add it to the `request` buffer. We send this request to the IFTTT service by calling `esp_mbedtls_write`. If the write operation completes successfully, we read the server response, as follows:

```
        if (ret > 0)
        {
            while (1)
            {
                ret = esp_mbedtls_read(tls, (char *)reply,
sizeof(reply) - 1);
                if (ret > 0)
                {
                    reply[ret] = 0;
                    ESP_LOGI(TAG, "%s", reply);
                }
                else
                {
                    break;
                }
            }
        }
        esp_tls_conn_delete(tls);
```

```
    }


    vTaskDelete(NULL);
}
```

We read the server response with the help of `esp_mbedtls_read` and print it on the serial monitor. We delete the TLS connection and the loop starts over again with a new temperature reading from the queue.

We have completed the application. We can flash the devkit and test it:

```
(penv)$ pio run -t upload && pio device monitor
```

We then check whether it really works. The Google spreadsheet should have the temperature records:

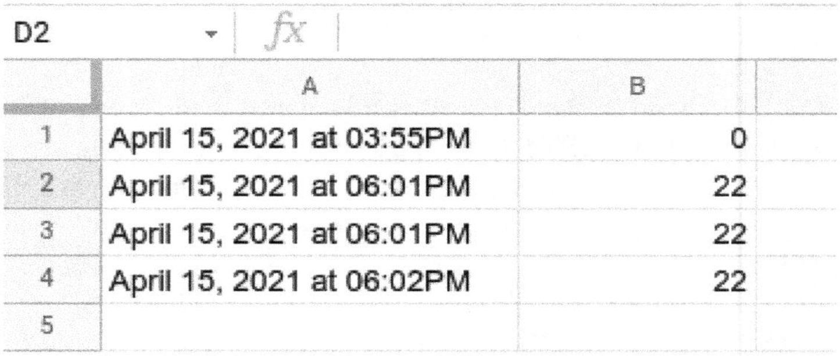

D2	▾	_fx_	
	A		B
1	April 15, 2021 at 03:55PM		0
2	April 15, 2021 at 06:01PM		22
3	April 15, 2021 at 06:01PM		22
4	April 15, 2021 at 06:02PM		22
5			

Figure 11.49 – Temperature records on the spreadsheet

It works, but it seems that the IFTTT service throttles our web requests. We read from the DHT11 sensor every 2 seconds, but we see only 2 temperature records in a minute.

IFTTT provides more features, with more than 600 services. If you want to use IFTTT in your next project, you can read the documentation here: `https://platform.ifttt.com/docs`.

This was the last example of this chapter. We have discussed two important online services that we may need in IoT projects. In the next chapter, we will practice what we have learned so far by developing a full-fledged project.

Summary

An IoT product is more effective and more valuable when it is integrated with other products and online services. In this chapter, we have learned how to integrate our ESP32 devices with Amazon AVS. This integration requires many steps to accomplish the task. We created a smart home skill and developed a Lambda function as the backend handler. AWS IoT Core was the glue between the ESP32 sensor and AVS. We created a device shadow on AWS IoT Core to hold the state of the ESP32 sensor. We have seen that all data exchanges are in the form of JSON documents and the document structures are available in the online Alexa documentation as the main reference. When we look at the products on the market, we can understand that voice interfaces are becoming more common among IoT products. Therefore, it is important for us to learn how to use voice services and integrate them within our solutions.

We have also experimented with IFTTT. It is an online rule engine, not only for IoT solutions, but also many other software products as well. IFTTT presents a great opportunity when we need to design our IoT products to work with other online services and products. As IoT developers, we have many options on the market that we can leverage when we need to add new features. The only thing to do is to select the right one.

The next chapter is the final chapter of the book. We will develop another complete project to improve our ESP32 skills to work with cloud platforms and integrations.

Questions

Let's try to answer the following questions as an overview of the subject:

1. Which of the following is not among the main technologies employed in voice assistant services?

   a) Microservices

   b) Speech recognition

   c) **Natural language processing (NLP)**

   d) Speech synthesis

2. Which of the following makes a voice user interface different from an ordinary graphical user interface?

   a) It is a human-machine interface.

   b) A user can provide inputs by using it.

c) A device can provide output by using it.

d) Users need more guidance since there is no visual element.

3. What is the use of a wake word for a voice assistant?

a) To make it more engaging.

b) To give it a personality.

c) To activate it.

d) To wake it up in the morning.

4. Which of the following doesn't count as an example of a voice assistant?

a) Amazon Alexa

b) Google Assistant

c) Microsoft Azure

d) Apple Siri

5. Which of the following is not a benefit of integrating with third-party services?

a) Access to an ecosystem

b) Longer time to market

c) Increased effectiveness

d) Fast development cycle

Further reading

- *Hands-On Chatbot Development with Alexa Skills and Amazon Lex, Sam Williams, Packt Publishing* (https://www.packtpub.com/product/hands-on-chatbot-development-with-alexa-skills-and-amazon-lex/9781788993487): Although the main subject of the book is chatbot development, it explains the basics of the Alexa skill development well, especially in *Chapter 2, Getting Started with AWS and Amazon CLI*, and *Chapter 3, Creating Your First Alexa Skill*. The book also covers several other Amazon services, such as Amazon S3 and Amazon DynamoDB, to develop complete cloud applications.

12
Practice – A Voice-Controlled Smart Fan

In this final chapter of the book, we are going to develop another smart home device, a smart fan. We will take an ordinary fan that has mechanical buttons on it to control the fan speed and we will convert this fan into a smart one where we can set the speed by voice in addition to its buttons. The fan that I am going to hack in this project has four buttons, where one button is for stopping the fan and the other three are for three different speed modes, from slow to fast. The idea is to intercept the button presses by connecting the speed buttons of the fan to GPIO pins of ESP32 and control the speed via relays when a button press is detected. It will also respond to voice commands by changing the relay states. The voice assistant will be Amazon Alexa and we will use Amazon IoT Core and Lambda as the backend services to handle the voice commands.

This chapter introduces a great opportunity to practice what we have learned throughout the book:

- We will configure the GPIO pins of ESP32 to collect button-pressed events and react to them by setting/resetting another set of GPIO pins to control the relays.

- We will connect the smart fan to the local Wi-Fi network to make it accessible from anywhere in the world.

- We will develop the backend service of the solution on the AWS cloud. Amazon Alexa will enable the device with voice control.

In this chapter, we will cover the following topics:

- Feature list of the smart fan

- Solution architecture

- Implementation

Technical requirements

You can find the chapter code in the GitHub repository here: `https://github.com/PacktPublishing/Internet-of-Things-with-ESP32/tree/main/ch12`.

The external libraries can be found here: `https://github.com/PacktPublishing/Internet-of-Things-with-ESP32/tree/main/common`.

When we prototype on a breadboard, we need the following items as hardware:

- An ESP32 devkit

- A breadboard, four tactile buttons, and jumper wires

- A relay module with at least three relays on it (5 V DC input to drive 230 V AC output)

- A logic converter, 3.3 V to 5 V (for example, an AZ-Delivery TXS0108E logic level converter module)

- A power source (for example, the power supply module from the ELEGOO kit)

After developing and testing the code, we can move the hardware setup to a universal PCB so that we can mount the assembled hardware on a fan. You don't need to do this part of the project if you're happy with the prototype on the breadboard. However, if you want to have a final working smart fan, here is the component list:

- A fan with three levels of speed (for example, a Daewoo 12-inch table, portable desk fan)
- A power module (for example, an AZ-Delivery 220 V to 5 V mini power supply module)
- The components from the first prototype: the ESP32 devkit, the relay module, and the logic converter
- A universal PCB to assemble the components, wires, and headers

> **Important note**
> You need to have soldering equipment and some soldering skills to assemble the components on the universal PCB in the second prototype. It also requires working with high-voltage electricity; therefore, take all precautions while testing the fan powered by the mains.

If you have completed the examples of *Chapter 11, Connectivity Is Never Enough – Third-Party Integrations*, you should already have Amazon and Alexa developer accounts, but if you don't have them, you can follow the steps here to create your accounts: `https://developer.amazon.com/en-US/docs/alexa/smarthome/steps-to-build-a-smart-home-skill.html#prerequisites`.

Check out the following video to see the code in action: `https://bit.ly/3xsLbdI`

Feature list of the smart fan

The smart fan will have the following features:

- It has a button switch to stop the fan.
- It has three other buttons to change the fan speed: low, normal, and high speeds.
- It is Alexa-enabled. It responds to voice commands to change the fan speed.

We also need to keep track of its current state on AWS IoT Core to maintain consistency. When the user sets the fan speed by physically pressing the speed buttons of the fan, the cloud backend will be updated with this information.

Solution architecture

In the solution architecture, we need to discuss two different parts: the firmware and the cloud backend. Let's talk about the firmware first.

The device firmware

The following diagram shows the main components of the firmware:

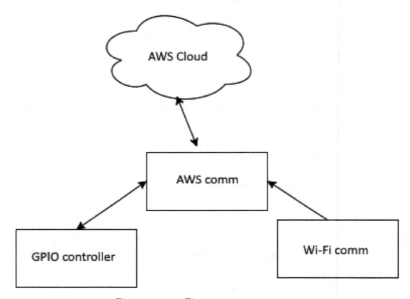

Figure 12.1 – Firmware components

The GPIO controller will configure and drive the GPIO pins of ESP32. There are four pins to be used as inputs and three other pins as outputs. The input pins will read from the tactile buttons (or the speed buttons of the fan in the second prototype) and the output pins will control the relays. When the stop button is pressed, all relays will switch off. If any one of the speed buttons is pressed, the corresponding relay will switch on. The GPIO controller also communicates with the AWS module to send the button state information and to receive voice commands from Alexa.

The Wi-Fi communication module connects to the local Wi-Fi network as specified by the SSID and password. After a successful connection, it will notify the AWS module to connect to the AWS cloud.

The AWS communication module has a central role in the design. It monitors requests from the cloud and passes them to the GPIO module to set/reset the relay pins. It also passes the fan speed information to the cloud when the user presses any of the buttons.

The cloud architecture

The cloud application provides voice support in our project. We will create an Alexa smart home skill and bind it to our device through AWS IoT Core. The services in the cloud solution and how they are related to each other are displayed in the following diagram:

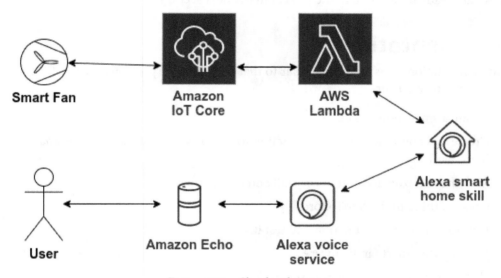

Figure 12.2 – Cloud architecture

We will create a thing on Amazon IoT Core as the cloud representation of the smart fan. Any status change will be synchronized on both the smart fan and the thing.

A Lambda function will be the glue between the thing and **Alexa Voice Service (AVS)**. The function will parse the requests coming from the Alexa skill and reply to them according to the context. It will also update the thing's state with Alexa commands, which will eventually cause a speed change on the physical device. In the Lambda function, we will implement the `Alexa.PowerLevelController` interface as defined in the AWS documentation here: `https://developer.amazon.com/en-US/docs/alexa/device-apis/alexa-powerlevelcontroller.html`.

We will also create and configure an Alexa smart home skill. As we discussed in *Chapter 11, Connectivity Is Never Enough – Third-Party Integrations*, smart home skills provide ready-to-use voice interaction models, which means we don't need to design a voice interface with utterances since it is already built for us to be used in our products. A device with the `PowerLevelController` interface allows its users to control the power level of the device. The user gives a voice command in percentage form, such as *Alexa, set the smart fan to 40%* or *Alexa, increase the smart fan by 10%*. These utterances are all included in this voice interface.

Now, we are ready to implement the project in the next section.

Implementation

The implementation steps are very similar to that we did in the previous chapter for the smart temperature sensor:

1. Create a smart home skill.
2. Create and configure a Lambda function to handle the requests from the smart home skill.
3. Link the Amazon account to the skill and enable the skill.
4. Create a thing in AWS IoT Core.
5. Develop the Lambda function and test it.
6. Develop the smart fan firmware.
7. Test the smart fan with voice commands.

Since we have already examined this procedure in detail in *Chapter 11, Connectivity Is Never Enough – Third-Party Integrations*, I will fast-forward through them and discuss the application code more. Let's begin by creating the smart home skill.

Creating the skill

As of the time of writing this book, the AVS command-line tool (version 2.22.4) doesn't support smart home skills, so we will stick with the web GUI for the skill operations. Here are the steps to create a skill:

1. Log in to the Amazon Developer Console at `https://developer.amazon.com/alexa/console/ask`.
2. Create a skill with the name `myhome_smartfan` and **Smart Home** as the model.

3. Take a note of the skill ID on the page. It will be something like `amzn1.ask.skill.<unique_id>`.

We will return to this web interface after creating the Lambda function to link the Lambda handler and the skill, so it is better to keep the page open. Let's deal with the Lambda function next.

Creating the Lambda function

We will create a function and attach a policy to allow logging and operations on IoT Core. We will also set the skill as a trigger for the Lambda function. We can use the AWS command-line tool for this purpose in the following steps:

1. We first need to have a role for the Lambda function. Edit a file with the following content as the assume role policy document and save it as `lambda_trust_policy.json`. This file describes the trust relationship between the Lambda service and AWS Security Token Service:

```
{
    "Version": "2012-10-17",
    "Statement": [{
        "Effect": "Allow",
        "Principal": {
            "Service": "lambda.amazonaws.com"
        },
        "Action": "sts:AssumeRole"
    }]
}
```

2. Create the role with the following command:

```
$ aws --version
aws-cli/2.1.31 Python/3.8.8 Linux/5.4.0-65-generic exe/
x86_64.ubuntu.20 prompt/off
$ aws iam create-role --role-name smartfan_lambda_role
--assume-role-policy-document file://lambda_trust_policy.
json
```

This command will output the information about the role that we have just created. Take a note of the **Amazon Resource Name (ARN)** of the role. It will be something like this: `arn:aws:iam::<your_account_id>:role/smartfan_lambda_role`. We will use it while creating the function.

3. Edit a file with the following content as the policy and save the file with the name `lambda_permissions.json`. It defines what the Lambda function can do:

```
{
    "Version": "2012-10-17",
    "Statement": [{
        "Effect": "Allow",
        "Action": [
            "logs:CreateLogGroup",
            "logs:CreateLogStream",
            "logs:PutLogEvents",
            "logs:DescribeLogStreams"
        ],
        "Resource": "arn:aws:logs:*:*:*"
    },
    {
        "Effect": "Allow",
        "Action": [
            "iot:*"
        ],
        "Resource": "arn:aws:iot:*:*:*"
    }
    ]
}
```

This policy allows logging and IoT operations.

4. Create the policy defined in `lambda_permissions.json` as follows:

```
$ aws iam create-policy --policy-name smartfan_lambda_
policy --policy-document file://lambda_permissions.json
```

Take a note of the policy ARN in the output of this command. The ARN will be similar to this: `arn:aws:iam::<your_account_number>:policy/smartfan_lambda_policy`.

5. Attach the policy to the role with the following command:

```
$ aws iam attach-role-policy --role-name smartfan_lambda_
role --policy-arn <the_policy_ARN>
```

6. Create a source code file with the following content and name it `lambda_function.py`. This is temporary code that is necessary to create the Lambda function:

```
import json
def lambda_handler(request, context):
        pass
```

7. Create a source package by compressing `lambda_function.py` with any `zip` utility:

```
$ zip lambda_package.zip lambda_function.py
  adding: lambda_function.py (stored 0%)
```

8. Create a Lambda function with the name `smartfan_handler`. The following command does the job:

```
$ aws lambda create-function --function-name smartfan_
lambda \
--zip-file fileb://lambda_package.zip \
--handler 'lambda_function.lambda_handler' \
--runtime python3.8 \
--role <the_role_ARN>
```

Again, take a note of the ARN, of the Lambda function this time. It should be similar to this: `arn:aws:lambda:<default_region>:<your_account_number>:function:smartfan_lambda`.

9. Create a trigger for the Lambda function. The trigger will be the smart home skill that we created before. Unfortunately, we don't have a command-line option for this. Therefore, we need to log in to the AWS web console (`https://aws.amazon.com/console/`) and navigate to the `smartfan_handler` function in the Lambda service. Copy the skill ID from the Alexa Developer Console that we kept open and use the skill ID as a configuration parameter for the trigger after clicking on + **Add trigger**.

10. Copy the Lambda ARN and return to the skill configuration page. Paste the Lambda ARN in the textbox that is labeled **Default endpoint***. Don't forget to click on the **Save** button on the configuration page. With this step, the skill knows where to send the request when the user utters a command for the smart fan.

We have the Lambda function ready. Next comes the account linking.

Account linking

We need to link our account to the smart home skill and then enable the skill to be able to use it. We can follow these steps to accomplish the account linking:

1. Navigate to **ACCOUNT LINKING** for the skill in the Alexa Developer Console and fill in the form with the following information:

   a) **Your Web Authorization URI**: `https://www.amazon.com/ap/oa`

   b) **Access Token URI**: `https://api.amazon.com/auth/o2/token`

   c) **Your Client ID**: The client ID from the security profile

   d) **Your Secret**: The client secret from the security profile

   e) **Your Authentication Scheme**: `HTTP basic`

   f) **Scope**: `profile:user_id`

   The client ID and secret come from the security profile in our developer accounts. You should have a security profile in your account if you have completed the example of *Chapter 11, Connectivity Is Never Enough – Third-Party Integrations*. The direct link to the **Login with Amazon** console is `https://developer.amazon.com/loginwithamazon/console/site/lwa/overview.html`.

2. Click the **Save** button on the configuration page to complete the account linking.

3. To enable the skill, log in to `https://alexa.amazon.com/` and find **myhome_smartfan** in **DEV SKILLS**. After clicking on the **ENABLE** button, the page shows a success message if we have configured the skill correctly. Just skip the discovery process that pops up when we close the success page.

We are done with the skill configuration. Now, it is time to create a thing in the AWS IoT Core service for the smart fan.

Creating the thing

As I mentioned earlier, a thing represents a physical device in the cloud. All cloud services interact with the thing and the physical device also interacts with the thing to synchronize its status in both directions. Let's create the thing with the following steps by using the AWS CLI tool:

1. Create a thing with the name `myhome_fan1`:

```
$ aws iot create-thing --thing-name myhome_fan1
```

2. Create the following policy file with the following content and name it `myhome_fan1_policy.json`. This will give all IoT-related permissions to the thing:

```
{
    "Version": "2012-10-17",
    "Statement": [{
        "Effect": "Allow",
        "Action": [
            "iot:*"
        ],
        "Resource": "arn:aws:iot:*:*:*"
    }
    ]
}
```

3. Create the policy by using the policy file from the previous step:

```
$ aws iot create-policy \
    --policy-name myhome_fan1_policy \
    --policy-document file://myhome_fan1_policy.json
```

4. Create the certificate and private/public key pair:

```
$ aws iot create-keys-and-certificate \
    --certificate-pem-outfile "certificate.pem.crt" \
    --public-key-outfile "public.pem.key" \
    --private-key-outfile "private.pem.key" \
    --set-as-active
```

The command output will have the certificate ARN. We will use it to attach the certificate to the policy in the next step. We will also embed the keys into the device firmware to keep them in a safe place.

5. Attach the policy to the certificate:

```
$ aws iot attach-policy \
    --policy-name myhome_fan1_policy \
    --target <certificate_ARN>
```

6. Attach the certificate to the thing:

```
$ aws iot attach-thing-principal \
    --thing-name myhome_fan1 \
    --principal <certificate_ARN>
```

We have the thing configured and ready to interact with other components in the solution. We can now move on to coding the Lambda function that implements the `Alexa.PowerLevelController` interface for the skill and makes a bridge between the thing and AVS.

Developing the Lambda function

In the Lambda function, we will reply to the following requests from AVS:

- A discovery request from the `Alexa.Discovery` namespace to find the fan associated with the user account
- An `AcceptGrant` request from the `Alexa.Authorization` namespace to obtain credentials that identify the user to Alexa
- A `SetPowerLevel` request from the `Alexa.PowerLevelController` namespace to set the power level of the fan
- An `AdjustPowerLevel` request from the `Alexa.PowerLevelController` namespace to change the power level by an amount
- A `ReportState` request from the Alexa namespace to send the device state
- The connectivity status from the `Alexa.EndpointHealth` namespace

> **Tip**
>
> The endpoint health interface is a mandatory interface if your device is a
> sensor or you are planning to apply for the **Works with Alexa** certification. The
> connectivity property of the interface shows the status of the device and
> can have OK or UNREACHABLE as the value.

The Alexa Skills Kit supports many other interfaces to help developers and vendors. You
can learn more about the framework at this link: https://developer.amazon.
com/en-US/docs/alexa/ask-overviews/what-is-the-alexa-skills-
kit.html.

Let's develop the Lambda function in lambda_function.py as follows:

```python
import logging
import time
import json
import uuid
import boto3
from fan1_responses import import *

logger = logging.getLogger()
logger.setLevel(logging.INFO)
client = boto3.client('iot-data')
```

We start by including the Python modules that we refer to while developing the Lambda
function. fan1_responses contains the response templates that we modify and return
to AVS requests. Now we can define the request handler next:

```python
def lambda_handler(request, context):

    try:
        logger.info("Directive:")
        logger.info(json.dumps(request, indent=4, sort_
keys=True))

        request_namespace = request["directive"]["header"]
["namespace"]
        request_name = request["directive"]["header"]["name"]
        corrTkn = ""
        if "correlationToken" in request["directive"]
```

```
["header"]:
            corrTkn = request["directive"]["header"]
["correlationToken"]
```

`lambda_handler` is the entry point for the Lambda function. The Lambda service will invoke this function when a trigger happens. We extract `request_namespace` and `request_name` from `request` to understand its type and reply properly. Some of the responses need a correlation token coming in the request, so we have a variable for this as well. Next, we check the request types:

```
            if request_namespace == "Alexa.Discovery" and
request_name == "Discover":
                response = gen_discovery_response()
            elif request_namespace == "Alexa.Authorization" and
request_name == "AcceptGrant":
                response = gen_acceptgrant_response()
            elif request_namespace == "Alexa.PowerLevelController"
and request_name == "SetPowerLevel":
                response = set_power_level(request["directive"]
["payload"]["powerLevel"], corrTkn)
            elif request_namespace == "Alexa.PowerLevelController"
and request_name == "AdjustPowerLevel":
                response = adj_power_level(request["directive"]
["payload"]["powerLevelDelta"], corrTkn)
            elif request_namespace == "Alexa" and request_name ==
"ReportState":
                response = gen_report_state(corrTkn)
        else:
            logger.error("unexpected request")
        return response
```

This is the code snippet where we check the request type and generate a proper response. I will not list the contents of the JSON responses since they are quite long, but you can find them at this location in `fan1_responses.py`: https://github.com/PacktPublishing/Internet-of-Things-with-ESP32/blob/main/ch12/smart_fan/aws/fan1_responses.py. The response for the `Discover` request contains the capability information of the smart fan. The `Alexa.PowerLevelController` interface has two specific directives, which are `SetPowerLevel` and `AdjustPowerLevel`.

We include the correlation token when we reply to these requests. The last request type is `ReportState`. AVS sends this request to learn the power level of the fan and we return the power level with the correlation token of the request. The endpoint health information is attached in the `ReportState` response, so we don't handle it explicitly here. The remainder of the Lambda handler function is just the boilerplate code, as follows:

```
        logger.info("Response:")
        logger.info(json.dumps(response, indent=4, sort_
keys=True))


        return response


    except ValueError as error:
        logger.error(error)
        raise
```

We simply log the response and return it if there is no exception. Any exception is also logged and raised if it happens while executing the handler.

There are several other helper functions to accomplish the task; however, it is enough for us to discuss the important ones. Let's see how we reply to a `SetPowerLevel` request:

```
def set_power_level(power_level, tkn):
    power_level = update_power(power_level)
    set_power_level_shadow(power_level)


    response = init_response(set_power_level_response, tkn,
power_level)
    return response
```

In `set_power_level`, we first normalize the power level to one of the following values by calling `update_power`:

- `0` (zero) when the user specifically sets the power level to 0. This power level means power off the fan.
- `33` if the user input is between 1 and 33, which corresponds to the low-speed mode of the fan.
- `66` if the user input is between 34 and 66, which is for the normal-speed mode.
- `100` if the user input is greater than 66, for the high-speed mode.

After the power level normalization, we update the shadow desired state with that value by calling the set_power_level_shadow function that we implement. In the init_response function, we simply set the correlation token and the power level of the JSON response and return it to the Lambda handler to be passed to AVS. set_power_level_response is the JSON response template that is defined in fan1_responses.py. Let's discuss how we implement the set_power_level_shadow function next:

```
def set_power_level_shadow(power_level):
    payload = json.dumps({'state': { 'desired': { 'powerlevel':
power_level } }})
    response = client.update_thing_shadow(
        thingName = endpoint_id,
        payload =  payload)
    logger.info("update shadow result: " + response['payload'].
read().decode('utf-8'))
```

We prepare a JSON payload for the desired state of the powerlevel property of the shadow and call the update_thing_shadow function of client. It will update the thing's shadow and this information will be shared with the application on ESP32 over MQTT. When the handler in the ESP32 application runs upon receiving the desired state request, it will update the fan state accordingly by switching the relays on/off. An example shadow state is given as follows:

```
{
  "desired": {
    "welcome": "aws-iot",
    "powerlevel": 0
  },
  "reported": {
    "welcome": "aws-iot",
    "powerlevel": 33
  },
  "delta": {
    "powerlevel": 33
  }
}
```

desired denotes the new state value requested by the user. reported is updated by the device, and delta is calculated by AWS IoT Core. If you want to learn more about device shadows, AWS provides great documentation here: https://docs.aws.amazon.com/iot/latest/developerguide/iot-device-shadows.html.

We take a similar approach to reply to the AdjustPowerLevel request, but this time we calculate the new power level for a given delta input.

For the rest of the helper functions, you can see the code here: https://github.com/PacktPublishing/Internet-of-Things-with-ESP32/blob/main/ch12/smart_fan/aws/lambda_function.py.

We have completed the Lambda handler implementation. Let's now update it and test it with the sample requests as follows:

1. Update the Lambda code package. The package should contain both source files:

```
$ zip -u lambda_package.zip *.py
updating: lambda_function.py (deflated 73%)
  adding: fan1_responses.py (deflated 83%)
```

2. Update the Lambda code on AWS:

```
$ aws lambda update-function-code --function-name
smartfan_lambda --zip-file fileb://./lambda_package.zip
```

3. Test for all request types. The sample requests are found at this location: https://github.com/PacktPublishing/Internet-of-Things-with-ESP32/tree/main/ch12/smart_fan/aws:

```
$ aws lambda invoke \
    --cli-binary-format raw-in-base64-out \
    --function-name smartfan_lambda \
    --payload file://./discovery_request.json \
    response.json
{
    "StatusCode": 200,
    "ExecutedVersion": "$LATEST"
}
```

All tests should pass with a status code of 200.

4. Since we have the backend service by the Lambda function ready, we can run the device discovery in our Alexa account by visiting `https://alexa.amazon.com/`. We navigate to **Smart Home | Devices** and click **Discover**. In 20 seconds, the smart fan should be listed as a new device.

We are done with the development on AWS and we can implement the ESP32 application next.

Developing the firmware

As a quick recap, the ESP32 application will detect which button is pressed on the fan and switch the corresponding relay on to set the fan speed. The state of the thing on the AWS cloud will be updated as well. When a voice command changes the desired state of the thing, this information will also be captured and reflected on the physical fan by the application running on ESP32. The Fritzing diagram of the hardware setup is as follows:

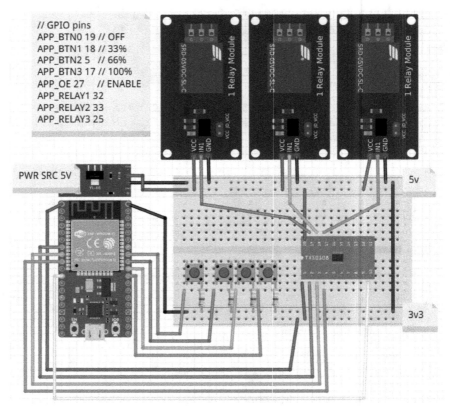

Figure 12.3 – Smart fan circuitry

For the second prototype, we connect the fan buttons to ESP32 instead of the buttons on this diagram. We open the bottom lid of the fan, cut the button cables off, and connect the buttons to the GPIO pins of ESP32. The relays will control the fan speed, replacing the fan buttons. We connect the other ends of the cables to the relay loads.

> **Important note**
>
> Please take all necessary precautions while working with high voltage. This website explains neatly how to use a relay with a load: `https://ncd.io/relay-logic/`. You may also want to use an RC snubber around the relays to protect them from inductive kickback coming from the fan motor. Wikipedia has an article about inductive kickback and snubbers at this link: `https://en.wikipedia.org/wiki/Snubber`. One example of such snubbers that you can use in this project is XE1201 from Okaya, which is available worldwide (`https://okaya.com/product/?id=9716226e-c62c-e111-a207-0026551ab73e`).

The next figure shows the TXS0108E logic converter module from AZ-Delivery:

Figure 12.4 – TSX0108E module

There are two ports on the module. Port A (the bottom row) supports any voltage between 1.4 V and 3.6 V, and port B (the top row) is for 1.65 V to 5.5 V. The rule is that **VA** should be less than **VB**. **OE** enables port B output when it is set to high. The online datasheet is here: `https://www.ti.com/document-viewer/TXS0108E/datasheet`.

We will use four buttons to control the fan speed. The first one will stop the fan by switching all the relays off and the other three buttons are for different speeds. The GPIO pins of the buttons will read high when no button is pressed since we enable the internal pull-up resistors for these GPIO pins.

Having the circuitry ready, we can move on to the application. Let's start by creating a new PlatformIO project with ESP-IDF as the framework:

1. Edit the `platformio.ini` file of the project with the following content:

```
[env:az-delivery-devkit-v4]
platform = espressif32
board = az-delivery-devkit-v4
framework = espidf

monitor_speed = 115200
lib_extra_dirs =
    ../../common/esp-idf-lib/components
build_flags =
    -DWIFI_SSID=${sysenv.WIFI_SSID}
    -DWIFI_PASS=${sysenv.WIFI_PASS}
    -DAWS_ENDPOINT=${sysenv.AWS_ENDPOINT}

board_build.embed_txtfiles =
    ./tmp/private.pem.key
    ./tmp/certificate.pem.crt
    ./tmp/AmazonRootCA1.pem
```

The AWS device SDK is under `../../common/esp-idf-lib/components`, so we include this path in the project. We define `AWS_ENDPOINT` as an environment variable. The application will connect to this endpoint to communicate with the thing that we have created in AWS IoT Core. We also specify the paths for the cryptographic files of the thing. We will copy them to the `tmp` folder, which is excluded from the GitHub repository so as not to expose the cryptographic files publicly.

2. Edit `src/CMakeList.txt` with the following content:

```
FILE(GLOB_RECURSE app_sources ${CMAKE_SOURCE_DIR}/
src/*.*)
set(COMPONENT_ADD_INCLUDEDIRS ".")

idf_component_register(SRCS ${app_sources})

target_add_binary_data(${COMPONENT_TARGET} "../tmp/
```

```
AmazonRootCA1.pem" TEXT)
target_add_binary_data(${COMPONENT_TARGET} "../tmp/
certificate.pem.crt" TEXT)
target_add_binary_data(${COMPONENT_TARGET} "../tmp/
private.pem.key" TEXT)
```

We also need the cryptographic files known to ESP-IDF. We use the `target_add_binary_data` directive to specify the file paths.

3. Copy the cryptographic files to the `tmp` folder in the project root:

```
$ mkdir tmp && cp <thing_cert_files> tmp/ && cd tmp
$ wget https://www.amazontrust.com/repository/
AmazonRootCA1.pem
$ ls
AmazonRootCA1.pem   certificate.pem.crt   private.pem.key
public.pem.key
```

We have also downloaded the Amazon root certificate, which is located here: https://www.amazontrust.com/repository/AmazonRootCA1.pem.

4. Copy the library files from this GitHub location: https://github.com/PacktPublishing/Internet-of-Things-with-ESP32/tree/main/ch12/smart_fan/lib. Once we have all the files in place, we should have the following directory structure in our project:

```
$ ls -R
.:
CMakeLists.txt   include   lib   platformio.ini   sdkconfig
src   test   tmp
./lib:
aws   hw   README   wifi
./lib/aws:
app_aws.c   app_aws.h
./lib/hw:
app_hw.c   app_hw.h
./lib/wifi:
app_wifi.c   app_wifi.h
./src:
CMakeLists.txt   main.c
./tmp:
```

```
AmazonRootCA1.pem  certificate.pem.crt  private.pem.key
public.pem.key
```

5. Activate the PlatformIO virtual environment and set the environment variables:

```
$ source ~/.platformio/penv/bin/activate
(penv)$ aws iot describe-endpoint --endpoint-type
iot:Data-ATS
{
    "endpointAddress": "<your_endpoint>"
}
(penv)$ export AWS_ENDPOINT='\"<your_encpoint>\"'
(penv)$ export WIFI_SSID='\"<your_ssid>\"'
(penv)$ export WIFI_PASS='\"<your_password>\"'
```

Before developing the application code, let's see what we have in the project libraries. There are three of them:

- `lib/wifi/app_wifi.{c,h}`: Implements the Wi-Fi connection

- `lib/aws/app_aws.{c,h}`: Handles AWS communication

- `lib/hw/app_hw.{c,h}`: Handles button presses and manages the relays

In `app_wifi.h`, we have only one function declaration, as follows:

```
#ifndef app_wifi_h_
#define app_wifi_h_

typedef void (*on_connected_f)(void);
typedef void (*on_failed_f)(void);

typedef struct {
    on_connected_f on_connected;
    on_failed_f on_failed;
} connect_wifi_params_t;

void appwifi_connect(connect_wifi_params_t);

#endif
```

`appwifi_connect` tries to connect to the local Wi-Fi and it runs a corresponding callback function according to the success status.

Next, we have the GPIO-handling API in `app_hw.h`:

```
#ifndef app_hw_h_
#define app_hw_h_

#include <stdbool.h>
#include <stdint.h>
#include "driver/gpio.h"

// GPIO pins
#define APP_BTN0 19 // OFF
#define APP_BTN1 18 // 33%
#define APP_BTN2 5  // 66%
#define APP_BTN3 17 // 100%
#define APP_OE 27   // ENABLE
#define APP_RELAY1 32
#define APP_RELAY2 33
#define APP_RELAY3 25
```

We first define the macros for the GPIO pins. We have four buttons, three relays, and a pin for enabling the logic converter output. The API functions come next, as follows:

```
typedef struct
{
    gpio_num_t btn_pin;
    gpio_num_t relay_pin;
    uint8_t val;
} btn_map_t;

typedef void (*appbtn_fan_changed_f)(uint8_t);

void apphw_init(appbtn_fan_changed_f);
uint8_t apphw_get_state(void);
```

```
void apphw_set_state(uint8_t);


#endif
```

The `apphw_init` function initializes the GPIO pins as inputs or outputs based on the purpose. The button pins provide inputs and the relay control pins are outputs. `apphw_init` also takes a function parameter to be called when a button is pressed and the state of the corresponding relay has been changed. The thing needs to be updated with this information. `apphw_set_state` is the function to change the relay state externally. When a voice command is issued by the user, the AWS library will use this function to set the relay state.

Let's continue with the AWS communication API in `app_hw.h`:

```
#ifndef app_aws_h_
#define app_aws_h_


#include <stdint.h>


#define AWS_THING_NAME "myhome_fan1"


typedef void (*fan_state_changed_f)(uint8_t);


void appaws_init(fan_state_changed_f);
void appaws_connect(void *);
void appaws_publish(uint8_t);


#endif
```

In `app_hw.h`, we declare a macro that indicates the thing name. It is the parameter to the shadow connect function in the library implementation. The `appaws_init` function initializes the library internals. It takes a callback parameter to be called when a user request comes to change the fan state. The library holds a reference for this callback inside and it will be run when the thing's state has been changed by the voice request. `appaws_connect` is called when the local Wi-Fi is connected. It also monitors the thing changes after connecting to the AWS cloud. The last function, `appaws_publish`, is used to update the thing's state when the fan speed changes by a button press. All the interesting things happen in this library and we will discuss the implementation a bit later in this section.

Let's see how we glue all these parts together in `main.c`, as follows:

```c
#include <stdlib.h>
#include "freertos/FreeRTOS.h"
#include "freertos/task.h"
#include "esp_log.h"

#include "app_wifi.h"
#include "app_hw.h"
#include "app_aws.h"

#define TAG "app"
```

We first include the necessary header files as usual, including the library headers. Then, we define the Wi-Fi state handlers:

```c
static void handle_wifi_connect(void)
{
    xTaskCreatePinnedToCore(appaws_connect, "appaws_connect",
15 * configMINIMAL_STACK_SIZE, NULL, 5, NULL, 0);
}

static void handle_wifi_failed(void)
{
    ESP_LOGE(TAG, "wifi failed");
}
```

`handle_wifi_connect` is the function to be called when the Wi-Fi is connected. It will start a FreeRTOS task to connect and monitor the thing by running `appaws_connect` inside the task:

```c
void app_main()
{
    apphw_init(appaws_publish);
    appaws_init(apphw_set_state);

    connect_wifi_params_t cbs = {
        .on_connected = handle_wifi_connect,
        .on_failed = handle_wifi_failed};
```

```
    appwifi_connect(cbs);
}
```

In the `app_main` function, we start with the library initializations. The hardware library takes `appaws_publish` as the callback function to be called when a button press happens on the fan, and the AWS library takes `apphw_set_state` as the callback function to be called when the thing's state changes on the AWS cloud. Both libraries update each other when something changes on their sides. Finally, we call `appwifi_connect` with the handler functions to connect to the local Wi-Fi.

As I promised, we can now discuss the more interesting parts inside the AWS communication library, which is implemented in `lib/aws/app_aws.c`. Let's see the `appaws_connect` function first:

```
void appaws_connect(void *param)
{
    memset((void *)&aws_client, 0, sizeof(aws_client));

    ShadowInitParameters_t sp = ShadowInitParametersDefault;
    sp.pHost = endpoint_address;
    sp.port = AWS_IOT_MQTT_PORT;
    sp.pClientCRT = (const char *)certificate_pem_crt_start;
    sp.pClientKey = (const char *)private_pem_key_start;
    sp.pRootCA = (const char *)aws_root_ca_pem_start;
    sp.disconnectHandler = disconnected_handler;

    aws_iot_shadow_init(&aws_client, &sp);
```

We initialize the thing's shadow by calling `aws_iot_shadow_init`. It takes the connection parameters and cryptographic keys to get access to the thing. Then, we will connect to the thing:

```
    ShadowConnectParameters_t scp =
ShadowConnectParametersDefault;
    scp.pMyThingName = thing_name;
    scp.pMqttClientId = client_id;
    scp.mqttClientIdLen = (uint16_t)strlen(client_id);

    while (aws_iot_shadow_connect(&aws_client, &scp) !=
SUCCESS)
```

```
    {
        ESP_LOGW(TAG, "trying to connect");
        vTaskDelay(1000 / portTICK_PERIOD_MS);
    }
```

`aws_iot_shadow_connect` establishes the connection to the thing by trying in a loop until it succeeds. Our next goal is to register a function for the changes on the thing's shadow, so that we can update the fan speed accordingly. Any voice request causes a change on the thing. Here is how we register a delta callback:

```
    uint8_t fan_powerlevel = 0;
    jsonStruct_t fan_controller;
    fan_controller.cb = fan_powerlevel_change_requested;
    fan_controller.pData = &fan_powerlevel;
    fan_controller.pKey = "powerlevel";
    fan_controller.type = SHADOW_JSON_UINT8;
    fan_controller.dataLength = sizeof(uint8_t);
    if (aws_iot_shadow_register_delta(&aws_client, &fan_
controller) == SUCCESS)
    {
        ESP_LOGI(TAG, "shadow delta registered");
    }
```

`aws_iot_shadow_register_delta` is the function for this purpose. In its parameters, we provide which field delta MQTT topic we subscribe to and also a callback function to be called when a message comes from that delta MQTT topic. In our case, `powerlevel` is the delta field, and `fan_powerlevel_change_requested` is the callback function for `powerlevel` changes. `fan_powerlevel_change_requested` informs the hardware library about the `powerlevel` updates:

```
    IoT_Error_t err = SUCCESS;
    while (1)
    {
        if (xSemaphoreTake(aws_guard, 100) == pdTRUE)
        {
            err = aws_iot_shadow_yield(&aws_client, 250);
            xSemaphoreGive(aws_guard);
        }
        if (err != SUCCESS)
```

```
        {
            ESP_LOGE(TAG, "yield failed: %d", err);
        }
        vTaskDelay(100 / portTICK_PERIOD_MS);
    }
}
```

At the end of the `appaws_connect` function, we monitor the AWS messages in a `while` loop by calling `aws_iot_shadow_yield`. According to the AWS documentation, the shadow functions are not thread-safe, so we need to protect them via a semaphore.

The next function that we will talk about is `appaws_publish`. It is called by the hardware library when a button press is detected, which means the current state of the fan has been changed manually by the user and the thing also needs to be updated on AWS IoT Core. It is as follows:

```
void appaws_publish(uint8_t val)
{
    jsonStruct_t temp_json = {
        .cb = NULL,
        .pKey = "powerlevel",
        .pData = &val,
        .type = SHADOW_JSON_UINT8,
        .dataLength = sizeof(val) };

    char jsondoc_buffer[200];
    aws_iot_shadow_init_json_document(jsondoc_buffer,
sizeof(jsondoc_buffer));
    aws_iot_shadow_add_reported(jsondoc_buffer, sizeof(jsondoc_
buffer), 1, &temp_json);
    if (desired_state != val)
    {
        aws_iot_shadow_add_desired(jsondoc_buffer,
sizeof(jsondoc_buffer), 1, &temp_json);
    }
    aws_iot_finalize_json_document(jsondoc_buffer,
sizeof(jsondoc_buffer));
```

We prepare a JSON message to update the thing's state on AWS IoT Core. `aws_iot_shadow_add_reported` attaches the fan speed information to the message. We also want to update the desired section of the thing's shadow when the desired state is not equal to the current state, because if we don't do this, AWS IoT Core recalculates the delta when it receives the update message from the device firmware and finds out that there is a difference between the desired state and the current state. It results in a delta message on the firmware side requesting the previous state to be set again, which means the user cannot change the fan speed by using the physical buttons on the fan, which is not a great user experience. So, we update the desired state as well. We have the JSON message ready to be sent. Let's do it as follows:

```
    IoT_Error_t err = SUCCESS;
    if (xSemaphoreTake(aws_guard, portMAX_DELAY) == pdTRUE)
    {
        err = aws_iot_shadow_update(&aws_client, thing_name,
jsondoc_buffer, NULL, NULL, 4, true);
        xSemaphoreGive(aws_guard);
    }
    if (err != SUCCESS)
    {
        ESP_LOGE(TAG, "publish failed: %d", err);
    }
}
```

We simply call `aws_iot_shadow_update` to update the thing's shadow. We also check whether the semaphore is available to operate on the shadow since this function is not thread-safe, as we discussed before.

Alright, we are ready to test it after flashing the devkit. We have two major tests. The first one is that when we press a button, the thing's shadow should also be updated. The other one is the opposite; when we send a voice command from the Alexa Developer Console, the relays should be switched on or off accordingly.

Let's do the tests in steps as follows:

1. Press the full-speed button at GPIO17 and observe that `powerlevel` of the thing's shadow is updated to `100` on the AWS console. The AWS Management Console can be accessed at this link: `https://aws.amazon.com/console/`:

Shadow state:

```
{
    "desired": {
        "powerlevel": 100
    },
    "reported": {
        "powerlevel": 100
    }
}
```

Figure 12.5 – Full power

2. Press the off button at GPIO19 and observe that `powerlevel` is updated to `0` on the thing's shadow:

Shadow state:

```
{
    "desired": {
        "powerlevel": 0
    },
    "reported": {
        "powerlevel": 0
    }
}
```

Figure 12.6 – Power off

3. Navigate to the Alexa Developer Console in the browser at this link: `https://developer.amazon.com/alexa/console/ask`. Then, go to the test page of the myhome_smartfan skill. Enter `set smart fan to 50` in the Alexa simulator and observe that the normal speed relay (the one in the middle) is switched on. The thing's shadow should have the value of `66` as `powerlevel`:

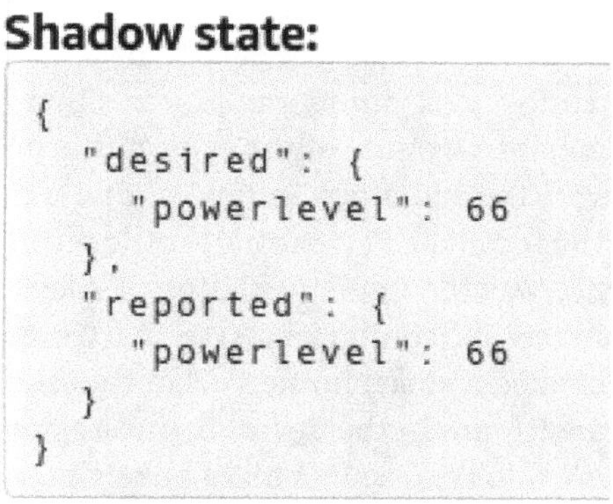

Shadow state:

```
{
  "desired": {
    "powerlevel": 66
  },
  "reported": {
    "powerlevel": 66
  }
}
```

Figure 12.7 – The normal speed

You can repeat the test with other power levels to confirm that the firmware works as expected.

Congratulations! It was not an easy project, but I think it was worth developing it to understand how we can employ ESP32 in a real-world IoT scenario. We covered all the layers of a typical IoT project, including sensors and actuators, networking, and cloud integration.

What is next?

We can improve the smart fan by adding more features, such as the following:

- Integration with a temperature sensor. Then, it can be possible to add an auto-mode feature so that the smart fan can set the fan speed automatically based on the readings from the temperature sensor.

- Implementation of the tower fan device template as explained in the Alexa documentation here: https://developer.amazon.com/en-US/docs/alexa/smarthome/get-started-with-device-templates.html#tower-fan.

- **Over-the-air (OTA)** firmware update.

- BLE **Generic Attribute Profile (GATT)** server for local communication.

I strongly suggest you implement these features to hone your ESP32 skills. As we all know, it is all about practicing.

Summary

In this final chapter, we put almost everything into practice that we have learned throughout the book. On the hardware side of the project, the buttons were the sensors of the solution and the relays were the actuators. In the Wi-Fi library, we used ESP32 in the station mode to connect to the local Wi-Fi network for the given credentials. The most interesting part of this practice was the implementation of Alexa support, which required the utilization of cloud resources. We configured AWS IoT Core, developed the backend code in AWS Lambda, and created a smart home skill in the Alexa Developer Console to add a voice interface to the smart fan. In the device firmware, we used the AWS device SDK to communicate with AWS IoT Core. It is highly likely that you'll face similar challenges in any kind of IoT project. Therefore, this chapter provided a great opportunity to gain experience of the complete picture.

I want to thank you for coming so far and developing the projects together with me. I really enjoyed them, and I hope you enjoyed them as well. For the rest of your ESP32 journey, I recommend you try different ESP32 chips. Espressif Systems launches each of them for specific purposes to fulfill industry needs. For example, ESP32-S2 has a USB OTG interface to develop USB hosts or devices. ESP32-C3 has an RISC-V MCU in its design with a world controller that provides a **trusted execution environment** (**TEE**) as an extra security layer in the applications. ESP32-S3 targets the AIoT market with its AI acceleration support. IoT is a fast-paced, vast area with many different types of applications. It introduces countless opportunities as long as we keep up with the changing technology.

Answers

Chapter 2

1. (b) – sdkconfig. ESP-IDF uses sdkconfig as the project configuration file, which is based on the Kconfig system, which provides a compile-time project configuration mechanism. For more information, see https://www.kernel.org/doc/Documentation/kbuild/kconfig-language.txt.

2. (b) – TSL2561. It is an ambient light sensor. For more information, see https://ams.com/tsl2561.

3. (c) – Button. It is a sensor. We read the status of a button (on/off) from the connected GPIO pin.

4. (c) – **PWM**, or **pulse-width modulation**. PWM is a way to control analog actuators with a GPIO pin. For more information, see https://www.analogictips.com/pulse-width-modulation-pwm/.

5. (a) – Data and clock. An MCU needs a clock and data line to communicate with an I2C device. For more information, see https://learn.sparkfun.com/tutorials/i2c/all.

Chapter 3

1. (c) – OECD. It is not a display technology.

2. (a) – OLED, TFT, LCD. Although there are some exceptional products, this is the order that we usually evaluate displays in terms of energy consumption.

3. (c) – TFT, OLED, LCD. Again, there are some exceptions, but this is the order that we usually evaluate displays in terms of graphic capabilities.

4. (a) – The vanilla FreeRTOS is designed for a single core, whereas ESP-IDF supports multiple cores. See https://docs.espressif.com/projects/esp-idf/en/latest/esp32/api-guides/freertos-smp.html.

5. (b) – portENTER_CRITICAL_SAFE/portEXIT_CRITICAL_SAFE. They identify the context of execution (ISR or non-ISR) and call other critical section functions accordingly.

Chapter 4

1. (c) – The start bit. It starts a UART frame and is not configurable while setting up a UART connection. See more here: https://www.analog.com/en/analog-dialogue/articles/uart-a-hardware-communication-protocol.html.

2. (d) – UART has two different lines for transmitting and receiving, while others use a single line for data. This is not true. SPI also has two different lines for sending and receiving data packets. See https://www.analog.com/en/analog-dialogue/articles/introduction-to-spi-interface.html.

3. (b) – They need the same number of pin connections. This is not true. I2S has a **word select** (**WS**) line, which doesn't exist in I2C communication. See more here: https://www.allaboutcircuits.com/technical-articles/introduction-to-the-i2s-interface/.

4. (a) – Modem sleep and light sleep. In these modes of operation, ESP32 preserves its RAM state. See more here: https://lastminuteengineers.com/esp32-sleep-modes-power-consumption/.

5. (d) – Deep-sleep; employ the ULP coprocessor.

Chapter 6

1. (a) – STA or AP. You can run a web server on ESP32 in any of these Wi-Fi modes.

2. (c) – Web URL. It is not related to setting up a Wi-Fi connection.

3. (c) – mDNS. Multicast DNS is a zero-configuration service to resolve hostnames in small networks. It is also a means to expose services on a machine. See https://en.wikipedia.org/wiki/Multicast_DNS.

4. (d) – ICMP. **Internet Control Message Protocol** (**ICMP**) is an error-reporting protocol. There are some diagnostic utilities, such as ping and traceroute, to check hosts in a network. For more information, see https://www.techtarget.com/searchnetworking/definition/ICMP.

5. (a) – SNTP. The **Simple Network Time Protocol** (**SNTP**) is a time synchronization protocol of the TCP/IP protocol family. See more here: https://www.ionos.co.uk/digitalguide/server/know-how/sntp-simple-network-time-protocol/.

Chapter 7

1. (a) – Starting a secure web server on ESP32. This option provides a secure communication channel between the parties, not related to the field installation of a physical ESP32 device. A good reference is here: `https://www.iotsecurityfoundation.org/wp-content/uploads/2019/12/Best-Practice-Guides-Release-2_Digitalv3.pdf`.

2. (b) – Embedding the key in the encrypted flash. The application would still have access to the private key.

3. (d) – OTA updates. With an **over-the-air (OTA)** update mechanism, we can update the firmware of a wireless device.

4. (b) – Secure data exchange. Secure data exchange happens after setting up a secure communication channel. This article explains the TLS handshake process: `https://www.cloudflare.com/en-gb/learning/ssl/what-happens-in-a-tls-handshake/`.

5. (b) – Difference in version file content. An update happens if the versions are different. See the Espressif documentation explaining the OTA process here: `https://docs.espressif.com/projects/esp-idf/en/latest/esp32/api-reference/system/ota.html`.

Chapter 8

1. (c) – Link layer. The link layer resides on the controller side of the BLE stack. Read this article for more information about the BLE basics: `https://www.novelbits.io/basics-bluetooth-low-energy/`.

2. (a) – **Generic Access Profile (GAP)**. This layer is responsible for the advertisement and connection establishment.

3. (b) – **Generic Attribute Profile (GATT)**. This layer defines the format of the data shared between BLE devices

4. (b) – It is a point-to-point protocol. This is not true. In a BLE mesh network, there are many nodes, and each node can communicate with the others.

5. (b) – Model. A model defines the functionality in a BLE mesh network. A good reference is here: `https://www.novelbits.io/bluetooth-mesh-tutorial-part-2/`.

Chapter 10

1. (d) – MQTT. The MQTT protocol defines a broker as a central element in the architecture, where clients can publish and subscribe to topics. Refer to this link for more information: `https://mqtt.org/`.

2. (c) – Only runs on top of UDP. This is not true. CoAP is a service layer protocol so it can run on top of any transport layer. Wikipedia explains this well with examples: `https://en.wikipedia.org/wiki/Constrained_Application_Protocol`.

3. (a) – Polling server for status updates. The WebSocket API provides a two-way communication channel between a browser and a server, removing the necessity to poll the server for status updates. See here: `https://developer.mozilla.org/en-US/docs/Web/API/WebSockets_API`.

4. (b) – Security is an optional feature. On the contrary, most IoT platforms force security at each level of communication.

5. (c) – A policy file is automatically generated when a thing is created. This is not true. A policy and a thing are independent of each other in AWS.

Chapter 11

1. (a) – Microservices. Although we can employ microservices architecture while developing a voice service, it is not one of the main technologies behind voice assistants.

2. (d) – Users need more guidance since there is no visual element.

3. (c) – To activate it. Wake words are used to activate voice assistants. A good article about wake words on Medium is here: `https://medium.com/@rowantrollope/7-things-you-didnt-know-about-wake-words-d4e9e041d11d`.

4. (c) – Microsoft Azure. It is the cloud computing service by Microsoft, not a voice assistant.

5. (b) – Longer time to market. Third-party services shorten the time to market since they free us from the development effort that they provide in their services.

Packt.com

Subscribe to our online digital library for full access to over 7,000 books and videos, as well as industry leading tools to help you plan your personal development and advance your career. For more information, please visit our website.

Why subscribe?

- Spend less time learning and more time coding with practical eBooks and Videos from over 4,000 industry professionals

- Improve your learning with Skill Plans built especially for you

- Get a free eBook or video every month

- Fully searchable for easy access to vital information

- Copy and paste, print, and bookmark content

Did you know that Packt offers eBook versions of every book published, with PDF and ePub files available? You can upgrade to the eBook version at packt.com and as a print book customer, you are entitled to a discount on the eBook copy. Get in touch with us at customercare@packtpub.com for more details.

At www.packt.com, you can also read a collection of free technical articles, sign up for a range of free newsletters, and receive exclusive discounts and offers on Packt books and eBooks.

Other Books You May Enjoy

If you enjoyed this book, you may be interested in these other books by Packt:

Practical Internet of Things Security - Second Edition

Brian Russell, Drew Van Duren

ISBN: 978-1-78862-582-1

- Discuss the need for separate security requirements and apply security engineering principles on IoT devices
- Master the operational aspects of planning, deploying, managing, monitoring, and detecting the remediation and disposal of IoT systems
- Use Blockchain solutions for IoT authenticity and integrity
- Explore additional privacy features emerging in the IoT industry, such as anonymity, tracking issues, and countermeasures

- Design a fog computing architecture to support IoT edge analytics
- Detect and respond to IoT security incidents and compromises

IoT and Edge Computing for Architects - Second Edition

Perry Lea

ISBN: 978-1-83921-480-6

- Understand the role and scope of architecting a successful IoT deployment
- Scan the landscape of IoT technologies, from sensors to the cloud and more
- See the trade-offs in choices of protocols and communications in IoT deployments
- Become familiar with the terminology needed to work in the IoT space
- Broaden your skills in the multiple engineering domains necessary for the IoT architect
- Implement best practices to ensure reliability, scalability, and security in your IoT infrastructure

Packt is searching for authors like you

If you're interested in becoming an author for Packt, please visit authors. packtpub.com and apply today. We have worked with thousands of developers and tech professionals, just like you, to help them share their insight with the global tech community. You can make a general application, apply for a specific hot topic that we are recruiting an author for, or submit your own idea.

Share Your Thoughts

Now you've finished *Developing IoT Projects with ESP32*, we'd love to hear your thoughts! Scan the QR code below to go straight to the Amazon review page for this book and share your feedback or leave a review on the site that you purchased it from.

https://packt.link/r/1838641165

Your review is important to us and the tech community and will help us make sure we're delivering excellent quality content.

Index

9 781838 641160